THE AUSTRALIAN PEOPLE

Other books by the same author

CRITICISM

The Lucky Country
God Is An Englishman
The Next Australia

NARRATIVE

The Permit
The Education Of Young Donald
But What If There Are No Pelicans?

THE AUSTRALIAN PEOPLE

Biography of a Nation

Donald Horne

ANGUS AND ROBERTSON

First published in 1972 by
ANGUS AND ROBERTSON (PUBLISHERS) PTY LTD
102 Glover Street, Cremorne, Sydney
2 Fisher Street, London
107 Elizabeth Street, Melbourne
167 Queen Street, Brisbane
89 Anson Road, Singapore

© *Donald Horne* 1972

This book is copyright. Apart from any fair dealing for
the purposes of private study, research, criticism or
review, as permitted under the Copyright Act, no part
may be reproduced by any process without written permission.
Inquiries should be addressed to the publishers.

National Library of Australia
card number and ISBN 0 207 12496 5

Registered in Australia for transmission by post as a book
PRINTED IN AUSTRALIA BY WATSON FERGUSON AND CO., BRISBANE

*Dedicated to
the historians
of Australia*

Foreword

HAVING A GO AT THE WHOLE THING

All histories have a bias. The bias of this history is to tell the story in a way that may suggest some answers to the question: *How did Australians become what they are?* Some histories leave this as a puzzle, perhaps because their authors wanted Australians to be something else. When Australian society is judged by the standards of some other society parts of it may seem irritatingly unfamiliar, even perverse: it is almost recognizable, but some things are missing and others are in the wrong places. It might help the understanding of contemporary Australia to accept that what happened in its history *did* happen; we can't go back over it all again and undo its peculiarities.

Looking for first signs of trends towards modern Australia does not mean, of course, that one ignores events that seem to move in some other direction. As in a novel, a small early incident later becomes more significant. But in many cases contradictory trends can all move towards the present society. Like any other nation, Australia is a society of contradictions. This is why it is possible to agree with practically all the contradictory interpretations given by Australian historians: almost all of them are right—to some extent.

Private analysis and self-argument stretching, on and off, over six years went into writing this book, but I hope all this has been cleared away so that the flow of narrative is not interrupted. It is meant to be a story. There are disadvantages in this approach: you can't argue your case, not even in footnotes. But you can't have everything. I have tried to provide a general history in which matters like education, living styles, religion, economic activity, politics, leisure pursuits, art, ideas, attempts at self-definition, are all woven together into 'the whole cloth''. I have had a go at the whole thing.

It is a story about people, but not about personages. The

names of individuals crop up where they are part of the narrative, but the real participants are types of people, not individuals. I have tried to turn these types of people into the kind of "characters" who make up the biography of a nation. Perhaps one of the functions of history-writing is to bring new types of people onto the stage and describe the interplay.

The book is composed of overlays of themes. It is chopped up into chronological divisions, but within each division one theme is developed right through the period, then another, then another. The cumulative effect is intended to provide a memory rather like the kind of memories we have of our own lives: we know that we go on year by year, but we also know that the themes of our lives have histories other than those suggested by the calendar.

There was a particular difficulty in writing the last two chapters, covering the period 1950 to 1970. Once it would have been possible to end twenty years earlier: now it is fashionable to try to give closing scores at the end of the day's play. This can't be done with quite the same apparent detachment as can be summoned for the earlier part of the story: as he packs the puppets away the puppeteer shows his hand.

There was a different difficulty in writing the first chapter, on the period 1788 to 1820, because this period is usually the one most familiar to the general readers. (For some time historians found it difficult to get past it.) I have tried to deal with it lightly and quickly, sketching a general framework that gets the story going without too much detail and, I regret to say, without going into too much argument.

Not having footnotes has one embarrassment. It is not possible to make acknowledgments. In the case of the direct quotations this doesn't matter. They don't come from historians. They are merely contemporary voices chattering away, and who they are (or whether they are right or wrong) is of no significance; they are just conversation. Some are named. Some are not. Since the writing of this kind of book necessarily depends on exploiting the devoted work of a great number of historians, it seems unfair not to be able to acknowledge them. But to do so in the text would impede the book's narrative style. The best I can do in individual tribute is the bibliography at the back; and in general I can add the observation that history-writing seems well in advance of most other aspects of investigation into Australia. If that were not so, this book could not have been written.

Sydney, 1972   DONALD HORNE

CONTENTS

Part 1
THE AGE OF AUTHORITY 1788-1850

PROLOGUE: TWO BEGINNINGS	xv
Brown beginnings	xv
White beginnings	xvi
1: NEW WORLD—OLD WORLD (1788-1820)	1
A European city	1
The sardonic frontier	5
The rebels and the respectable	9
2: THE NOBS (the 1820s and early 1830s)	19
A second England	19
The new "Natives"	23
A seaport civilization	25
3: THE IMPROVERS (1830 to early 1850s)	28
A life of his own	29
Holding things together	35
The faith of the improvers	38
The black hats	42
4: THE LAND GRABBERS (1830 to early 1850s cont'd)	45
The rush to the grasslands	45
The destruction of the blacks	52
The squatters take over	55
5: THE AUSTRAL-ASIATICS (1830 to early 1850s cont'd)	60
4,000 miles of the Southern Hemisphere	60
The rise of "the people"	69

Part 2
THE AGE OF IMPROVEMENT 1851-1910

6: AUSTRALIA UNLIMITED (1851-1885)	79
The diggers	79
The New York of Australia	84
The blast of the trumpet	88
No class too poor to play	92

7: ALMOST EVERYONE A LIBERAL (1855-1885)	97
The liberals	97
The war on the squatters	104
The perils of the liberals	109
8: LOOKING FOR AUSTRALIA (1870-1885)	117
Members of the Empire	117
The gum-suckers	118
The pride of the colonies	121
9: THE NORMAL MARCH OF PROGRESS (1885-1910)	124
The fall of Melbourne	124
The commonplace rich	126
An exemplar to the old lands	129
Every worker a gentleman?	131
Every farmer a yeoman?	134
10: THE MODERN AGE (1885-1910 cont'd)	137
The rise of the professionals	137
The rise of the employees	140
The New Imperialism	142
The syndicalists	145
The coming of the parties	148
11: THEORIES ABOUT WHO THEY WERE (1885-1910 cont'd)	152
The other side of the range	152
Australia for the Australians	156
12: BIRTH OF A NATION (1885-1910 cont'd)	160
Coming together	160
The new protection	164

Part 3

THE AGE OF IMPERIALISM 1910-1970

13: BLOOD SACRIFICE (1910-1919)	173
14: THE END OF IMPROVEMENT (1919-1939)	186
The Returned Men	186
The first suburban nation	188
"Development", not Improvement	193
The improvisers	198
"The greatest Test Match of them all"	202
15: TUNING IN TO BRITAIN (1919-1939 cont'd)	206
The creed of the black hats	206
A nation without a mind	209
Not like last time	215

16: THE ORPHANS OF THE PACIFIC (the 1940s)	218
17: THE LUCKY COUNTRY (1950-1970)	230
The Australian style	230
An industrial society	236
The rise of the executives	240
The rise of the intellectuals	242
18: THE END OF IMPERIALISM (1950-1970)	248
The failure of politics	248
The afterglow of Britishry	252
Ten minutes to midnight	254
Becoming something	258
BIBLIOGRAPHY	262
INDEX	276

Part 1

The Age of Authority

1788—1850

Prologue

TWO BEGINNINGS

Brown Beginnings

Some brown people discovered Australia and settled in it something like 30,000 years ago when the last Ice Age had shrivelled the oceans sufficiently for men to walk some of the way from what are now the islands of South-east Asia to what is now the Australian mainland. A few thousand years later the ancestors of the American Indians were walking out of Asia into Alaska and then across the Americas.

We know little about the first Australians, but we know that the major part of the land they came to was to become almost rainless and that the rest of it had no seeds that could be cultivated and no animals that could be herded or used as beasts of burden. The adaptation of the Australians to these harsh circumstances is remarkable in the whole history of human stubbornness and inventiveness.

On the coasts they became fishermen; in the forest lands and mountains, bushmen; in the dry interior, plainsmen who had to travel so much to find something to eat that they owned only what they could carry and who, to drink, might collect the early morning dew from leaves or squeeze water out of the pouches of frogs. In the human manner, they all developed a culture, making sense of their existence: each tribe's own particular territory was justified by a special theory of creation which made it the sacred property of their ancestors, and their distinctiveness was maintained by a special language and special rituals.

Since the 300,000 or so Australians who were spread out over three million square miles were divided into hundreds of tribes, there were hundreds of Australian "nations", some of less than 500 people, few of more than 1,500, connected only by a complex system of barter in which a traded object could finally cross the whole continent. These tribes further broke down into smaller groups and it was in these smaller communities that the Australians spent most of their lives, leaving their food-gathering territories only to visit relations or to attend the occasional gatherings of the whole tribe for those games, feasts or ceremonies that gave them a sense of belonging to something bigger.

Each tribe was usually sure of its rights and habits without challenging the rights of others: there were no drives into alien lands to seize slaves or land and, although there were the personal satisfactions of large scale fights, complicated blood feuds, duels, and squabbles over women, there were no predatory wars. There were not even leaders. The old men of each small group were supposed to provide its wisdom, but their wisdom did not include the arts of organized warfare.

There was a common thread in many of the creation myths of the Australians, the belief that things began with the sudden materialization of creatures that did not look like humans but acted like them and that wandered aimlessly around the country. This was the kind of way, from the seventeenth century onwards, in which the Europeans materialized in Australia. To start with there were some apparently meaningless landings, followed by years of nothing. Then in January 1788 eleven strange ships anchored in a bay on the east coast and out of them came scarcely human creatures who began moving here and there for some unknown purpose.

White Beginnings

The purpose seemed clear enough to the scarcely human creatures. It was to found a prison colony at the bay where the English naval captain, James Cook, had first landed when, almost eighteen years before, he had voyaged along the east coast of New Holland and found it better favoured than the coasts already looked at by the Dutch. It was an age when any part of the world whose inhabitants could not fight the Europeans was considered European property; so later, as Cook was leaving the northern reaches of New Holland, he ordered the Union flag to be run up and, just as the brown Australians might clap bits of wood together to give special solemnity to an occasion, he ordered muskets to be fired to make his claim sound real. He announced that the whole east coast now belonged to Great Britain and for some unknown reason he gave it the curious name of "New South Wales". Soon Europeans began printing this new name on their maps.

With the Australians knowing nothing about what these people 12,000 miles away were doing, London gentlemen from time to time would urge that the unknown land be turned to some new English purpose. That purpose proved to be the emptying of the prison hulks that had been crowded since transportation of convicts to North America had ended in 1776. The hulks were a nuisance and transportation a habit: it seemed ridiculous that a country should house its own convicts; there were questions in the House of Commons and committees of inquiry. To a cocky, newly arrived power boasting that it ruled the waves, the decision became obvious: start another colony—it might also prove useful for trade or some strategic purpose.

As the eleven ships lay at anchor in Captain Cook's "Botany Bay" on 20th January 1788, there was self-congratulation that an eight-month voyage had ended with so few deaths, and curiosity as boats explored the bay and land parties gave beads to the natives; but it was obvious to Captain Arthur Phillip, governor of the colony, that he had been sent to the wrong place. Too much of its land was low and boggy. The supply of fresh water was poor. The grass was long and coarse. The soil was black sand. There was no shelter for the ships.

Phillip went up the coast with three boats to look for something better. He found "a large opening or bay", which at first seemed unpromising. But after the three little boats had passed between two high, rugged stone cliffs Phillip saw opening before him "the finest harbour in the world, in which 1000 sail of the line may ride in the most perfect security". His main difficulty was to decide at which of the inner harbours he should found his colony. He chose a bay into which a stream ran down through the red gums and with water deep enough for ships to anchor close to the shore. He named it "Sydney Cove" after the English politician who had sent him to New South Wales, and by 26th January the whole colony was anchored off it. Early in the morning a party began clearing a space for a flagstaff. Shortly after noon the officers and a party of marines landed. The Union flag went up. Possession was taken for King George. At sunset a salute was fired. Phillip and his small staff drank to King George's health and the colony's success.

The next day Phillip marked out lines for an encampment. His portable house was to be on one side of the stream; most of the encampment was to go up on the other. Some parties netted for fish; others cut down trees; others unloaded the blacksmith's forge, the cookhouse and tools, and some of the colony's flour, rice, beef, pork, peas and butter. Tents went up. Two days later the Governor's house was erected, a convict had been lashed for insolence and the colony's 9 horses, 6 cattle, 44 sheep, 3 goats, 28 pigs and diverse poultry were landed.

It began to thunder, with lightning and rain. For the next eight days there were thunderstorms, except on the Sunday, when the chaplain preached under a tree on the text: "What shall I render unto the Lord, for all his benefits towards me?" There were complaints of the heat, of the indolence of the convicts and of the ineptitude of their overseers (who were also convicts); a party of natives threw stones at a fishing party; several convicts ran away; a number of others got drunk. The hospital tents were filled with people suffering from dysentery and scurvy.

On the night of 6th February there was the most violent of all the storms. The lightning, not letting up the whole night, killed five sheep and a pig; on the ships the sailors were excited to drunkenness ("some swearing, others quarrelling, others singing—not in the least regarding the tempest, though so violent that the thunder shook the ship") and on the shore the storm was background to a black carnival in which the men convicts got to the women, who had landed that day, and celebrated the birth of the colony, with lightning flashing and thunder roaring, in "debauchery and riot".

It was after this remarkable night that on 7th February the official beginning of the colony was proclaimed. Assembled around the governor or sick in hospital or in one of the ships were 736 male and female convicts, 17 convicts' children, 211 marines, with 27 wives and 14 children, and the few officials of the colony. After Phillip had been proclaimed Captain-General and Governor-in-Chief he warned the convicts that men found in the women's tents at night would be shot at, and that anyone who stole food would be hanged. Three volleys were fired. Phillip received the honours due to a Captain-General and retired to a large tent where he and the officers dined on a cold collation. "The mutton," said one of those who ate it, "was full of maggots. Nothing will keep 24 hours in this country."

Chapter 1

NEW WORLD — OLD WORLD
1788-1820

A European City

"I looked on the wonderful sight of a European city thriving in the bosom of a country all but wild," wrote a French explorer who came to Sydney in 1819. Some of the thousand or so buildings of this town of 12,000 people were still wooden huts but there were enough brick or even stone houses, and a sufficient sprinkling of bigger residences and public buildings, for it to have some small sense of presence. And it had a certain look of industry about it. Timber was being sawed, beer brewed, hides tanned, salt dried, shells were being burned into lime, clay turned into brick, wheat ground into flour, wool woven into cloth. The town even had a steam engine. Men and women had come from one part of the world to another, and so far as this new world allowed them had again built what they knew.

By 1819 the leaders of this small new community had learnt how to huddle together and comfort themselves with the familiarity of old diversions. They had to make do with kangaroos for hunting, but they retained what they could of the pleasures of a provincial English town—musical evenings, cricket, some picnics, horseriding, occasionally a ball. They had to do without a theatre—the first play went on in a mud hut decorated with coloured paper, and a playhouse was built in 1796, but later it was pulled down by order of the governor because there were too many robberies on play nights; they had only one newspaper, started in 1796, at first mainly for the governor to issue his instructions, and always subject to his censorship; and they had no general reading of their own—the first book printed in the colony was a summary of its standing orders and it was not until 1819 that a local periodical was contemplated; but there was a large supply of imported British periodicals and books to tell them about the part of the world they most cared about. The small pretension of the bigger public buildings was in the English style of the late eighteenth century, less well done than similar derivations in Virginia, but familiar. Sydney's main distinctiveness was how it spread out. With most houses on their own plots of land Sydney took up more space than towns of similar population in Great Britain. And the dominant veranda'd style was producing one of the first towns of predominantly single storey residences in the history of European urbanization.

By English standards society was thin. There were no aristocrats, no old gentry families. The best the colony could produce was the small gentry of the principal civil and military officers and a few others who had come to the colony to get something out of it; to these were added those who had *made* themselves gentry, and in a small community they could seem big. There was an extra distinction a man could boast of: in one generation a unique caste system had been created—between ex-convicts and others—that was already being applied to the children of its original members, an attitude not softened by the Church of England whose chaplain showed little Christian charity to the penitent. This new caste system could not work at the lower levels of the colony, but at the top it was pursued by some with an intemperance natural to a convict colony in which anger and fear could speak a language of extraordinary threats.

The higher officials were all placemen of English politicians; some, in the fashion of the day, held several offices at once; many squabbled with each other; most were not much good at their jobs; and at times almost all of them seemed to be arguing about what there was to be in it for them. Some disputed the governor's power, seeing themselves as directly responsible to particular authorities in London; the military and civil officers who sat in the courts sometimes used their independence as a weapon against the governor; and some of the colony's officials—most notably the chaplain—were in a state of almost continued campaign against him. The petty officials, nearly all convicts or ex-convicts, saw bribery and fraud as part of their natural reward.

As comforting in its familiarity as the administrative muddle was the parsimony of the time. Although New South Wales was a convict colony there was not enough government money to build even a jail. When the thatched wooden jail of one of the early governors was burnt down he had to impose special levies to finance the building of a stone one. Fed by special fees, levies and licences, the Gaol Fund he established became one of the colony's two sources of independent revenue, the other being the Orphan Fund, which was similarly provided. The Gaol Fund then became the principal source of money for public works, the Orphan Fund for public schools. It told something of the nature of the colony that its two departments of exchequer were called the Gaol Fund and the Orphan Fund. In one of the most desperate of other expedients Sydney Hospital was built by giving three contractors a semi-monopoly in the sale of rum. There was no purse for civic pride: for a while, using Francis Greenway, an ex-convict, as architect, Governor Lachlan Macquarie tried to give a sense of order to Sydney and its smaller towns by erecting public buildings; but attacks on such extravagance were among the reasons for his recall.

Whatever attacks there were on a governor, to be invited to dine at Government House was to have arrived (even if, as the colony's first brick building, put up at a time when the mysteries of turning Australian clay into true English bricks had not altogether been solved, it was in danger of falling down). A governor was something different from what offered in a provincial town back home, and if less than a lord he was more accessible. The colony was short on official ceremony and belief, but such official ritual as it had was the expression of its loyalty to the British monarch, and to the mysteries of this loyalty a governor, whatever one thought of him as a man, held the key. He presided over celebrations of the royal birthdays and national days: one governor ordered the colony into a week's inactivity to mourn the death of an English princess.

But a governor, since he had to get on with governing New South Wales, was less a social arbiter than were the transient English regimental garrisons, which could more easily despise any habits that had become peculiar to the colony. Boasted of as the biggest and best outside Britain, the newly built barracks was much larger than Government House and dominated the town; the garrison's band played in the park, its red coats gave colour to the streets; its officers defended their position at the top of the colony's hierarchy with a militant attitude of snubs to all colonial upstarts. In particular, although the officers, like their men, took convict mistresses and enjoyed the gambling dens, grog shops and brothels run by ex-convicts in the Rocks area of Sydney, they were the leaders of those who enjoyed the distinction of having come to the colony "free".

It was the officers of the five successive military garrisons who provided the governors' most public opposition. Only a few months after the settlement began a captain of marines wrote to an English lord saying of Phillip: "I do not think (*entre nous*) that your three kingdoms could produce another man, in my opinion, so totally unqualified for the business he has taken in hand as this man is"; and the especially formed N.S.W. Corps (the "Rum Corps") that followed the marines boycotted Governor Hunter and secured his recall; later it went so far as to depose Governor Bligh, and for a while itself ran the colony. When the Corps was disbanded and replaced in turn by three regular regiments, officers of each of these took sides against Governor Macquarie and attempted to humiliate him.

Nevertheless by 1820 the colony had more confidence in itself. For one thing, the House of Commons was beginning to take an interest, in 1819 appointing Commissioner Bigge to go to New South Wales and recommend what should be done about it. Amateur collectors sent plants to London, where they became exotics in English glass houses; birds were described and new specimens made known through European publications; hundreds of drawings were done of native plants, fish, insects, animals and humans; whole landscapes were painted, presenting the colony as an English nobleman's park or as a drab, monotonous wilderness. In 1819 the first book by a native born colonist was published in London. In the same year a colonial official who had been a friend of Leigh Hunt's and the Lambs published in Sydney its first volume of verse. He described the south land as not part of the work of initial creation but "... an afterbirth, not conceived in the Beginning ... but emerged at the first sinning."

The sardonic frontier

It had taken years for the colony to be sure it would not starve. The soil was mostly hungry sand or hard clay. The seasons were upside down. There were no native crops, and what there was of native game was difficult to shoot and fish were hard to catch. "In the whole world there is not a worse country than what we have seen of this," wrote one of the first officers. "The colony is never likely to answer the wishes and expectations of Government," wrote another. "The Nation would save money by feeding the convicts at home upon Venison and Claret—clothing them in Purple and Gold."

The plain that had limited the horizons of settlement ran about 40 miles along the coast, and at its widest 30 to 35 miles inland, all of it hemmed in by the foothills and cliffs of a bushy sandstone plateau. Within the plain, amongst the sand or clay, there were isolated stretches of useful soils, but they quickly lost their goodness and the richer river flats were often flooded. Settlement had hopped desperately all over the plain. As each new area proved disappointing another was tried. For a season the river flats of the Nepean-Hawkesbury, which wound in an arc almost completely around the landward side of the plain, were compared with the Nile, but when there were four floods in two years another hope was washed away. Dominant for thirty years, the inhospitable plain on which the Colony was established was a frontier of absurdity. Of the whole population of 24,000 in New South Wales, half stayed in town.

To the north of Sydney a couple of dozen farms had spread along the black flood soils of the Hunter River; to the south where timber-getters were felling the rain forests, there were a few grants for grazing, as there were in the west, opened up when a way had been found across the ridges of the sandstone mountains. But the interior was still a secret, the mystery of its westward-flowing rivers unsolved. Did they turn and flow into the ocean? Did they flow into a great inland sea? Two exploring parties lost their answer in swamps and reeds. There seemed an impassable limit to further expansion.

For farmers, there were the consolations or sorrows of a sardonic luck—the good luck of a governor's favour or of suitable soil, the bad luck of a flood or a drought. Many farmers failed, and lost their farms. Those who failed but stuck it out lived in tiny bark huts growing potatoes and running pigs and goats on their few acres, perhaps supplementing this by also working for wages. The majority lived in slab or weatherboard cottages, from which they ran small holdings, growing grain, but with some sheep or cattle as well, their sense of success or failure depending on their expectations. The few who had been favoured lived in comfortable veranda'd houses of brick or stone, surrounded by gardens and orchards, with their work done by convicts. All the land had begun as government grants—big grants for big men, little grants for little men—but how the land was first granted no longer mattered. Those who had lost their chances had lost them.

More immediate opportunity had come from the sea. To the south the islands of Bass Strait swarmed with seals; the business of clubbing and skinning tens of thousands of them had set small enterprises going in Sydney—shipmaking, providoring, trading. When most of the seals had been clubbed merchants looked to the cannibal islands of Fiji where muskets or axes could be bartered for sandalwood or trepang, or to Tahiti where there was trade to do for pork. They stirred the societies of these islands to new techniques of villainy.

Most of the expansion even of land frontiers had been by ship. In 1801, when Sydney decided to set up its own colony a hundred miles up the coast, it was by ship that the expedition had set off for what was to become Newcastle. The next two sub-colonies, established in fear of the French, were also on the coast, on the island of Van Diemen's Land, 500 miles south of Sydney. If the 27,000 people of New South Wales and Van Diemen's Land were to become anything, it seemed obvious that, in the British tradition, it would be as a maritime and trading people.

The habits of trading had been harsh, beginning with even a scarcity of coins. Since in the late eighteenth century Great Britain was generally short of coins it was more than ten years before any official consignments reached New South Wales and then they were only batches of pennies, halfpennies and farthings. Ducats, guilders and rupees drifted into the colony but it was not until 1813 that the first big consignment arrived—$10,000 worth of Spanish dollars from India—and these were so insufficient that the governor ordered that "dumps" be stamped out of the middle of them so that each coin could become two. For their own buying and selling the colonists had to rely mainly on IOUs, or on receipts from the Commissariat, the government store; receipts and IOUs passed from hand to hand, more or less as banknotes. In the early days rum was all that many would accept as wages and it became an important form of currency. When the use of spirits was later brought under control this reform produced a currency crisis. What was there worth working for now?

To buy foreign goods, foreign currency was needed and with hardly any exports the colony had hardly any foreign currency. This made the colony's officers its first traders: they were the main holders of internationally negotiable paper, in the form of Treasury bills from London, obtained privately, as pay, or by fiddling regimental funds; and with it they alone could buy the cargoes that came to Sydney. When it became clear that ships' captains were using their monopoly to extort high prices, the officers formed a buyers' ring, which forced down the price of cargoes by making only one offer for them; then they would split the cargoes, mark up the prices and, to avoid despoiling their rank as gentlemen, sell the goods through some of the "pedlars, dealers and extortioners" of the colony, who marked up the prices again. The success of this monopoly increased when, during an interregnum between governors, the officers helped themselves to other privileges. News of it attracted to Sydney a few merchants who were looking for new ways of making money.

By about 1800 the officers' ring began to break, partly because of the arrival of the professionals, partly because the Commissariat was now issuing more Treasury bills than the officers could monopolize and partly because some of the ex-convict dealers of the 1790s, formerly intermediaries for the officers, had accumulated enough money and skills and more than enough nerve and energy to emerge in their own right. From then on most military and civil officers tried to make or increase their fortunes by farming rather than by trading; of the significant exceptions most were only junior partners of the new men. Trade was becoming too tough for amateurs. When a slump in confidence slowed down the English trading world all the merchants of Sydney seemed ruined.

By 1820 the survivors of the colony's many commercial

disasters were grouped into twelve main mercantile houses. As well as trading they experimented in manufacturing and, by purchase or by supplying goods against secured mortgages and then foreclosing, they built up some of the biggest landed properties in the colony. They dined with each other in their town houses or on their country estates and their children tended to intermarry. An ex-convict was the most prominent of them, two other ex-convicts were important. Below them in the money scale there were several hundred petty dealers, shopkeepers, innkeepers, and self-employed tradesmen. Below these something like a fifth of the total work force (including convicts) claimed to know some sort of trade; then came the unskilled, who if free took their work where they could find it but were more likely than not to find it in building, timber-working or shipping.

In a colony which was half town, traders and dealers were an important part of its frontier. There was an unusually high amount of litigiousness, harshness and fretfulness as, to the black atmosphere of a convict colony, there was added the "prevailing impulse of truck and cavil" of a commercial society of enormous risk. A significant part of its tone was hardheaded and frenetically individualistic. This individualism further inflamed the colony's peculiarly autocratic character. There was no other colony with such a despotic constitution. New South Wales enjoyed none of the oligarchic freedom of the homeland. The rule of law was that of court martial; the governor was the sole legislator, the chief executive and the only court of appeal. He could forbid public meetings; there was no religious freedom; and the colony's one newspaper came out at his pleasure. He could parcel out land, and as the main controller of labour he handed out human beings like a slave-master. The Commissariat was the colony's largest trader and biggest employer; its buying, selling, price-fixing, lending and control of international currency made it the central part of the economy. Even if this had not been so, the baffling inadequacies of the soil and the seasons would have demanded strong action from the governors.

The masterful individualists of the colony did not oppose government; they saw it as something that was expected to assist them and be put to their purposes. In this they added to the frustrations of the governors. There had been four after Phillip, three naval officers and an army officer, each appointed to clean up the mess his predecessor had left, each frustrated and living out the rest of his time in England with a sense of resentment. To the shortage of money, the lack of experience of the principal labourers, the inadequacies of the land, the corruption of petty officers and the quarrelsomeness of great ones, the masterful individualists added an exploitation of a governor's greatest weakness: his despotism was limited by the fact that his proclamations had to be countersigned in London, and they were often queried because he was governing Great Britain's only penal colony. Before a reply was given it might have to take into account the demands of other departments of government, theories in the British Parliament about how the colony should be run, pressures from groups such as the whaling interest or the East India Company. Only then could the Governor of New SouthWales learn what they thought in London of some action he had taken more than twelve months before. And to these lobbying groups were added the conflicting factions of the colonists who were building the biggest stakes in the colony.

Even behind the local insults of the military there lay the disagreements among themselves of the traders and the larger landowners. Some would support the governor because he supported them, others would attack him because he did not take their side. Increasingly the insults offered by the passing military merely gave public colour to these domestic contentions. One of the true "frontiers" for the individualists of New South Wales was in the exploitation not of its soil but of its government.

The rebels and the respectable

Most of the hard work of transplanting Western European civilization to Australia was done by thieves. Eighty per cent of those transported had been sentenced for larceny, and by 1820 almost three-quarters of the total adult population were convicts or ex-convicts, and at least four out of five of the colony's young were the children of convicts.

The process of turning a thief into a colonist began when his convict transport sailed into Sydney Harbour. The convicts were formed up on the quarter-deck, questioned by the Superintendent of Convicts, exhorted to improve themselves by the governor or the Judge-Advocate and then sorted out. The few gentlemen convicts and convicts with special talents or money were usually given a ticket-of-leave as soon as they arrived, which considerably increased their prospect of self-improvement. Of the others, those judged most useful would be picked as petty officials, overseers, superintendents, police or clerks, or to work in the government establishments or construction gangs. (Thus, how a convict was treated depended not on his offence, but on his capacity to work.) Those expected to be most troublesome were usually sent to Van Diemen's Land. In their home cities most thieves understood best the criminal's morality: that virtue consists in trickery and sharpness of wit and its reward is the freedom of idleness. But although used to an aristocratic life of heroism and leisure in circumstances of extreme poverty and squalor, when they arrived in Sydney they were put to *work*. Since opposition to work was the whole ethic of many of them it is not surprising that there were complaints of their indolence. Many of their offences against the authority of the colony were those of cheeky, high-spirited young soldiers—they got drunk; they were absent without leave; they pretended to be sick when they weren't; they lay around in bed; they poked fun at people; they didn't salute; they refused to put out the light. The reaction of many to the system was to try to cheat it, or bribe it, or to thumb their noses at it; the reaction of the system was to flog them. About two out of five of the convicts were flogged at least once. A quick hearing before a magistrate and then a quick flogging cost the colony nothing and allowed the victim to be put back to work fairly quickly. About one in ten were not caught doing anything wrong and received no punishment; the majority offended authority a little and received some punishment, if only an admonition; about another one in ten did everything wrong. Lost in a hell of rebellion and retribution, they were flogged, sentenced to labour in road gangs, or abandoned in chains on the beaches of Newcastle to burn shells for lime. About one in a hundred was hanged.

Since only about one in seven were women, the convicts'

was a man's society, depending mainly on prostitution or homosexuality for its shared sexual pleasures. Its language was thieves' slang, providing some of the first contributions to the English that was spoken in the colony. (The dominant group were the cockneys, flash-talking "townies", adept at collective bullying.) It was a society of desperate gambling (convicts staking the clothes off their backs even stood naked while the game went on) and hard drinking: at a pint a week, average spirits consumption was four times that in Britain. It may have been one of the most drunken societies ever to have existed; it was seen by some visitors as one of the most foul-mouthed and licentious.

To these rebellions of the flesh there was added a rebellion of race. Within the suppression of the convicts there was another suppression—the suppression of the Irish. About a quarter of the convicts were Irish and, although in their court convictions they tended more than the English to crimes of violence and acts of insubordination against the State, even the jailers sometimes pitied their bewilderment and felt sympathy for their anxiety to oblige and their desire to make something more of their lives. There were fewer professional criminals among them; the predicament of many was that of destitute or near destitute peasants who lived in the most poverty-stricken country of Western Europe, in such deprived circumstances that it was natural for there to be an understanding and pleasantness between persons and also a violence. Of those transported in the first 15 years about 600 (three priests among them) had been sentenced for riot and sedition, most for taking part in the Irish uprisings at the end of the century. In the colony there were from time to time rumours that the Irish were assembling pikes and planning revolt: the rumours proved true in 1804 when it was heard in Sydney that a group of them had armed, seized a commanding hill, and was planning to take Parramatta, then Sydney. Fifteen were shot, nine hanged, a number flogged and fifty others sent in chains to the beaches of Newcastle.

Living as Irishmen under English laws, most of them illiterate and bereft of property, they saw themselves as Catholics: to many even this lacked much particular meaning, but it was what they had. Yet as Catholics they were forbidden the mass. Two priests had volunteered to go as chaplains to the colony at its beginning, paying their own expenses, but their offer was refused; apart from a brief period of toleration which ended with the 1804 mutiny the celebration of mass was illegal and Catholics could be forced to attend Church of England services. Probably with authority's connivance, ex-convict priests did perform some surreptitious masses, but after 1808 there were no priests until one arrived in 1817. He was without civil authority and in the next year he was arrested and deported. It was not until 1820, after the House of Commons had been stirred by this deportation and after Rome had got around to setting up a vicariate stretching across the Indian Ocean from Cape Town to Sydney, that two Irish chaplains arrived, their salaries paid by the British government. They were greeted with friendship. They might help keep the Irish in order.

Some convicts were insubordinate or indolent or drunken or Irish, but among others there was a contrary drive to respectability that was pursued with such success that the conformity of some received as much comment as the rebelliousness of others. The drive to respectability was aided by the opportunity for most convicts to live some sort of a civilian life. The majority were assigned to private masters, who provided lodging, food and clothing in return for their labour. (A married convict could be assigned to his wife.) If a convict was assigned to a well-to-do master he might live reasonably well, by the colony's standards; if the master was poor his assigned convict would live as badly as he did, but an assigned man could work for someone else in his spare time to add to what he was given by his master. Most convicts ate more and worked less than most working men in England. For most of this period even the government-employed convicts did not live in barracks in Sydney: they were given time off to do work for private masters, paying for their lodging out of whatever extra they earned. Convicts wore no uniform; there was no way for the innocent observer to judge by dress or place of living or by manners who were convicts, who were ex-convicts or who were the few who came free.

By being sent to New South Wales young criminals were given another chance to adopt the habits of the law-abiding, and this time it was made easier because of continuing labour shortages. Many were pardoned before their time was up and, like those who fully served their sentences, they could take up a small land grant, 30 acres, plus 20 for a wife, plus 10 for a child. Some paid their passages home; others absconded; most stayed. Of those who stayed almost all gave up crime. It is true that for most of them honesty had to be its own reward and they had to live out their lives on short measure—there were not enough wives to go round and they worked as labourers for masters, many of whom were themselves ex-convicts—but a significant minority did "better themselves" by becoming farmers or tradesmen. A very few, who arrived when the colony was full of pickings, did very well: one became the colony's second biggest landholder, another became one of its biggest merchants. (Having been transported for stealing muslin and calico, he ended his career as a textile manufacturer.) Some ex-convicts found it easy to make an honest living because they were really law-accepting people who had merely broken the law: others, though criminals by belief, accepted the opportunity to take up a working life. By 1820 these two classes of people had gained sufficient economic strength to provide an implicit challenge to the older standards of the colony; they included a few rich merchants, they provided most of the tradesmen, and although they held only about a third of the total acres granted they were producing nearly three-quarters of the colony's grain, half its cattle and a third of its sheep. Whether they were big men or small, those who had hoisted themselves up in the world of the colony's economic activity were now beginning to see its development as mainly *their* work and its future as mainly *their* business.

The greatest insult available was the word "ex-convict". The euphemism "Emancipist" had been coined, suggesting by its suffix not so much one on whom a freedom had been conferred as one who himself conferred freedom. It was to Emancipists with social pretensions that the garrison and its civilian associates were most hostile: the officers of one regiment bound themselves by oath to have nothing to do with successful Emancipists; when Governor Macquarie invited some of these Emancipists to his table the regiment snubbed the governor. But the Emancipist enjoyed a compensating pride in his overweening belief that it was the Emancipists who had made the colony what it was and the Emancipists who held an exclusive right to the possession of whatever it had to offer. If this was linked with the possession of nothing, or very little, it could be accompanied by a frustrated resentment. But when it was linked with financial success it created a unique concept of a self-made man. The Emancipist who had made it had made it twice over.

"On the whole, as a place of punishment, the object is scarcely gained; as a real system of reform it has failed, as perhaps would every other plan; but as a means of making men outwardly honest—of converting vagabonds, most useless in one hemisphere, into active citizens of another, ... it has succeeded to a degree perhaps unparalleled in history." Charles Darwin's comment was made at a later date, but it applied even more aptly to this earlier period. The English government had found a way of turning thieves into honest or more or less honest workers. Beneath the superciliousness and snobberies on top, there was underneath, as well as the drunkenness and gambling and whoring, a contrary drive to achieve a degree of respectability. In a society in which an officer of the colony who had not done particularly well for himself might find it tempting to allow his daughter to marry the son of a merchant who had come to the colony as a convict, or in which a man who had started well but grew wheat might find himself a lesser person than someone of the same type who had started badly but raised sheep, or in which an ex-N.C.O. who failed as a small settler might find himself in much the same boat as an ex-convict who also failed as a small settler, some were of necessity developing a tolerance of a man's past. It was a society in which it could not seem unusual that even the very least persons should achieve respectability.

There was little other impulse: in the whole history of European expansion there were few other European settlements founded with such an official indifference to Christianity as New South Wales. The Church of England held a monopoly, but this was merely a convention of State: in the style of a sceptical age no importance was given to religion as a mainspring. Only one chaplain came out with Phillip and he had to wait five years for a church. He conducted services under a tree, in a store room, in a boatshed, and when he was able to build a church it was only a wattle and daub affair with a thatched roof that convicts burned down five years later in protest against a new rule demanding compulsory church attendance. His successor was the only chaplain for nine years, making do with catechists until three assistant chaplains were appointed. But towards the end of the period there was a small flourish of church building. Other than this, the Wesleyans had a chapel, put up in 1819, and immigrants from the Scottish border built a Presbyterian Church, but it was without a minister. For most of this time the Catholic mass was banned.

Such official religious drive as existed was of the evangelical kind, and along with quarrelsome cavilling and anxious clinging to expatriate prestige, evangelical moralism began to set some of the tone of the colony, or at least some of its ambition. Two of the five governors and both the chaplains were evangelists; the headmasters of the two Orphan Schools were Wesleyans; there was a sprinkling of evangelists among other colonial officials; the one newspaper, when it moralized, did so with exhortations of self-improvement. Religion was a matter of reaching a state of personal grace by reading the Bible, respecting the sabbath and following abstemious habits: some of its main drives were regulation and prohibition. In the last ten years there were official attempts at an enforced sabbatarianism, rules against gambling, reduction in the number of inns, and attempts to reduce the use of women convicts as concubines.

In a convict colony a stress on self-improvement was understandable. Now, to the convenience of such a doctrine (reform made it easier to run the colony), there was added moral belief. Not a great deal else was added. There were three Benevolent Societies, a Sunday School movement was started, and in addition to the colony's 11 private schools there were 15 government schools—although only one in eight of the colony's children went to them. Perhaps the greatest success in the drive for self-government was the establishment of a savings bank in 1819, designed to tempt "poor settlers, mechanics, servants and labourers" not to waste their money on drink and gambling, which would leave them "poor, vicious and unmarried", but to bank it and so learn the pleasures of "economy, industry and matrimony". It was by such means, after a long silence, that the faith of the colony was proclaimed —as one of respectability.

Although most of the convict men died without leaving families the convicts were not to prove an extinct race. From their loins they were to found what was quickly accepted as a new kind of people. From the marriages into which about one in ten of them entered or from the taking of mistresses or from chance sexual acts or from prostitution there came the first generation of native-born white Australians, the "currency lads" and the "currency lasses" (so called to distinguish them from the "sterling" of the British-born) at once believed by observers to be a distinctive type.

As the children of the convicts grew into men and women they were, generally speaking, "self-respecting, moral, law-abiding, industrious and surprisingly sober". Whatever the changes in the convicts themselves, they were not as great as this extraordinary change between the generations. Perhaps this came partly from the not unusual reaction of the children of immigrants, that they should be ashamed of their parents: with, in this case, a special contempt for what was seen as vice and depravity, and with the special circumstance that a large minority of the children were illegitimate. Only a sixth of them went to school; a convict's child could be out in the world ten years old, earning good wages, and at thirteen "a perfect little man, learned in all the ways and byways of life". In this they were aided by the colony's almost continuous shortage of willing labour. Some of their sense of independence may have come from this economic opportunity for early self-reliance: but perhaps it was also part of their inheritance, freed of the shiftlessness of their parents.

The first native-born white Australians were soon being described as tall, slim, tough and active; although at times awkward and quick-tempered, they were taken to be well-meaning; they were believed to be at all times self-reliant and resourceful; to hear them talk you'd have thought they owned the place. They were the custodians of the colonial style. They knew how one was supposed to behave in New South Wales.

Colonists were now looking for some other name for the huge island in one little bit of which they were living. Naval men had begun to turn the old "Terra Australis" into the new "Australia", and by 1817 Governor Macquarie was using this word in his dispatches. At a party of forty people held in the house of a successful Emancipist on 27th January to celebrate the colony's foundation a song was sung to the tune of "Rule Britannia", which, after suggesting that Australia's rise was Neptune's wish, bore the injunction "Rise, Australia! with peace and plenty crowned, Thy name shall one day be renowned" and concluded with the boast that "While Europe's powers in conflict do Exhaust the Flower of the brave, Here peace shall flourish, shall flourish—None conspire with human blood their soil to lave."

The native born could hardly describe themselves cumbrously as "New South Welshmen". But they needed some way of talking about themselves beyond "currency lad" and "currency lass"; they began to find it in the new word "Australian". The belief began to stir that "Australians" were best.

The brown men whose ancestors had first discovered the continent were now being pushed out of the way. Since the British government considered that they had no title to the land they hunted over, there was no need even to exchange axes or blankets for marks on paper; their land belonged to the English king, his to dispose of as his governors decided. The general instructions were to try to gain the friendship of the "natives", but since they had no tribal organizations that could organize or sustain serious resistance to the invaders or even negotiate with them, the natives could be got out of the way without friendship.

It was usually incomprehensible to the natives that they could not still take whatever food, including the strangers' animals, they could find on their old hunting territories, and sometimes they speared a few white men for what was seen as their theft and generally dishonourable dealing. To the settlers, the natives were troublesome and sometimes destructive animals rather than human beings. By decision of the English king, the natives were British subjects, bound to the king's law, with their own laws unrecognized and largely unknown; so if they gave trouble they were treated not as landholders resisting invaders, but as criminals. In Van Diemen's Land some Royal Marines killed forty natives in 1804 because they were armed. They did not realise that they were armed for hunting, not raiding.

It had been the British government's theory that, as part of the lower orders of the colony, the natives would learn the benefits of a superior civilization and, with industry and sobriety, take their modest place as labourers or as small farmers, converted to Christianity and protected by British law. But what the natives most saw of the new civilization was its anarchy and barbarity: its land thefts, its peculiar internal institutions such as flogging, chaining men together, hierarchic social divisions, ritual drunkenness. It was not long before it became an alternative amusement to cockfights for the invaders to get a couple of natives drunk and set them against each other.

A Native Institution was set up at Parramatta for children to be introduced to the consolations of the new civilization that was all around them. But it did not work. For a few years annual meetings of natives were held with the governor bestowing insignia of chieftainship on representatives of a people who, since they did not have chiefs, could not understand what on earth he was doing. In the first year in which these meetings were held, after the murders of some white stockmen, the governor issued a proclamation, on the one hand offering land grants to natives and on the other permitting settlers to fire on them if they did not leave a farm.

Chapter 2

THE NOBS
The 1820s and early 1830s

A second England

In England estates had become larger; it seemed part of the rational order of things to "divide the country amongst opulent men". Yet here were the governments of New South Wales and now the separate colony of Van Diemen's Land still attempting to encourage small farmers; even worse, they were granting land to convicts, thereby threatening the fabric of British society by weakening the idea of punishment. Now small land grants were to be discouraged: land should go to men with capital. By the end of the 1820s a new kind of Old Virginia was being established in the colonies, with British and Irish convicts instead of African slaves.

To turn convicts into slaves it was necessary to treat them more harshly. Despite the disappointments of a puzzling country, the earlier system of land grants had had some sense of democratic pioneering: even if restricted, it gave unfortunate men a chance to hoist themselves up a bit in material reward or—if they failed—it at least offered the self-regard of not working for a master, and the recognition of a possibility of *reform* may have given at least a little idealism to a very hard-headed colony. Now, although a ticket-of-leave system still operated and a convict still had a chance to make good before his time was up, the granting of land to ex-convicts was abolished; and compassionate hope that men might change became even more constricted. For those "government men" who had to serve their time there were now to be no more easy jobs in town, apart from positions in the hospitals or as servants to government officials, or as constables (a much sought after post, because of the bribes, particularly from sellers of sly grog). Both the use of transportation as a deterrent and the material interests of the colony seemed best served by sending convicts to farms as assigned labourers. The slaves were ready for the plantations.

The masters of the plantations were also being assembled: the new settlers attracted by land and forced labour were men such as officers on half pay from the Army, the Navy or the East India Company, or Scottish or Irish small gentry, or sons of English large tenant farmers. In New South Wales the properties of men like these began to spread south from the Sydney plain, west from the mountains, and to the north along the Hunter Valley; in Van Diemen's Land they stretched across the country between Hobart and Launceston. A few of the colonial estates had display houses of the kind that denoted success in the British Isles. On the most ambitious estates little villages were set up by colonial squires. Even the less successful lived with the modest confidence of lesser gentry.

Now that the colonies were more appropriate to gentlemen it was useful to restrict the boundaries of settlement, for things to be made more orderly. Since the colonies were prisons, right from the beginning there had been an unusually cautious control of settlement, to which was added the stinginess of the soil, the caprices of the weather, and the limits of economic circumstance; with a movement out to the frontiers that was slow and constricted and had little aspiration about it except, for the well-to-do, the hopes of fore-closing, there was not much surprise when in 1829 the New South Wales government declared a limit to the area available for further settlement. Partly to keep things under control and partly to catch up with survey work which was years behind, a border was declared beyond which settlement was forbidden. Two years later land grants were abolished: if people wanted land they could buy it.

In the new colonial upper groups now being created there were divisions as to who was most gentlemanly. On one side were those who had got there first. Now derided by some as "the ancient nobility", they were the members of the "respectable establishments" set up by early military or civil officers, or N.C.Os, or merchants turned landowners, or the few early free settlers. They had shown such a quick sense of dynasty-founding that there was already talk of establishing a colonial Order so that with new titles the "ancients" could be distinguished from other men; but they also distinguished themselves from the antiquity of the rich Emancipist families by seeing themselves as "the pure merinos", taking the name of a fine-wool sheep to dramatize their freedom from convict taint. However, the social dominance of anciently noble pure merinos was challenged by the immigrant gentry. There were derogatory stories of the ungentlemenly origins of some of the ancients. ("Very strange tales are told of gentlemen of New South Wales".) But, since the aristocratic idea is based on being there first, in a few years even the less-than-ancient might pride themselves on an earlier arrival than someone else.

In the rest of New South Wales and Van Diemen's Land these divisions meant much less. The few hundred landed gentlemen, whether ancient or modern, pure merino or crossbred, made up most of "the nobs" of the colonies. They became justices of the peace; the few who imitated the great British landed "improvers" formed agricultural societies and experimented with viticulture, horticulture, the improvement of grain and stock, and methods of preserving meat; if public meetings were to be held they preferred to chair them. Power does not seem to have rested lightly on their shoulders. Complaining of their "supercilious intolerance", one observer warned would-be immigrants that the nobs had "... so long been used to dealing with the poor wretched convicts... and to taunt and mock them if they talk about seeking redress for any ill treatment, that... they would wish to treat free people in the same way."

Understandably, the nobs followed the ambitions of the upper classes of the homeland. They wanted to live like English gentlemen. This meant that, as well as establishing display country houses, they wanted the same leisure interests. But there was hardly any system of tenant farmers in the colony—even the least significant farmer preferred to own his few acres rather than to rent them; so, however much the nobs might put much of the work off onto overseers, they themselves usually had to pay attention to the control and working of their properties. Nevertheless they did their best to make the two colonies "a second England". Various kinds of honoured vermin were imported and let loose (joining as pests the house mice, ship rats and sewer rats that had been involuntarily introduced), and hunt clubs were formed to chase them across the bush.

The lesser orders were despised as un-British. A Sydney newspaper said of them in 1826: "They have lost their English spirit and have degenerated into *Australians*." However, of the nobs' determined Englishness it was said in London: "To form a clear conception of the 'upper classes' here, suppose all the natives of France annihilated, and the whole country belong to the English residents of Boulogne."

Associated with the landowners were the town nobs—the court of the governor, the "heads of departments", some of the leading professional men, the principal officers of the garrison regiments. Most of this upper group were invited more often than anyone else to Government House. Respectability still began at the governor's table. Connected with them was another (if lesser) town superior class—of civil officers, professional men, property owners and a few of the more ambitious merchants—who were conscious, sometimes for good reason, sometimes for none, of a sense of education.

Their habits deriving from an English society in which cultivated leisure pursuits were founded in economic classes, they were somewhat adrift in a colonial town in which economic classes were developing differently and in which already some of the well-to-do did not attempt—as *arrivistes* did back home— to heighten their respectability by education. Nevertheless those who saw themselves as the cultivated lined their studies with books, discussed Scott and Byron and went to lectures by gentlemen scientists. In Sydney the exclusive group to which they could belong was the Australian Subscription Library, a privately established lending library in which a blackball could create as great a scandal as in a gentleman's club in London.

It was an affront to these upper groups that the governor had so much political power and that, except by lobbying and factionalism, they had so little. In 1823 the British Parliament passed an Act for "the better Administration of Justice in New South Wales and Van Diemen's Land and the more effectual Government thereof", but nothing much was gained. A small Legislative Council was established, but the five members of the first council were all officials, their meetings were chaired by the governor, their business was decided by him, they had no control over his executive acts, and they were committed to an oath of secrecy. The Council's greatest use was the opportunity of inspiring officials to act against the governor. More hope came from the Supreme Court, now also established. There was provision for a beginning of trial by jury and before a law became effective it had to be "certified" by the Chief Justice as to its Britishness: when one of the governors instigated measures to restrict the freedom of the new newspapers now being started, the Chief Justice refused to certify them, thereby, in passing, granting the colony freedom of the Press. He was of the opinion that ". . . the people are far more intelligent, active and determined than in any of the older colonies; they are newly sprung from intellectual and enterprising England . . . to govern them, as one governs . . . our Indian possessions, is quite impossible." The Legislative Council was made a bit bigger; more officials were added to it and to them were added men who were not officials, but were nominated by the governor. As a matter of course, it was the most important of the nobs who were nominated.

The position was rounded off in the mid-1820s when the Church of England became the endowed Church of New South Wales. An Archdeacon was appointed at $2,000 a year; he was put on the Legislative Council, and the government schools were handed over to the Church. The Archdeacon announced that he would be the chief inspector and that teachers would provide detailed records so that he would know what they were doing. There seemed little doubt that he would be able to carry out his plans: for its income the Church was to be given one-seventh of all the settled lands of New South Wales.

The new "Natives"

The Englishness of this upper group was discounted among those in whom pride in colonial birth was extending. There was a magazine called *The Currency Lad*, a boat called *The*

Currency Lass and a cricket club called *The Currency Lads*, but now another name was developing for the locally born. The brown Australians were being called "blacks" instead of "natives", so the white colonial-born took the title and spoke of themselves as "the Natives". When asked in a magistrate's court what his religion was, a 12-year-old boy replied: "I am a Native."

It was hard to know what being "a Native" meant: there was not much attempt to dress the colonies up in the language of new human hope and such as there was usually derived its rhetoric from liberal or radical thought in England, or, more daringly, from America. However, W. C. Wentworth, a colonial-born nob, and many well-to-do Emancipists used aspects of Nativeness in their general push against the majority of the nobs, whether ancient or imported, who wanted to turn the colonies into a second England: there was particular derision for the idea of "an English gentleman, *Australian born*"; but the ideal they opposed to this was often merely that of "a new Britannia in another world", Britain all over again, with a few faults corrected, so that the colonial-born could become better at being British than the English. Thus, in the more articulate debate about what the colony was, perhaps the main distinction was between the *second* England of the nobs and the *new* Britannia of the better-off Natives and Emancipists.

Part of the pride of Nativeness was simply *being there* (a favourite toast at Native dinners was "The land, boys, we live in") and the most important part of this was that, like the ancients, Natives asserted their superiority because they had *been there first*. Unlike the ancients and other nobs, however, Natives hated newcomers from the British Isles ("the self-imported devils"). The convicts and ex-convicts felt that the colony should belong to them—they had earned their right to it by being transported and doing most of the hard work—and the Natives developed this belief even more stringently, especially after land policy became more restrictive and favoured the moneyed immigrant, with no particular provision for the native born.

Nativeness seems to have been a sub-culture of aggrieved ordinariness, its tone set to an unknown extent by convict influence: literate nobs wrote little about it except in disapproval: it found memorable expression mainly in ballads or exemplary tales of rebellion. When the robbers of the bush lost their first description as "banditti" and became "bushrangers", they were turned by ballads into heroes displaying some of the Native virtues. The ballad of the death of Bold Jack Donohoe, the wild colonial boy, later spread to other parts of the English-speaking world, even if it was to be banned for a while in public houses in New South Wales. ("I'd rather roam these hills and dales, like wolf or kangaroo, / Than work one hour for Government, cried bold Jack Donohoe.") The story was often retold of a convict who, when challenged by a nob as to who he was, replied "I am a man", shot his interlocutor dead, and then from the scaffold said: "Good-bye, my lads. I shot the Doctor not for gain, but because he was a Tyrant. . . . If any of you take to the bush shoot every tyrant you come across."

Visitors were increasingly detailed in giving their impressions of the Natives. Some found them as monotonous as the landscapes and as uniform as the seasons, but in the more favourable view Natives were tall, slender and fair; they had extremely good health; they showed a manly independence of disposition and a quality of downrightness that secured truthfulness and sincerity at least among themselves; they were free-hearted, generous, shrewd and good-natured; every man seemed to consider himself equal with all the rest: they were a race with whom one of the worst reproaches was to be a *crawler*. There were, however, times when they showed a taciturnity proceeding from natural diffidence and reserve. "They could do everything," said one writer, "but speak."

A seaport civilization

To begin with the British had claimed less than half of the three million square miles of the continent. Then in the mid 1820s, when more than a million square miles of what had already been claimed was still quite unknown to them, they drew a new line on the map and said they owned some hundreds of thousands of square miles more. On the northern edge of this new claim, on a tropical island off the mainland coast 2,000 miles north-west of Sydney, they built a log fort. The Union Jack was run up in front of an assembled 57 soldiers and 44 convicts; then, after five years of scurvy, tropical diseases and food shortages, and after two ships had been captured by Indonesian pirates and most of their crews slaughtered, the flag came down and the settlement was abandoned. In the meantime 200 miles to the east a stockade and a log tower were built, thatched huts went up and a palisade was constructed. This settlement of 77 people was perhaps intended to be another Singapore, but just when, in 1829, regular contact seemed possible with the Indonesian trepang-fishing fleets that visited the northern coast each year the settlement was closed.

In the south Union Jacks went up at two other little settlements—one near the south-eastern tip of the mainland, and the other 1,600 miles away near the south-western tip. Then the flags came down and the people in the settlements packed up and sailed away. Despite these failures the remaining million square miles of the continent were claimed and just before the end of the decade, on the west coast something like a month's sea voyage from Sydney, a new colony, the Swan River Colony, to be established without convicts, was set up on a five-year trial, on the prompting of a syndicate of speculators (who had broken up before the colony started). The new settlers raised the tents they had brought with them from England, abandoned some of their possessions on the beach, and waited for the surveyors to come back and tell them what kind of land they had come to. They did not know that they were on the edge of one of the biggest stretches of arid country in the world.

The first steamboat arrived in Sydney in the early 1830s. By plying up the rivers and along the coast small steamers began to help strengthen and then extend the coastal settlements. Newcastle had ceased to be a convict jail, becoming instead a company town controlled, with nob support, by an English company that had a monopoly of Newcastle's coal, and consignments of convicts to work it. In its place a penal settlement had been established at Moreton Bay, 450 miles north of Sydney, after an explorer found some shipwrecked sailors there who took him to the Brisbane River and displayed its commodiousness. To many people in Sydney and

Hobart the sea still seemed easier going than the land. Operating with a ruthlessness for which a few of them were killed and eaten, traders continued to infiltrate the South Pacific Islands and some adventurers joined the courts of the chiefs. Enough people moved into New Zealand as traders and settlers for a Resident to be appointed in 1832.

A big business for Sydney and Hobart became whaling. Prices were going up for the wax in whales' heads that could be made into candles, for the bones in their mouths that could be shaped into corsets and umbrella frames, and the blubber that could be turned into lamp oil. Sydney merchants now had enough money to go into the whaling business for themselves. Ships were built for deep-sea whaling; whaling stations, with whaleboats and boiling down works, were set up on southern Australian coasts and New Zealand. While exports of wool were increasing, whale products increased more; they were the colony's biggest export: the long eluded export staple seemed to have been found and the first impression of visitors when they landed in Sydney or Hobart was that the colonies represented a seaport civilization.

Dependent on government allocation neither of land nor of convicts, ships providers furnished the Australian whaling fleets and visiting whalers from America and Britain; shipbuilders constructed sloops, brigs, schooners, whaleboats; merchants bought and sold; and hundreds of families lived on the earnings of the whaling crews. To the oligarchic government-sponsored landed society with its forced labour, the "free enterprise" of the sea frontier was so distasteful that some of the nobs, like the governors, preferred, so far as they could, to keep out of town.

Chapter 3

THE IMPROVERS
1830 to early 1850s

"At last we anchored within Sydney Cove. . . . In the evening I walked through the town, and returned full of admiration at the whole scene. It is a most magnificent testimony to the power of the British nation. Here, in a less promising country, scores of years have done many times more than an equal number of centuries have effected in South America. My first feeling was to congratulate myself that I was born an Englishman." When Charles Darwin said this, after his visit to Sydney, it was not merely chauvinism that made him attribute Sydney's material success to its British origin, but the evidence of his own eyes—by a comparison between the material success of what he saw in New South Wales and the material failure of what he had recently seen in Latin America. The material achievements of the colonists of New South Wales did not come from new talents that sprang uniquely from colonial circumstances; they came because the colonists brought certain characteristics from the British Isles which reacted to those circumstances. They were part of a society that was on the move.

In Britain it was, along with other and opposite things, the Age of Improvement with its optimistic faith that things could be made better and better; there was enough of Britain in New South Wales for it to take over many of Britain's Improvements. Steam engines had been invented in Britain; so Sydney put steam engines into some of its flour mills and steamboats ran across Sydney's harbour as ferries; when roads were macadamized in Britain they were later macadamized in Sydney; when omnibuses were introduced in Britain they were later introduced in Sydney; when streets were lit by gas in Britain, streets were later gas lit in Sydney. By 1850 Sydney began to build its first railway. (One of the few Improvements that Sydney was able to export back to Britain was its invention of the pre-stamped envelope.)

The idea of Improvement expanded. As well as steamboats the colonies imported friendly societies, trade societies, temperance societies, building societies; as well as omnibuses they adopted Catholic emancipation; as well as using gas lamps and macadamized roads they contemplated new systems of education and government. Just as, by careful breeding, sheep could be made better wool producers, so by opening accounts at saving banks artisans could become better persons, and by education all mankind might reach excellence.

A life of his own

There seemed too many people in the British Isles: the unemployed were destitute, and at times in parts of Ireland and Scotland there was not enough to eat. The new use of coal and iron, the new ways of making textiles and the new steam engines were destroying old habits: in the new towns there were disorders and dangers of a kind no one knew what to do about. Periods of riot were followed by spasms of coercion. Except in Ireland there were pauses of reform (there was no pause in the coercion of Ireland), but dreams of redress or perfection faded; the imaginings of frustrated hope floated overseas. While in 1815 less than 2,000 emigrants left the British Isles, the average annual emigration was 65,000 in the 1830s; by the late 1840s a quarter of a million or more left each year.

In the first small rush of the 1820s, hardly anyone had emigrated to New South Wales or Van Diemen's Land; a four month voyage was too long and cost too much. North America was quicker, cheaper, and seemed to offer more. Then in the early 1830s it was realized that the decision to sell land in the Australian colonies would provide a fund to pay people to get out of Britain without expense to the British taxpayer. For the next twenty years there were various schemes of assisted emigration to the Australian colonies—for one period two different schemes were tried at once—and, although there were punctuation points when emigration was suspended because of depression in one colony or the other, 200,000 people emigrated to Australia. (During the same period 1,750,000 people emigrated to the U.S.)

Almost two-thirds were "bought" by assistance schemes; there was fear that the best immigrants would go to North America, leaving the Australian colonies to make do with second best. "Who, we ask, would be so foolish as to emigrate to New South Wales?" demanded an English magazine in 1835, comparing the uncertainties of Australia with the "decency of manners and comfortable life" of Upper Canada. (Perhaps the reply was contained in the heading of an Australian propaganda pamphlet: "Comfort for the Poor! Meat Three Times a Day!") Many assisted emigrants were paupers, gathered from workhouses, orphanages, mendicity societies, refuges for the destitute. For two years there was a special hunt for Irish orphan girls; at another time children were collected from the ragged schools (70 out of 178 children in one emigrant ship died of measles). Parish officers sometimes pushed off those they least wanted, and ships' brokers, keen for the bounty money, were not always careful about whom they picked—of the first of the special 14 shiploads of women sent out in the 1830s to redress the balance of the sexes a high proportion proved to be prostitutes.

The nobs, although wanting labourers, complained about what was coming out. But sometimes it seemed they were complaining that the quality of the immigrants was too high. Paupers were simply men or women made destitute by unemployment and many were trained for better jobs than those the nobs wanted to give them. It was said that to the nobs the ideal immigrant was "an able-bodied single man from an agricultural county—humble, ignorant and strong". For most immigrants the idea of working for wages on Australian farms was repulsive and many of them stayed in town. Paupers wanted to return to being human beings.

In twenty years, by outnumbering the convicts, the immigrants wiped out the freakishness of the convict system and the emphasis on female immigration soon began to balance the numbers of non-convict men and non-convict women (although most of the ex-convicts were left with no consolation but themselves). And some immigrants began to think they were the true makers of the colonies, a sense of importance that came partly from the sea changes that happened to them on the way.

Small bits of the populations of the three nations of the Union—some destitute, some poor, some lower-middling—were put into immigrant ships and for months subjected to the shocks of a crudely enforced equality and fellowship. They were mixed up on a steerage deck which, to begin with, had no dividing partitions; and even when bulkheads sorted out single men, single women, and the married into three odd lots, only a foot-high fence separated berths (sometimes with four people to a berth), and messing was done in further odd lots, groups of ten or so sitting on the deckboards to eat the food dished out from the galley. After a voyage which for many may have proved a critically self-defining period, these batches of haphazardly drawn together people were deposited in seaports in Australia and, either from spontaneous self-congratulation or from what they heard around them, could come to see their act of emigration as a sign of particular independence and enterprise, which now deserved some reward.

Perhaps even more important than this new sense of independence were the already established habits they brought with them. For a man who grappled with the harshness and oddness of rural life many of his old ways would be destroyed; but a man who got a job in town somewhat similar to his work at home might continue in some of his former habits of Improvement. Since so many stayed in the towns it was their Improving ways that helped change the colonies, because some of the ways of the immigrants were newer than the traditional ways of Van Diemen's Land and New South Wales.

In the eighteenth century "Irish temperament" was often attributed to the English poor, but in the nineteenth century the temperament of some of the working class was seen to be changing to new and more methodical habits, with new ideas of mutual-organization, perhaps matching the changes brought by the new industrial machinery and quite different from the traditional attitudes.

Until mass immigration started, the colonies' population

seems to have been more traditional than methodical. Thieves were a highly traditional class, and, whether Irish or not, given to "the Irish temperament". But free immigration brought a much bigger proportion of those who represented change in the British Isles. To some of them improvement was to be found in the "mutuality" of collective action. The habit of getting together to do something in common had been established in English manufacturing towns, and immigrants from these towns brought to Australia this new sense of group morality, in which those who did not conform (either through treachery or eccentricity) were treated with intolerance. In certain ways this was a repetition of convict exclusiveness. But the institutions of thieves' honour did not have chairmen or secretaries, minute books or points of order.

Of the "mutual" groups the oldest were the friendly societies. A small group of men would contrive to try to protect themselves against the costs of sickness, unemployment and funerals. From meeting together in an orderly way, in arranging to keep funds safe, in working out rules by which they could disagree without splitting up, they would learn much self-discipline and collective purpose. In the new "mutuality" even having a good time was made more methodical—with organized club nights and annual outings. There were more than a million friendly societies in Britain before mass emigration to the Australian colonies, and in the colonies small friendly societies soon grew beyond measure, in little groups of men who worked together, or lived near one another, or shared some other common interest. When the big amalgamations of friendly societies began in Britain, great names began to echo in the southern hemisphere: the Manchester Unity Independent Order of Odd Fellows was established in Sydney in 1839 and members began meeting immigrant ships to help British members of the order; the 1840s saw the foundation of the Independent Order of Rechabites, the Ancient Order of Foresters, the Grand United Order of Odd Fellows. Native improvisation waited until 1849 for the formation of the Australian Mutual Provident Society.

There was a similar transplanting of the early institutions of trades unionism. In the first half of the nineteenth century the early trade clubs and trade societies of Britain, probably growing out of the habits of mutuality of the friendly societies, were organized by skilled artisans who wanted to keep their status while things around them were changing; such organization was not known to the farm labourers or domestic servants who made up the larger part of the British work force or to most of the workers in the new factories. Their skills were not scarce enough, nor their wages high enough for them to be able to take a stand against their masters. In the Australian colonies, where a workshop might consist of only ten hands, the trade societies were equally confined to the traditional skilled trades, but they were active on questions of status, work conditions and margins. Individual trade societies came and went, but they were replaced by others. By the late 1840s there were a couple of dozen trade societies in Sydney, with others in Hobart and Melbourne, and at one of the protest meetings that had become popular in Sydney a Chartist immigrant was able to say with some meaning to his audience: "I belong to the largest class of men in the colony—the working class."

Starting in the United States at the beginning of the nineteenth century, Temperance Societies, devoted to the ideal of mutual Improvement, spread to Ireland and then to England; in the 1830s they were transferred to the colonies. Temperance Halls were built, providing general community centres; magazines were produced; festivals and processions were arranged (in which, to symbolize the universality of the movement, the marchers might wear rosettes made up of the national colours of England, Ireland and Scotland). Oratory was one of the entertainments of the age and a special temperance oratory developed, promising a brighter future for mankind. To show that "rational enjoyment and merry-making can be kept up well without the aid of stimulants", "tea parties" were held, sometimes with dancing till dawn. In the 1840s the battle within local temperance movements between adherents of moderation and the newly powerful Total Abstainers provided one of the greatest issues of the times, with opportunity for group activity, political contest and the display of rival views of the meaning of life.

The immigrants were called "Emigrants" (often "bloody Emigrants") as if they were remarkable more for their leaving than for their arriving. But since, except during the great depression of the early 1840s, jobs were not scarce, the hostility of the Natives was practised mainly against those Emigrants who did remarkably well out of the colony. The Improving ideas and methodical habits that the Emigrants brought were also known to some of the Natives, but the huge increase in the proportion of Emigrants probably made the growth of a methodical and institutional approach to "mutuality" stronger than if it had been left to the Natives, and it may have strengthened that faith in respectability that had already emerged alongside the licentiousness of the colony.

Sydney, said Charles Darwin, "may be faithfully compared to the large suburbs which stretch from London". And while in the bush the Natives might begin to seem to have special wisdom, and to provide metaphors of independence that seemed to give a unique sense of locality, in the towns it was the Emigrants, expressing the hopes of the suburbs of London, who seemed to express wisdom. Prompted by impulses that came from Britain and were perhaps in some sense "artificial", they strengthened the institutions of mutuality, while what mainly prevailed in the bush was bondage or nomadism, dominated by men who showed the crassest kind of individualism.

A sense of moral shock was common to both Emigrant and Native: that in a colony it required money to be a farmer. The Natives thought the land was "theirs by right". The Emigrants thought not getting land easily an affront to the myth of a happy time when every true man was his own landowner that had quickly grown in the new manufacturing towns of the British Isles. A town worker in England might dream of working his own farm land; his son might transfer that dream to Sydney. It was a dream of the right of the common man to lead some life of his own, on land that was his own, and escape the rest of the world. In Sydney, his dream might seem almost as hard to realize as in Britain.

But now he could at least grow things. In the new softening of leisure pursuits, with amusements such as cock fighting yielding to gentle pastimes, gardening was taken as morally good; and if they could not be yeomen farmers Emigrants could at least tend their gardens. Although speculators were cramming terraces on the hills of Sydney, there was still a detached cottage style, a veranda in front, a paling enclosure and a backyard where a man could grow flowers and vegetables.

Even more important, if an Emigrant could not own a farm, he might now begin to think of owning the cottage he lived in. The building society movement had been slowly developing in England, mostly in the midlands and in the north, but it exploded into popularity in the mid 1840s. In the colonies building societies began to form from 1847. Meanwhile savings banks had opened in all the main towns. In Sydney, through this form of self help, artisans were already financing the building of "the humble cottages springing up in thick clusters in the Surry Hills, at Chippendale, at Pyrmont, at Balmain".

A few years later the British economist W. S. Jevons saw how a labourer or mechanic might have "his own residence on freehold or leasehold land", a couple of rooms often built by himself, to be added to later. A suburb of that period might have looked like the wooden huts of a military encampment, but nevertheless "unpretentious as it is to any convenience or beauties, it yet satisfied him better than the brick built, closely packed, and rented houses of English towns". With a framed certificate of his membership of a friendly society, perhaps also of a temperance society, on his walls, a sense of his right to the dignity of independent existence in his heart, and of the right to respectability of every person in the society around him, a man could walk out into his own backyard and feel that an ambition had been met: he owned some land.

Holding things together

New South Wales and Van Diemen's Land were England, Ireland and Scotland all mixed up into one, and it was feared that maintaining old divisions would provoke new disasters. It was this dread of division that caused the *No religion! No politics!* rules in some of the mutual societies; the rosettes worn in processions sometimes included all three of the national colours of the colonies' three founding nations. For the same reason Improvers' ideas of tolerance as a creative force in human conduct achieved much faster realization in the colonies than they did in Britain. Tolerance was a useful way of holding things together.

A most remarkable result of the new tolerance was the

quick destruction of the special position of the Church of England. Even when it was the established church some of the nobs had worshipped with more than one denomination, not finding religious dogma and denominational disputes important enough matters to split a colony. It was only within the church itself that there was much concern when in the early 1830s it ceased to be the State church: to have kept it as the monopolistically endowed government church would have risked dangerous tension. Even in the British Isles the Church of England was "in danger", so, with a government of Whig Improvers in London and the Improving Governor Bourke in Sydney, there was a chance to display the now fashionable religious tolerance.

The government cancelled the grant to the Church of England of a seventh of the colony's lands and the monopoly of its public education, and instituted instead a system in which Anglicans, Romans, Presbyterians and Wesleyans— the four main divisions of religion of the British Isles—were all to be subsidized by the government with stipends to "duly appointed" clergymen and grants to match money voluntarily raised for the construction of church buildings. There were now to be four "established churches". (The Independents and the Baptists later also took government money.) There were envious complaints against "turtle and port for the over-fed preacher", and in 1842, because of a depression, a limit to the total amount was fixed, but the subsidy was to last for another twenty years. Each new suburb and country town could look forward to four churches going up, from which, if it wanted to, it could take its pick.

Governor Bourke also tried to set up a system of non-sectarian government schools, with non-denominational scripture lessons. The Church of England defeated him, but the governor replied with a system of subsidy for *all* church schools that lasted for fifteen years. At the end of the 1840s non-denominational "national" government schools were finally established, but the subsidized church schools were kept as well. Two boards were set up, one for each kind of school. Now New South Wales had one of everything.

With its sense of monopoly outraged, the Church of England seemed to lose its self-possession. It set up a hierarchy of bishops, but the first of them was humiliated at Government House by having to contest his precedence over the Catholic bishop. He had both to write a complaint to a tolerant government in London that Anglicans, not Wesleyans, should have been sent as missionaries to the blacks and then to his own tolerant flock ("A letter of Vindication of the Principles of the Reformation") warning them that they should not contribute money to help put a roof on an unfinished Catholic church.

It was now the emancipated Catholic Church that began to prosper. Its growth helped change the colony. In the 1820s the Catholic Church had not one proper church building, no prominent laymen, and for a while only one priest. By 1850, although its congregation was still predominantly poor and mainly Irish, a few of its best-known members were among the nobs and, helped by government money, its churches, schools and clergy had grown to match its position as the denomination of more than a quarter of the colonists. With an archbishop in Sydney and bishops in other towns, it had established the first Catholic territorial hierarchy under the British crown since the Reformation. The Catholic Mrs Caroline Chisholm was one of the most influential private persons in the colony; priests were in the forefront of movements for self-improvement and respectability.

In Melbourne's biggest procession the Father Mathew Total Abstinence Society was followed by the Rechabites; after the German Union came the St Patrick Society. After the masons came the priests. The Catholic Church saw itself as an integrated (if different) part of the community, even if the Protestant Irish had set up Orange Lodges; and now that the Anglican ascendancy was destroyed the Catholics had become the main enemy of the other denominations. The growth of the Catholic Church led many non-Catholic clergy to believe that Rome was planning domination of Australia, a hypothesis that seemed confirmed when the Catholics, although professing, and in other fields practising, a determination to join community activities, set up their own temperance societies which flaunted their independence in street processions, with brass bands and regalia. The Romanist plot seemed even more fully established when the Catholic bishop came back as Archbishop of Australia, and was escorted from wharf to cathedral by 2,000 Catholics, with a temperance band playing "See the Conquering Hero Comes". Nevertheless, despite whatever hostility existed, and however wide or narrow it was, the priests could follow the masons in a procession. Pius IX was not yet causing the Church to atone for his own earlier liberalism.

It is difficult to estimate how much of the anti-Catholic agitation was a matter of pulpits and clerical pamphlets that did not reach far into the community. There may not have been much readership, for instance, of a pamphlet one Anglican clergyman produced under the title "Are the Catholics of Port Phillip Tridentine Romantists?" What at first may have been more significant than anti-Catholic feeling was feeling against the Irish of "Pat-*riot*-ism". As one Sydney newspaper put it: "The Irish are ignorant, turbulent, mentally debased and totally unqualified for the elective franchise." Nevertheless here, too, there was integration. The Irish may not have been liked by some, but they were sharing the colonial experience; they did not see themselves with quite such separateness as did the floods of Irish immigrants who were coagulating in the cities of the United States.

The faith of the improvers

It was an age when the Press was of more interest than the pulpit. Some of them half-magazine, some denominational, some temperance, some political, newspapers came and went at a rate that usually had ten existing at once in Sydney, but even by 1850 the number of people of New South Wales likely to be at church on Sundays was about half that in the British Isles. The Legislative Council had no prayers, an innovation that caused one critic to complain that the Council was "under the stigma of being the only legislative assembly in the world which, as such, makes no recognition of Divine Providence". There was no new sustained religious enthusiasm like the revivalism that gave Methodists and Baptists big new congregations in the United States and caused the creation of new sects on the North American frontiers.

To the official indifference to religious impulse that had marked the colony's founding was added the private indifference of many of the convicts, and of the immigrants who came from the "heathen" cities thrown up by industrializing Britain. In this climate the transplanted churches seemed to loose some of their sap. To the more tolerant nobs the clergy could appear mere chaplains of respectability, their emphasis on respectability both reflecting a newly growing belief in the British Isles and meeting the needs of a convict colony. Diaries and letters show that some of the prominent persons in the colony did not lack individual faith, but their faith was often almost private.

It was only when the government began subsidizing the churches that the number of church buildings began to match the population. Within five years the number of church buildings doubled. Then it doubled again. But faith remained thin. The churches struggled bitterly between themselves for pupils and school subsidies, but it seemed mainly a matter of possession; there was not much religious instruction given in the church schools and the poorer people who were their main customers often did not care whether the school a child attended was run by the denomination to which he belonged. Often the Presbyterians were favoured because of their better reputation as teachers.

The Catholics provided the greatest community sense of religion, providing not only religious faith but also, although the Church was led by English Benedictines, a sense of Irishry. As "the Church of the Penitent" the Catholic mission to the convicts combined old compassion (even if at times affronting with what seemed an overzealous soul-snatching at the gallows) with some of the new Improvements. The Catholics achieved some reach into the otherwise almost religion-less country areas: so did the Anglicans; but while Irish shepherds were likely to respond to Irish priests English shepherds were likely to see an English parson as a master.

The Anglicans and the Presbyterians had fallen into the same internal divisions that were straining them in England and Scotland. The English Church was not sure whether it was Catholic or Protestant. Did it rely for its spiritual power on consecration or conscience? Congregations of largely Evangelical origin were puzzled by the tolerance of the ancient nobility who saw *any* religion as useful in a prison. The other Established Church of the British Isles, the Presbyterian Church, fell into four pieces, partly because of the turbulence of personal relations, but mainly as a reflection of the schism in Scotland.

What religious revival there was came mainly from "shopkeepers' Methodism". The Wesleyans had four good years from 1840 to 1843, during a depression, and they trebled their numbers; but their usual state was summed up by a Methodist Minister who said: "We have at times appeared just on the eve of revival amongst the people, and then something has transpired that has appeared to put an extinguisher upon the gracious flame."

Next to the thinness and divisions of religious belief the Improvers juxtaposed the faith that only the spread of knowledge would improve the general human condition. In discussion on colonial education the view that elementary education was mainly a matter of preparing the poor for suffering the indignities of this life with hope of reward in the next had quickly yielded to views such as that it was a "sacred and necessary duty" to use education for moral reform in a convict colony, or that "a child must be taught to reason", so becoming a better or more useful person (a view expressed as early as 1803), or that "the diffusion of knowledge" was good in itself or a basis for "good citizenship" or for success in an occupation.

Views like these were most clearly expressed by the colony's Scottish schoolmasters. In England education was more backward than in most other parts of Western Europe, but Scotland had had an education system for more than a century, and it was probably no accident that in New South Wales, despite their smaller numbers and their schisms, the Presbyterians ran the second biggest proportion of church schools, and about a third of the pupils were not Presbyterians. The most notable of these Scottish schoolmasters, Carmichael, a Benthamite who had experimented with several ambitious private schools in New South Wales including an *école normale*, saw the teaching of religious opinions as "no part of the duties of an ordinary schoolmaster"; the Bible should be present in schools, but only as "a book of reference and voluntary perusal".

On his voyage out, he found that after shipboard lectures some immigrants had mastered logarithms, the first six books of Euclid, and the first two books of *The Wealth of Nations*. Impressed by this industry, he responded to the Improving Governor Bourke's invitation to help found a Mechanics' School of Arts in Sydney, the idea of Mechanics' Institutes and Schools of Arts having become popular in Scotland, then

England. It was opened in 1833 and by 1841 it was reckoned that one in every fourteen adult males in Sydney belonged to it. Mechanics Institutes or Schools of Arts were to be established in almost every town in the colonies, often, in the colonial manner, with government subsidy. In Britain the idea, growing out of the growth of manufacturing, was "to impart instruction to workers in the rules and principles which lie at the basis of the arts they practice"; but with so few industrial arts practised in the colonies there was not much occasion to explain the theory that lay behind them. Instead, at their most ambitious, the institutes concerned themselves with public lectures, at first with a leaning towards science, and then with a dominant concern for the literary. It was as much the age of the public lecture as the age of oratory and the age of the procession, and lectures were part of the amusement available.

The Sydney School of Arts became the strongest intellectual institution in the colonies. Attacked by Charles Harpur, a Native intellectual, as the "School of Charlatans" because it was controlled by Emigrants, it reflected the changing nature of immigration: at its beginning it was dominated by non-political sections of the superior town class and reflected their cultivated interests; with the immigrant rush it became more a means of diversion for the middling, but from it, and reflected in some of the other institutes, came a hope of a national civilizing mission that, by improving minds, would improve morals and spread the gospel of an enlightened humanity. In this sense its function, like that of the temperance movement (despite the backing of the latter by clergymen) was in effect an attempt to provide a secular substitute for religious faith and a sense of community.

A minority belief grew that a sense of common purpose was to be found in a common culture, or, more narrowly, in a national literature. Carmichael said: "If we mean to rise in the scale of nations, we must possess a literature and science of our own." There were suggestions that to this end the arts should be given government support, although to some the moment of national liberation through cultural achievement seemed already at hand: "We do not believe there is a town or province in Europe possessing the same number of inhabitants . . . that can boast of more extended benefits accruing from literary institutions than can we of New South Wales."

In 1845 it was predicted that the colony was "on the verge of a glorious cultural advance".

The black hats

It took New South Wales sixty-two years for the Legislative Council to pass an Act to incorporate a university in Sydney (spoken of by some, in the Sydney manner, as "the national university"). Perhaps even more to the point: while the first of the U.S. public high schools started in 1821, by the end of the century most Australian colonies did not have one public high school. Between the language of the Improvers and their achievement there was a hiatus.

Even in the elementary schools little was achieved. Many teachers were themselves scarcely educated. About half the schools had insufficient books; three-quarters did not have enough furniture. The usual schooling period averaged only two years, with irregular attendance even within that short time; in any case, fewer than half the children attended school. Most elementary schools still practised the old system in which pupils of different ages sat in one class, learnt off set questions and answers, and went up one by one to the teacher's desk to be catechized, although some larger schools, particularly in Sydney, were using the newer monitorial system whereby a teacher taught his brightest pupils and they taught the others. Something was known of more experimental methods being tried in parts of Western Europe—for a while infants' schools were run on a principle of "gentleness rather than coercion"— but on the whole not much. Attempts to introduce vocational training failed.

There was a general drive in the United States in the 1830s for people's schools subsidized by taxes, but there could be no parallel in Australia, because of the lack of local government. It irritated the British that in the colonies the central government accepted such unusual functions as constructing all the roads, controlling all the police, subsidising all the schools and churches, and even giving money to the mechanics institutes. To save money and to introduce what was seen as the basis of all civil liberties the idea of local government with local taxes was regularly pushed from London. The colonists preferred to express their civil liberties by boycotting attempts to make them use them, which they saw as a trick to make them pay extra taxes. By 1850 it was clear that education would remain a central responsibility. Among other things, this meant that not enough money was spent on education.

In the colonies there was not much drive towards the education of the children of even the better-off. Most of what did exist was served by the 250 or so little schools, most of them bad. Parents often treated them with contempt, sometimes speaking in front of their children scathingly of their teachers, sometimes telling the teachers (with a "low-bred malice") how to run their schools. In the United States there was no lack of parents who despised education, but there was a contrary attitude that was based on a sense of religious mission derived from a very different beginning of settlement, and that found one of the symbols of human aspiration in the schoolmistress. There may have been something else: the idea of accepting one's station in life as a matter of divine providence was being discarded in the colonies, but its replacement by the idea of success as the reward of industry and merit was not altogether accepted. It was spoken about and written about because it was a growing idea in the English-speaking world: but the history of the colony, so different in its land settlement from the United States, seemed to suggest that success might be also a matter of special government favour, or of cheating, or gambling, or luck.

Perhaps there was an influence even more profound. The United States was an independent nation; seeking its own character was essential to its survival. Australia was a series of British colonies. In the main cities gentlemen's clubs had been set up on the London pattern and for most of those who ran the colonies they provided the true standards of existence. It was said of the one in Sydney that "all the aristocracy of the colony belong to it." In an appealingly exclusive dream the "Black Hat" life of the Government House set and of the clubs gave to the powerful the truest indication of what life was about. But if their standards were to affect the schools there was a serious weakness: if education were to be a matter of learning the manners and cultivated interests of those of higher status, most of the colonists were not interested. There were experiments in setting up corporate schools to turn Native sons into English gentlemen, but although there were usually three of these at any one time they survived only feebly. Ambitions of imitating the gentlemanly uselessness of the English schools did not come off because colonial hardheadedness sensibly preferred imitations of the Scottish or nonconformist academies as more appropriate to the colonies, but unlike the United States, where the public schools soon became comprehensive schools, there was no official sponsoring of the idea of useful vocational education in the Australian colonies.

Even if the standards of the Black Hats and superior town classes had been more suitable to the colonies, they had themselves been weakened. The manners and cultivated pursuits of an upper class were only feebly represented and they were in any case very largely swept away by colonial economic circumstance. Those of the superior town classes who wished for some of the life of a cultivated gentleman were often frustrated. "Amongst the higher orders, wool and sheep-grazing form the constant subject of conversation," said Darwin. Cultivated aspiration remained: but, instead of spreading the gospel of humanity, the mechanics institutes became libraries for lending light novels. What most strongly survived were the stiff, outward forms of exclusiveness—invitations to Government House, membership of the gentlemen's clubs, black hats.

Chapter 4

THE LAND GRABBERS
1830 to early 1850s (cont'd)

The rush to the grasslands

Cedar cutters opened up much of the coastal settlement of New South Wales. They would establish a camp; the logs would be hauled by bullocks to the nearest river and then rafted to a port from which they would be shipped to Sydney and finally perhaps even to London. As the trees were felled, small farmers, often dairy farmers, would move into the cleared spaces. But the settlement of the grasslands beyond the mountains was the scene of something more dramatic than this: in fifteen years or so—over roughly the period of the immigrant rush to the towns—there was one of the greatest pastoral rushes in history. This was to create a unique society within the general society of the colonies, a society whose leaders were to challenge the existing order and whose very existence was later to provide new metaphors of Australianness.

The scouting parties of this advance were the ex-soldiers, naturalists, surveyors, geologists or bushmen who took up exploring, a tedious, debilitating, and, on several occasions, fatal task in a country where looking for water could take up much of the time and where familiar food was so hard to find that the early explorers took live sheep and cattle to eat on the way, while the later explorers, although travelling lighter, allowed for the possibility of eating their pack horses or camels on the way back.

What first impelled them was the puzzle of the rivers that flowed away from the ocean. When they discovered that these flowed into two main rivers that joined together and headed south-west to an outlet on the southern coast there appeared on the map a river system that looked almost as extensive as those on the maps of other continents; but there was not enough water in it. Nevertheless, by the mid-1830s the unravelling of these rivers led the way to what was to prove much of the most useful land in Australia. The explorers were to have few more successes. They searched for an inland sea, and found deserts; they searched for a great river system in the tropical north, but it did not exist. In the south, one explorer, E. J. Eyre, travelled west for 1,500 miles without passing any running water.

Even some of those who were successful were often melancholy in their reports; because of the unfamiliarity of the strange continent or because it was a time of drought, some dismissed as difficult or useless territories that were among the best Australia had to offer. But whether the explorers were optimists or pessimists, pastoralists were soon driving sheep and cattle into the new country: in one case they followed tracks left by an explorer's bullock drays. By the 1840s sheep and cattle were eating the grass over a huge crescent in the south-east, 1,400 miles along in its inner curve, 400 miles broad at its widest, with the south-east coast on one side and the arid regions on the other. By the middle of the century there were 16 million sheep and 2 million cattle on what was to prove the better part of the hospitable acres of the continent.

At a time when 100,000 sheep might be moving to new runs on the same track, the most heroic form of this expansion was that of the "overlanders", a pastoralist and his men and a whole pastoral property moving on the hoof and on bullock drays; perhaps thousands of sheep, hundreds of cattle, several score of horses and working bullocks, and drays packed with boxes of tools, and sacks and chests containing twelve months supply of food. The driving belief was that there was "something better further out". Some of the pastoralists moved everything, looking for new and bigger runs; others split their flocks or herds, dispersing them in different parts of the colony. More cautiously, others would ride off to the borders of settlement, notch some trees, try to get their new neighbours to take this as meaning something, and then go back for their animals.

What moved them was not the romance of empty spaces but the excitement of a gambler's avarice: flocks of sheep could quickly double and re-double, and an ambitious man might try to snatch twenty times as much land as he needed to be ready for the later re-doublings of his stake. As the runs spread along the river banks those who had staked claims became apprehensive of "run hunters" attempting to bluff their way into part of a run. Scouting parties found information harder to get. It was like a gold rush.

Many of those who raced each other across the wilderness knew nothing about sheep until they had set up their runs. The pastoral rush in Australia arose from a limiting problem, and a sudden opportunity. The limiting problem was that the main form of land transport consisted of drays pulled by teams of six or more bullocks yoked in pairs, and these were too expensive to transport grain more than forty or fifty miles. However, meat could be driven to market on the hoof. And so, to begin with, expansion meant sending cattle or sheep to graze on up-country runs. The smaller settlers went off on their own; the nobs might have several runs in different parts of the colony, looked after by overseers and a few shepherds while the proprietor stayed on his comfortable estate nearer town. Then in the late 1820s came the seizing of sudden opportunity: mills in Yorkshire were increasing their demand so quickly that sheep farmers in Australia, 12,000 miles away, began switching from mutton to wool. A dray load of wool could be worth ten times a dray load of wheat, sometimes twenty times: it could be produced profitably almost any distance from the ports. At the same time sea freights came down so that it was cheaper to ship wool to Britain from Australia than from Germany. From 1830 to 1850 British imports of wool trebled and the Australian share of this increasing market went up by six times. By the middle of the century Britain's principal supplier was Australia.

To some, money from wool seemed as quick and easy as finding gold: it was only necessary to have enough cash to "put it into four legs" and then watch it grow. In the 1830s when the volume of bank loans increased by 600 to 700 per cent gamblers floated on a sea of English credit: they put all their own money into sheep and borrowed up to three times as much again. According to theory, receipts from wool would cover costs, and rapid increases in flocks would make a gambler's fortune. Apart from the merchants and other speculators in town, many of those who went out and controlled their own runs often saw this as just a quick bet: they would make a killing and then go back to Great Britain. But fortunes were lost on the sheep runs like stakes at cards. The oddities of flood, bushfire and drought, the diseases of sheep, the uncertainties of credit, and plain ignorance, led to many disasters. With such a reliance on credit, a man was usually ruined if something went wrong, and his creditors would take over his run; if *they* were also ruined, *their* creditors would take over. In a world of get-rich-or-bust more may have been ruined than got rich.

A depression hit New South Wales in the early 1840s. Banks failed or shut down. In its own exaggerated view of itself the whole colony seemed bankrupt. Total wool production continued to go up but those whose credit had flown too high fell down. In the panic that followed, sheep brought as little as sixpence each. When colonial ingenuity set up "boiling down establishments" which bought sheep at five shillings a head and turned them into tallow, in one year pastoralists who needed cash sold $2\frac{1}{2}$ million sheep to be boiled down. A moratorium and more sensible credit arrangements saved those who were not in too much of a mess, but many pastoralist-speculators had been cleaned out. The rush to the grasslands had seized millions of acres—both within the official borders of settlement and beyond them—and respectable men had become land thieves or, as it was put, "squatters". The most audacious land-grabbing episode occurred when groups of men in Van Diemen's Land sailed sheep over to the southern coast of the mainland where, for blankets and other trading goods, they had claimed 600,000 acres from the blacks. Mainland squatters also drove sheep south into this new area, and soon ships of immigrant squatters, many of them Scottish, arrived. In a few years almost all of southern New South Wales was settled. The government of Sydney had to accommodate itself to this illegal settlement. It declared the area the "Port Phillip District of New South Wales" and appointed a Superintendent with his headquarters in the new town of Melbourne. When squatters moved into pastoral lands outside Brisbane, the Sydney Government declared Brisbane the administrative headquarters of the "Moreton Bay District of New South Wales". New South Wales now had an official area of settlement, two special "districts", one in the south and one in the north, neither of which was intended to have been settled, and between them "the squatting districts", where there was also not supposed to have been any settlement. A large part of the most valuable land in Australia had gone for grabs.

A portion of the sheep owners were city credit institutions or absentee speculators (one of whom piled up 47 runs totalling five million acres) with overseers working for them, and most of the working squatters had started with some money. It is true that some had begun as prudent overseers who had raised their own stock on the side, or been staked by a city investor, and others had established themselves by stealing someone else's animals. But most had started with money. Money was needed to buy sheep and provisions, and to cover costs for the eighteen months or two years before the first wool cheque, and credit went only to those who had cash to begin with. The colonial dream that a propertyless man could get some land and lift himself up in the world by his own efforts became weaker still.

Some of the colonial-born got into the rush—mainly the sons of successful officials and settlers—but the typical squatter was an Englishman, a Scotsman or an Irishman with some money and some education who had come out from Great Britain with the intention of getting rich and then going home again. The discomforts of life on a run were regarded as "a few years of banishment". On the other side of the picture, almost two-thirds of the bush workers in 1840 were assigned convicts, ex-convicts or colonial-born. The pastoral society was dominated by new arrivals who hoped to get rich quickly and go home, but most of the work was done by those who were stuck in the place. Just as the brown Australians were pushed aside in the first invasion, the sons of the first white Australians, the new "Natives", were pushed aside in the second.

The centre of this society that had been created in a few years was made up of several thousand up-country huts. These were the "head stations" where the working squatters lived, or, in the case of runs belonging to absentee speculators, the overseers. If the head station hut were distinguishable from others on the run it was because it was a few feet bigger, and perhaps because it had a veranda (a bark awning over an earth floor). It was made of slabs of timber and a bark roof: its furniture might consist of a bush bedstead with sheepskins or possum rugs, a sea chest, a few iron pots and tin plates. According to the ethos of the wool rush, all a working squatter needed were something to eat and something to lie on while waiting for his new wealth. The human part of his domain consisted of the "out stations", other bark-roofed slab huts. each usually with two shepherds and a hutkeeper, and with a rigid demarcation of duties: each shepherd had a flock to watch during the day while the hut keeper did whatever cooking or cleaning suited his personal style, and at night when the sheep were folded in hurdles made of split palings the hutkeeper slept near by in a simple shelter of laced-up hide, with collie dogs beside him to give warning of native dogs or blacks. Shepherds were despised by other bushworkers as "crawlers after sheep". Shepherds, however, often despised hutkeepers, although they had to be polite to them because the hutkeepers did the cooking.

For most shepherds, squatters and hutkeepers life tended to be lonely and male and monotonous (except when monotony was relieved by catastrophe); breakfast, lunch and supper were all the same meal—mutton, damper and tea. Pannikins of sweet tea, brewed in quart pots and drunk through the haze of pipe tobacco, seemed all that a man needed for solace. The impermanence of the squatters' tenure led to a stylization of improvisation: the expected thing was for a squatter to live on his run like a tramp putting up for the night and to do no more than was necessary for survival. Whatever old aspirations he had to English standards of landed gentlemanliness were washed away by new colonial circumstances. A run might have been established for years without anyone bothering even to dig a vegetable garden: it was as if the huts were tents, the run a nomad's camp, and everyone would later pack up and go away. In such a cult of crudity and impermanence there was no place for display mansions or cultivated leisure interests, nor even for wives or fences.

The same sense of movement impelled other members of this new society. Timber-splitters, hurdle-makers, shearers and dealers roamed through the bush from one run to the next. The main representatives of government in the areas beyond the officially settled territory, the Commissioners of Crown Lands, dressed like officers in the irregular mounted rifles and sometimes adjudicated from the saddle. Attached to them were the border police, dragoons whose concern with blacks and bushrangers kept them on the move. In the ballads that began to celebrate this society, naming its parts and making it real, the heroes were usually going somewhere else. At times it seemed the only people who stayed still were the keepers of the grog shanties. The pastoral expansion did not throw up significant inland towns: A "town" might be little more than a court house, an inn, a store, a few huts, a police barracks. What mattered were the bullock drays, filled with wool as high as a hay stack, and the city ports where the wool was shipped for England and where the intricate social webs of credit and middlemen were being spun, giving extra texture to the cities. Now, as well as sending off the commercially desired parts of whales, the city could also send off the commercially desired part of sheep.

Crudity was the fashion: even in Sydney or Melbourne the squatters might still dress as bushmen, and back on the run sloveliness was an essential part of style. Getting away for a while was one of life's rewards. Working squatters would sometimes hang around in town from the Squatters' Ball in January to the races in March; in the same way, when a contract was up, the shepherds might "drink their cheques", sometimes a matter of a walk of up to a hundred miles to the nearest grog shanty where a week's drinking (and being cheated) could get rid of six months' wages.

Hospitality was equally obligatory, and whether with a squatter or with shepherds it might be much the same, an evening in a hut with pannikins of tea, pipes, yarns, ballads (clean and dirty), chaffing, bush news and talk of the performance of bullocks, horses or dogs. The required approach between two men meeting for the first time was one of frankness and cordiality, but for the convicts and ex-convicts there might be some reserve behind this outward openness. According to observers their *esprit de corps* was an exclusive one, with a reckless internal generosity but a readiness to despise those outside the group.

Homosexuality was common among the convicts, and presumably it spread to some of the others. Usually the only other shared sexual activity available was with black women, who were paid in tobacco and food (and sometimes further rewarded with syphilis and a half caste baby that might be murdered for the sake of tribal purity). What affection existed was usually that between men, particularly that between a man and his "mate", who was usually the man he worked with, with whom he might even divide his earnings. It was said "that a man ought to be able to trust his own mate in everything", and these occupational associations, based on the habit of working in pairs, could become so permanent that although shepherds were always on the move ("a full two thirds of the labouring population of the country is in perpetual migration") they often moved in pairs. They could leave a run, drink their cheque, hump their blankets and clothes onto their backs, and walk off to another part of the colony.

The squatting area made nonsense of orthodox classifications of frontiers: since it relied partly on forced labour it began as something of a "plantation" frontier (yet with many modifications and quick changes); it was also something of a "small farm" frontier because, although its units were big, its manpower was small and, except for the properties controlled by absentees, the owners of the flocks themselves worked; and, in a strange way, it was also something like the "camp" frontier of a gold rush—a temporary settlement in search of quick wealth, ready to get up and go.

Farming was seen as a gamble for quick profits, with something approaching contempt for the land itself. Expansion had meant not improving the land or flock techniques, but getting more land. The squatters saw themselves not as farmers, but as something bigger. The sheep and cattle runs were not called farms. "Farmers" were little men who grew wheat or maize or ran dairy herds, the most despised being the "dungaree settlers", men so poor that they wore clothes of cheap, blue Indian cotton and lived scarcely above the level of barter, selling their wheat for enough meat to keep them going and enough tea and rum to give them solace. The only big advance in agricultural technology was replacing the hoe with the plough. Out on the pastoral runs the cattle and the sheep trod down the native grasses and weeds flourished.

The destruction of the blacks

A rate of economic progress that was greater than in any other British possession was made possible by taking land from the blacks, and by the use of convict labour. It is difficult to see how the pastoral rush could have kept up its thrust without the supply of ex-convicts and assigned convicts. The wool rush coincided with the period of mass transportation of convicts and these extra labourers increased production out of all proportion to their numbers: while fewer than 30,000 convicts were sent out in the first thirty years, four times that number were transported in the following thirty, at the time that Australia was becoming Great Britain's greatest single supplier of wool.

The convicts also built roads, important in reducing graziers' transport costs. The Great North Road, the Great West Road and the Great South Road stretched across New South Wales, built out of human anguish. Some convicts worked on the roads in "iron gangs", iron bands riveted around their ankles and connected with a foot chain suspended from their belts; but even if without irons they could be yoked like cattle to pull their own carts, and were sometimes shut up at night in stockades or in large portable boxes on wheels. Ring bolts were driven into trees to fasten the chains of recalcitrants; flogging posts were put up along the roads. In one month in 1833, 9,000 lashes were ordered in New South Wales and 4,250 in Van Diemen's Land. It became a children's game to lash a tree, pretending it was a convict. For a time there was a fashion for treadmills, then for solitary confinement. Discipline at the penal settlements became more deliberately degrading.

But discontent with the convict system in the colonial towns, along with doubts in London, had political effects. Transportation to New South Wales was suspended in 1840, although it continued in a different form and with greater numbers to Van Diemen's Land. Almost at once the graziers complained of a labour shortage. There was an experiment with a small consignment of Indians; then with some Melanesians; then a couple of thousand Chinese. The anti-transportation cry extended to *No convicts! No coolies! No cannibals!*, but the squatters complained that none of these new labourers were as satisfactory as the convicts they had complained about so bitterly.

For "the blacks" the rush to the grasslands was a guerilla war in which the enemy seized the key rivers, creeks, lagoons and waterholes, drove away the native game, despoiled sacred places, set up dissension by pushing one tribe into the territory of another, and killed insidiously by spreading new diseases.

To the *Sydney Morning Herald* it was clear that it was not the Creator's intention when he caused "this great continent" to rise from the seas that it should remain "an unproductive wilderness". The British people took possession ". . . under the Divine authority, by which man was commanded to go forth and people, and *till* the land". God had not allowed for nomads. To the blacks, the continent was merely "a common—they bestowed no labour upon the land—their ownership, their right, was nothing much more than that of the Emu or the Kangaroo".

If the blacks killed animals or men, the settlers formed armed patrols which in reprisal might slaughter whole groups, perhaps quite innocent, in the scrub; when a force of Native Police was formed it became a new instrument of murder. It was almost impossible to get court evidence against killers of the blacks since blacks were not permissible court witnesses; settlers might shoot blacks in the scrub without anyone knowing, or leave them gifts of flour mixed with arsenic, or sheep carcasses spiced with corrosive sublimate. There were promptings to greater kindness from London and in Sydney protests against the spilling of "black blood", but there was only one significant case when evidence could be brought against the murderers: seven settlers who killed a group of blacks were brought to Sydney, tried and hanged.

In Van Diemen's Land, in an attempt to clear the blacks away from settled areas, a governor organized a drive lasting seven weeks and costing £35,000, but this human hunt found only a woman and a boy: what was left of the Tasmanians was later placed on an island. In New South Wales some settlers were charitable; others found the blacks more useful in odd jobs than they cared to admit; but usually any benevolent policies of government were taken as meddling softness, likely to encourage an ungrateful violence. Towards the end of the 1830s the settlers saw themselves in danger along an 800 mile front from what they saw as an organized "rising" (a type of activity impossible in the fragmented societies of the blacks). This mirage of fear was a mirror projection of their own conduct. It was the blacks who were the victims of a "rising".

In London in 1837 a Select Committee, having examined means of protecting the civil rights of those who had been displaced by the spread of British power and of introducing them to British Christian civilization, recommended that in Australia there should be protectors, missions, reserves, schooling and special interim codes of law for the blacks. Protectorates were set up in the Port Phillip district in 1838: the blacks would be taught how to work and in return they might get rations and clothing. At the same time Christian missions were to be given government money. Turned sober, industrious and God-fearing, the blacks might after all rise to the lower orders.

The remains of tribes, often the remnants of several different tribes, were put together in the protectorates and missions. But, dispossessed, their society shattered, and their new masters determined to take the young away from the old, many of the blacks responded with cynicism and despair. By the mid-century it was decided that the experiment had not worked. By that time whole populations were obliterated as surely as the Tasmanians and, in effect, brown Australian society was destroyed in New South Wales.

The squatters take over

At first there were only five high officials—the Commissary, the Head of the Convict Department, the Judge Advocate, the Surgeon-General and the Surveyor-General. Then a Colonial Secretary was appointed . . . then an Inspector of Government Works . . . a Postmaster . . . a Superintendant of Police . . . a Colonial Treasurer (for a while he kept some of the colony's money in his bedroom) . . . an Attorney-General . . . a Solicitor General . . . a Controller of Customs . . . a Collector of Internal Revenue . . . an Auditor-General . . . a Government Printer. A Superintendant went to Port Phillip, and a Resident to Moreton Bay; Land Commissioners, with the Border Police, ran things in the squatting districts and police magistrates, with the Rural Constabulary, in the districts of official settlement. For the more spectacular work (bushrangers, blacks, cattle thieves) there was the Mounted Police. These new officials created around them their own small departments of clerks, copyists, attendants and messengers, as well as those with specialist roles.

A governor exercised direct patronage for all government jobs of up to £100 a year, and recommended to the Secretary for the Colonies in London appointments to jobs of from £100 to £200 a year. Sheafs of papers moved backwards and forwards between heads of departments and the governor as part of the compromises of patronage; an appointment once made might give its holder an opportunity to enjoy "gross and outrageous corruption". The Secretary for the Colonies still appointed all the top officials, his choices sometimes so disastrous that one governor described New South Wales as not only a colony of convict "rogues and vagabonds" but also, so far as some of its civil officers were concerned, "an excellent asylum for fools and madmen".

"HE'S OFF! THE REIGN OF TERROR ENDED", said a Sydney newspaper when an unpopular governor was recalled. Attacking governors was one of the most exciting political activities the colonists had, and throughout the 1830s public meetings, deputations, petitions and newspapers enacted a drama of protest, threat and intrigue, that was followed by continuing concessions.

In these uproars there were two main factions: the Emancipists and the "exclusives". The "exclusives" hated convicts, Emancipists, Catholics, Irish and anybody else who upset their nobbish ideas. Although in some way they could be Improvers, the interest in constitutional reform of most of them was merely that they alone should enjoy all of what they saw as the rights of Englishmen. They wanted to take over so that they could live like English gentry. In distinction from them the Australian Patriotic Association, formed in 1835, put up a Native and Emancipist view of life, with some touches of democracy. The Patriots wanted full civil liberties for ex-convicts and general social acceptance of their children, and from some of them came the belief that Emancipists and Natives were the only true Australians. (*Australia for the Australians. . . . The land is theirs by right*). But poor Emigrants ("working emigrants") were sometimes accepted as honorary Natives and in general the Patriots also became for a while one of the main vehicles for liberal ideas brought from Great Britain.

As a political force the Emancipists and their allies made

up a city connection. Most of the Emancipist factions belonged to the town, and they attracted other self-made townsmen, including Emigrants who came to the colony low but rose high in the town. This grouping of forces had its greatest success with the incorporation of the Sydney City Council. It gained control in the first council elections in 1842, overwhelming the nobbish interests, the first check to the nobs' idea that it was they who should take over. Their second check came in the same year, but this time from the squatters.

On the face of it the nobs were to gain much of what they wanted now that the greatest of the changes that had followed colonial uproar was about to be put into practice: although the governor would still control the bureaucracy and the colony's land policy and could also veto the Legislative Council's measures, the council was now to be given the power to determine its own proceedings and there were to be elections to it, the elected members having a majority over those put in directly by the governor; at the same time there was to be no great experiment with democracy—in fact on the day of the polls the unenfranchized in Sydney were so outraged that for an afternoon their riots seemed to give them control of the city.

Despite fear of the votes of some "Romanists and liberals", it was to prove an assembly of the well-to-do, with a useful bias against Sydney which, with a quarter of the colony's population, secured only a twelfth of the representation. But the new Legislative Council was not the body the nobs had hoped for in the 1830s. It was a squatters' council. The squatters' men won most of the seats, and so many members were themselves squatters that the council usually adjourned for the wool-shearing season.

The political idea of the rebellious squatter now swamped all other political activity. The Australian Patriotic Association disbanded, broken after the success of the squatters, and, when the squatters formed the Pastoral Association in 1844 to fight Governor Gipps's land policy, most of the colony's best-known political animals trooped into it as auxiliaries to the squatters' rebellion. The insults governors had previously suffered now seemed small. The word "humble" was cut out of the Legislative Council's first "humble address" to the governor, and on the first day of the Budget debate it was moved (although there was no seconder) that the governor's salary be reduced from £5,000 to £3,000.

Most townsmen hated the squatters, but the squatters were too strong for them. Against town hostility, and despite their own divisions between absentee and resident, and large and small, the squatters were an efficiently functioning collectivity demanding special government protection for their self-interest. Believing themselves surrounded by envy and malice, they would meet to discuss common action or to make threats, and they had the support of some city spokesmen who shared in their interests. Rather like desperadoes taking over a town and appointing their own sheriff, they now wished to become the government; they channelled other feelings of discontent to serve their purpose.

In the mid 1830s the government had tried with a makeshift system of licences to give some legality to the squatters' land grab. In the 1840s when Governor Gipps wanted the squatters to pay more for the land they were using they used their monopoly of political power—grabbed as quickly and spectacularly as their land—to defeat him. Governor Fitzroy, his successor, gave in. The squatters got what they wanted, a combination of grazing licences and rights to purchase strategic lots within a run. There was a last scramble and in the rush for the new leases some squatters lost their runs. Then, except for those who had been thrown in this last gamble, the squatters had secured both tenure of land and political power. At first some nobs, believing that a gentleman should own his land rather than lease it, had opposed the squatters. But nobs also speculated in squatting—if they did not they lost their significance in the rush—and, as a distinct and significant economic class, by 1850 they had largely dissolved.

Once the squatters had what they wanted they moved from rebellion to conservatism. Out on the runs life had already lost some of its peculiarities as the new hands from Britain began moving in as bush workers among the old hands. The new hands were less restless: many would stay put on the one property, and they did not disdain taking an interest in its future. Married couples were sometimes hired—the squatters found them cheaper—and children began to appear amongst the sheep. With a security of tenure that was an asset they could sell, some squatters sold out to go back to Britain, but most stayed; they saw greater wealth "further out" into the future. "Head stations" became "home stations", huts were replaced by weatherboard cottages and plans were made to build comfortable houses, some as ambitious as those of the disappearing gentry. Native trees and plants around home stations were cut down or pulled out and exotics planted in their place.

In town the squatters looked forward to a complete self-government with a restricted and country-biased voting system giving them the main power. The successful ones tended to enjoy club life and some joined the Government House set, putting on black hats and taking over many of the attributes of the nobs they had helped to destroy; but the special circumstances of the strange frontier where they had gambled and won meant that even if they wore the black hats of nobbishness they did not usually wear its gentlemanly sense of culture or responsibility.

Chapter 5

THE AUSTRAL-ASIATICS
1830 to early 1850s (*cont'd*)

4,000 miles of the Southern Hemisphere

Whether all the inhabitants of all the Australian colonies wanted to be called "Australians" was not decided by the mid-century. And in any case the term did not include the New Zealand settlers. There were other possibilities. That Australia, New Zealand and the smaller islands were south of Asia seemed obvious enough; to some they seemed the southern part of it. A publication called the *South Asian Register* had been started in Sydney in 1827 and the terms "Austral-Asian" and "Austral-Asiatic" were invented to encompass the Europeans who lived in this imagined South Asia. By mid-century there were more than 400,000 Austral-Asiatics in five colonies that, including deserts and ocean, stretched from tip to tip across nearly 4,000 miles of the Southern Hemisphere.

When the Swan River Colony had begun in Western Australia in 1829, the hope had been that a well-to-do squirearchy would appear almost at once, with large estates, fine houses to live in and plenty of willing labourers to do the work. But they found themselves in "a miserable region, scarcely more valuable for the purposes of cultivation than the deserts of Africa". Some of the settlers went home. Others moved to the convict colonies. When better land was found most of those remaining had run out of resources. There were no convicts to build roads and bridges; there was no Commissariat expenditure; much of the trading was barter; wages were often paid in kind; there were too few land sales to subsidize immigrants. Throughout the 1830s the colony was a settlement of "sand, sorrow and sore eyes"—the "scarecrow colony".

British colonial reformers of the new school were delighted. Now *their* theories could be tried. So that it could start all over again with a proper scheme the British Government attempted to get back much of the land it had granted. But the colony's main success was not planned. Although there was reluctance to create "a nation of Bedouins", sheep runs began to spread out and they made money for those who ran them. However, after twenty years there were still only a few thousand people in a colony whose potential stretched across a million square miles. They suffered from a unique sense of isolation: in a settlement separated from the others by desert, it was not only London that was far away; it took up to a month's sea voyage to get to Sydney. Sceptical of new schemes, the colonists went back to an old one. They petitioned for convicts. In 1850 the British Government obliged them.

In 1838 there was another attempt to set up a "second Singapore" on the intractable northern coast. A flat piece of land on the extreme north-central tip of the continent was chosen and named Victoria Town. Its sea frontage was called Port Essington. Troops were sent; a commandant appointed; a wooden fort was built; flag poles went up; a jetty went out. After eleven years it was acknowledged a failure.

On the southern coast, under a big gum-tree on an alluvial plain, a proclamation was read in 1836 announcing the establishment of the "British Province of South Australia". The assembled immigrants sang the British National Anthem and "Rule, Britannia!", and then, as had happened at Sydney Cove in 1788, went off to eat a cold collation. This time the collation was better prepared. And this time there was high formal hope. The word "colony" was not used. South Australia (by which was meant only the central strip of territory of the continent) was to be a "Province" of Britain.

It was also to be an Improvers' model of rationality and liberty. Its rationality was to lie in its practical expression of the new theories of "systematic colonization": land would be divided neatly into adjoining lots and devoted to agriculture, which sharpened men's minds, rather than straggle out in sheep runs, which depraved their manners. The province's liberty was to lie in the absolute equality of the various denominations of the Christian religion; there would be neither monopoly for one, nor the corrupting equality of government subsidy for all. And there would be no convicts. Overall, the province suggested a return to the seventeenth century, when chartered companies started colonies in North America and there was an expression of religious conviction (although not necessarily of religious equality). Perhaps this was why, as an expression of hope, the province failed.

When confronted by a new environment and the old Adam, systematic colonization became mainly a way for speculators to make money. Too many people stayed in the new town of Adelaide; there was not much development of agriculture; in 1841 the province was pronounced bankrupt, and the British declared it a mere colony after all. Expenditure was cut, immigration was suspended, Adelaide was partly emptied. But towards the end of the 1840s South Australia began to assume a more ordinary form of success. Its wheat growing was close enough to town to be profitable and wheat was exported to Singapore as well as Sydney. A mechanical stripper was invented, Australia's first contribution to the industrial revolution. But South Australia's new success also lay in the unplanned expansion of squatters, and in the good luck of finding copper and silver-lead deposits. From 1845 to 1850 the value of its exports quadrupled (more in wool and minerals than in wheat) and by the mid-century its European population was more than 60,000.

In its expression of religious liberty, South Australia achieved no more than New South Wales; and the opposition to government subsidy led at first to a state of "religious destitution" and then to years of bitter dispute, after which, for a while, all except the most dissenting denominations accepted the government money for which the Church of England had been fighting, prepared to let the others have some so that it could have more. The colony's political practice was such that although Adelaide was the first colonial town with a Municipal Council, two years after its incorporation the council collapsed because of lack of interest.

South Australia continued to see itself as different, and in a more complex manner than did the Swan River colony with its grudging sense of neglect and isolation. The pastoral interest was not so dominant as in New South Wales—it was offset by the developing agricultural interest; whaling, shipbuilding and so forth were less significant; and there was less manufacturing. South Australia was less Catholic and less Irish than New South Wales, and minor denominations, including a large fraction of German Lutherans (as large a group as the Catholics) were more evident. It was the only colony with a sizeable proportion of immigrants not from the British Isles.

But the pickpocket colonies would not be denied. Immigrants from New South Wales and Van Diemen's Land—stockmen, shepherds, whalers, builders—came to teach South Australia how to do things in the colonial manner. Some time-expired and pardoned convicts were among them, even a few runaways. South Australia got its own back: some of those found guilty of crimes in Adelaide were transported to Van Diemen's Land.

At first European settlement in New Zealand was part of the expansion of the settlements in eastern Australia. There was a township, and elsewhere sawmilling camps, whaling stations, mission settlements, small traders, totalling about 2,000 Europeans by the end of the 1830s. When plans for "systematic colonization" spread to New Zealand it became a colony on its own. By the mid-century, there were about 25,000 Europeans in the six main settlements, more than half of them in Auckland and Wellington.

There was something of South Australia all over again in the southern settlements. Once again colonists saw themselves as seventeenth century North American settlers and in fact three settlements were sponsored exclusively by individual Protestant churches. Wellington had three times as many Methodists as Catholics. The north, however, was seen (and by the south despised) as "Australian"; Auckland was described as "a mere section of the town of Sydney transplanted to the shores of New Zealand", and when a New Zealand pastoral movement began, the sheepmen's clothes were those convention demanded for squatters in New South Wales. On their runs they acted in some of the same ways, although their huts were an adaptation of Maori dwellings, and they were more likely to let their Maori women live with them instead of fornicating and then dismissing them.

The strongest differences between settlement in New Zealand and in Australia were enforced by the Maoris. Perhaps this was where the parallel with North America lay: like the American Indians and unlike the Australian "blacks", the Maoris had traditions of war. Their lands were not seized by the Europeans as were those of the Australian blacks. There were instead attempts to cheat them with respect, paying for land purchases with blankets, nightcaps, pipes, beads, sealing wax, or with what the Maori chiefs most prized—muskets, kegs of powder, casks of shot, boxes of cartridges, the possession of which produced an immediate technological revolution. Many of the Maoris picked up reading and writing from the missions (they would sometimes scorn illiterate whites) and the adoption of the new religions gave inter-denominational rivalry some of the zest of tribal disputes. In some districts Maoris took up European-style farming and trading. They soon learnt the enormous profits to be made from the resale of land; some became shrewd salesmen.

From the beginning of systematic colonization people theorized about racial amalgamation, sometimes suggesting that the Maori chiefs should be turned into nineteenth century English landed gentry. Land was allotted to Maoris in some of the new systematic settlements, but in a way senseless to them. A Commissioner appointed by the British Government to inquire into land disputes found for the Maoris, but with 4,000 Europeans spread over the disputed territory, nothing was done. By the mid-1840s the Maoris and the whites were at war in some districts. Garrison troops from New South Wales were rushed to New Zealand and a local militia was raised. The final act occurred when the Lieutenant-Governor reduced a Maori stockade with a force of 60 officers, 1,100 troops, 450 Maori auxiliaries, five cannons, four mortars and two rocket tubes.

The second oldest of the colonies, the island of Van Diemen's Land, was, with 70,000 people, the second largest in European population; it was also the whitest, since the natives had been almost obliterated.

As a whaling and shipbuilding centre Hobart rivalled Sydney, but the island was too small, and much of its land too rugged, for the same pastoral expansion. Some of its pastoralists expanded right out of Van Diemen's Land and most of those who stayed mixed wheatgrowing with their sheep raising; to increase production they did not seize more land but tried to make better use of what they had. Throughout the 1840s, at a time when transportation to New South Wales was suspended, convicts still flooded Van Diemen's Land. It remained a "plantation" economy.

Melbourne quickly grew from a few huts into a town of merchants and dealers, servicing the squatters of the Port Phillip District of New South Wales, living on them, and, by and large, hating them. Its Town Council, made up mainly of Scots and Ulstermen, professed a radicalism less Native and more Emigrant than Sydney's. The pastoral districts had more worker-owners than the rest of New South Wales, more middle-sized men with less of a gambler's wastefulness. But the squatters, whose actions had created the Port Phillip District, appeared even more dominant than in Sydney, which had been created by other means.

Whatever the tensions between Melbourne and the Port Phillip squatters, both detested rule from "the Sydney side". The Port Phillip District elected six men to the Legislative Council but since Sydney was 600 miles away it was almost impossible to find candidates other than absentees. In derision, in the 1848 election, Port Phillip elected the British Secretary of State for the Colonies as one of its representatives.

Things moved more slowly in the Moreton Bay District of New South Wales. Until 1840 there was a penal settlement among the mangroves and mosquitoes of Brisbane, but even when a Prison Commandant was replaced by a Government Resident Brisbane still languished. The Moreton Bay squatters despised it and attempted to set up their own rival port. They were still on a frontier of expansion. To the unoccupied north there seemed prospects of *something better further out*.

In Sydney, Anniversary Day, the celebration of Phillip's landing at Sydney Cove, had early taken on a significance given previously only to royal birthdays, and in 1838 it became the first public holiday of colonial origin, kept up by a race meeting, pigeon-shoots, cricket matches and a regatta on the harbour watched from the foreshores by a crowd with their picnic lunches, or watermelon, peaches, nectarines, or pies bought from vendors. Anniversary Day did not mean much anywhere else. There was concern in New South Wales and in Van Diemen's Land (where 80 per cent of the colonists lived) about what it meant to be an Australian. National anthems were written (and forgotten) and there was an assumption in Sydney (shown for example, in the choice of "national" to describe Sydney's institutions) that it was, somehow, the "capital of Australia" and that if there were to be a nation, it would be a development of New South Wales. Such ideas could seem remote in the Port Phillip District, which had fewer Natives and sought its freedom from Sydney; in Western Australia and in New Zealand, so far away, they seemed irrelevant; in South Australia, proud of its purity from convicts, they were insulting.

Nevertheless Sydney at least thought it time for a definition of "national character" or "national opinion". But what kind of a "national character" was it to be? What sense of special destiny was there for an enterprise that began with the founding of a penal settlement? If God had a purpose in arranging this act, it could only have been that of salvation through penitence; but this view affronted respectability. Nor could any sense of history be respectably appealed to. To those who controlled the debate Bold Jack Donohoe was not an acceptable hero. Nor were there any great national ideals embodied in the State, since it consisted of London-appointed officials.

Looking back to English history was enough for some, although it could be an affront to the Irish and Scottish. Black-hat life was taken as an indication of what existence was about. Or could the colonies adopt a fictitious "British" history, disguising its Englishness, and rename institutions "British"? Or was it to be "the land, boys, we live in", a new society? Natives and Emancipists had impulses towards this, but it was hard for them to say what they meant. Or was it possible to be a nation that, though lacking a past, could look to the future for its history? This was the Improvers' view. Everyone could be made better. But with what distinctiveness? Would the answers come, as the Improvers who looked to education believed, in the development of a distinctive national culture? If so, it had not yet arrived. In the 1830s several magazines had deliberately concerned themselves with the idea of establishing a national consciousness through a literary culture. But the waves of Emigrants in the 1840s drove this hope away. To meet their tastes, the new magazines were direct imitations of

English magazines, some put together by scissors and paste. Novels were written about the colonies, using the tricks of the day, but giving some description of colonial life; in verse, following the trend in Britain, there was a switch from the Augustan to the Romantic and some attempts to accommodate the European vision to the Australian landscape, but a great deal of the verse might as well have been written in Manchester. Esteem seemed to be sought more by approximation to the fashions of the homeland than by native experiment.

Despite concern that colonial society might be "unfitted, and wholly unprepared, for the establishment of a theatre" a theatre had started in Sydney in 1833; it was patronized by the reforming Governor Bourke and welcomed as a diversion preferable to "horse-racing, cockfights, bull-baiting, skittles, billiards and gaming of every description". Other theatres went up in the main colonial towns, each with some variation on the royal name, a "Theatre Royal", a "Royal Victoria Theatre", a "Royal Theatre", a "Victoria Theatre", a "Queen's Theatre Royal". Italian opera was introduced in the 1840s; some plays, at least three with bushranger themes, were written by colonists. In self-congratulation one newspaper suggested that colonial theatre was "at least equal if not superior to any of the second-rate London theatres" and entrepreneurs went to England to seek suitable second-rate talent. Concerts became popular in the 1830s in Sydney; music schools opened; there were music festivals; arrangements were made of aboriginal songs. Several good second-rate English painters passed through the colonies, and several others stayed. Some of their more ambitious work, particularly of landscapes, had to be shipped to England to sell.

Even the first colonial architectural style—Georgian with verandas—was losing self-confidence. Single-storey houses with verandas on three or all four sides survived as "homesteads" in the country, but when blocks of two- or even three-storey terraces began going up in town in the late 1830s there was pleasure that many of them did not have ungainly verandas. It is true that shops and hotel verandas spread over the pavements, but what seemed more important was that churches were now in Early English Gothic and court houses had Classical facades.

Of the poets, Charles Harpur made serious attempts to import Wordsworth and adjust the English romantic vision to the Australian continent; he was also ambitious in seeking a history for Australia in a future where there would be an extension of the ideas of liberty and human brotherhood. The son of an ex-convict schoolmaster, he led a life inhibited by lack of conversation and frustrated by lack of recognition. (One of his sonnets was "On the Fate of Poetical Genius in a Sordid Community".) He was contemptuous of the power of the Emigrants and regretted the failings of the Natives. He said: "I am not one of the present men of Australia, nor could I mass myself down, endeavour to do so as I might, into the dead murky level of their intellectual grossness."

Even those who sought a proud future for the colony sometimes expressed despair that the colonials were excessively concerned with drinking, sport, gambling and money-making. In particular the "fatal facility" for making money was usually taken to be the root of all the other evils. The gentlemanly pursuits of money-making, gambling, sport and drinking were now becoming democratized. The same process was occurring in the British Isles, but in the colonies there was no hiding it. The poorest classes lived with less evident destitution than in the British Isles; they could eat more and engage more freely in some of the amusements of the rich (they could, for instance, get as drunk as lords); and they seemed to have more opportunity to make money and, if they made it, to buy items previously associated with status. These unusual events seemed so severe an attack on the moral order that some took the 1840s' depression as a judgment.

In the late 1840s the Colonial Office began to consider giving South Australia and Van Diemen's Land the same system of partly elected legislative councils that New South Wales already possessed, and to turn the Port Phillip District into a separate colony (with a similarly elected Legislative Council), to be named "Victoria", as if it were a theatre. It also considered allowing the four colonies to make their own constitutions at some suitable future time.

The Secretary of State for the Colonies was determined that New South Wales, Van Diemen's Land, South Australia and Victoria should become a federation, with a federal assembly appointed by the four colonial legislatures. This idea achieved its most precise opposition in South Australia which wished to keep clear of the pickpocket colonies, and to keep its own land policy; and in all three of the smaller population areas there was suspicion of the likely domination of New South Wales. However, lukewarmness or indifference was the overriding reaction. The great distances separating the four main cities gave the scheme a sense of impractibility and, apart from the tariff disputes already begun between New South Wales and Van Diemen's Land, there did not seem any special purpose to be served by a federation. Surrounded by apathy, the Secretary of State stuck by his plan for three years, but when the Bill reached the House of Lords there was a great deal of opposition, ranging from allegations of impractability to allegations that this kind of arrangement would usurp the power of the British government and lead to the dissolution of the British Empire. The government was weak in Parliament and, to save the rest of the measures, it gave in on federation. As the next best thing, the Governor of New South Wales was to be called the Governor-General, but nobody knew what that would mean. Each colony was to go its own way. Except as a geographic term, there would be no Australia.

The rise of "the people"

Divisions as to what life should seem to be about give existence a sense of shape and urgency and ennoble the itch to struggle. To many of the colonists the great division of the day, for which one group of men would contest with another, was whether a man should drink alcohol only in moderation, or whether he should totally abstain. To others it was whether the mechanics' institutes should be controlled by the Emigrants or the Natives. To others what mattered was the humbling of the ascendancy of Canterbury; to others the frustration of Rome's invasion of the colonies. For a short season in Sydney, the only colonial town with elected politicians, once concern with the rebelliousness by the squatters had subsided, the most significant sense of political difference lay in the Legislative Council of New South Wales and the City Council of Sydney. They were rival political arenas contesting what men should seem to be.

In aggregate, despite its internal disorders and factional formlessness, the Legislative Council still stood for black hats and an English view of life. The squatters had been graceless in their declarations of self-interest, but there they were, members of the gentlemen's clubs and, if anything, their political ambitions were even more oligarchic than those of the old nobs. On the other hand, the first Sydney Council included three butchers, two publicans, two builders, a druggist, a cabinet maker, a merchant tailor, a linen draper, a tanner and a miller. About half of them were Natives. Several were sons of Emancipists, and the first mayor was married to the daughter of the colony's richest Emancipist. When one prominent alderman who had come to the colony as a mere sergeant in a garrison regiment, and had grown rich and become associated with gentlemanliness by marrying the daughter of a lieutenant, went to a Queen's Birthday Ball at Government House, he was asked to leave, because of his earlier non-commissioned rank. (The affronted alderman subsequently got his own back by attending the Mayor's Fancy Dress Ball dressed half as a sergeant, half as an alderman. The next year he was made mayor.)

The governors complained of the quality of the debates of the Legislative Council. But the Legislative Council looked down on the debates of the Sydney Council as "noisy, contentious and meaningless"; its language was "indecent"; its meetings were like "the burlesque and beer garden ruffianship of American legislatures"; it was considered to be in the hands of the liquor interests; it put too much emphasis on equality; it was shameless in its use of patronage as a way of helping the needy. It was considered excessively and crudely chauvinistic, and spoken of contemptuously as Emancipist and "Australian" —second-rate, non-British. To the scorn for the idea of the Emancipist as self-made man was added scorn for any fellow who had risen above his station.

Along with their sense of brotherhood found in the institutions of mutualites, the immigrant Improvers had also brought with them the view that Jack might not only band together with the other Jacks in a friendly society or as total abstainers but he might also consider that perhaps in some way he might begin to seem as good as his master. It was a view already present in a colony where bushrangers were becoming examples of rugged independence; but while the sense of equality of Bold Jack Donohoe was expressed by roaming hills and dales like wolf or kangaroo, some immigrants brought with them more ordered and institutionalized ambitions for equality: the secret ballot, manhood suffrage, payment of M.Ps. Some of the new idealism of political equality in the British Isles emigrated to autocratic Australia and tried to set itself up in the same forms, with some wish to realize in the new world the frustrated idealism of the old. Although taken up now and again, the question of separation from Britain lacked wide appeal. It did not seem as familiar an idea as the secret ballot.

In the towns in the 1840s the phrase "the people" began to be used to harness to political ambition the dreams of those who hoped to go up in the world. In the manner of the age, "the people" did not include domestic servants or unskilled labourers. "The people" were roughly those in that part of the economic scale stretching from skilled workers and clerks to small "masters" and shopkeepers. As the decade went on there was a growing belief that "the people" were frustrated only by the power of the squatter "monopolists" and that their simple goodness was corrupted by this one single evil.

In 1843 the Mutual Protection Association, formed during the economic depression to express liberal and radical opinion, supported the Sydney Council as a true voice of "the people", but the Association collapsed when the squatters had their short season as leaders of rebelliousness. However, liberal and radical newspapers continued, if sporadically, and in 1848, with the squatters satisfied, the Constitutional Association was formed, with a full, if orthodox-English, programme of radical political reform. By now there were two populist impulses: the older, deepest-felt and more original, if less coherent and articulate, was based on Nativist ideas of a true Australianness; in political rhetoric it was now being replaced by the Emigrant idea of "the people", defined in orthodox-English terms and combined with ideas of mutuality and political equality.

"Revolution in France. Flight of the King. Republican Government Elected." When the news came on 19th June 1848 of a new European disorder there was fear that a European war might mean the French would attack the colonies, particularly New Zealand. For that matter, what effect would a successful uprising in Ireland have on the Irish in the colony?

A week after reading reports of the overthrow of the French King Governor Fitzroy issued writs for the second Legislative Council election which were not due until September: he wanted the elections out of the way before there was more inflammatory news from Europe.

It was in this election that some of "the people" began to imagine that they might rise higher than the City Council and perhaps go so far as to put a man into the Legislative Council. There was a meeting in the Royal Hotel to discuss it. A few of those there had connections with the Sydney Council—one was an ex-mayor, a leather, soap and candle manufacturer who was the son of a minor official in the Commissariat; but others were entirely new to official politics—shopkeepers, tradesmen, a Scottish schoolmaster, a few radical journalists. A few were Chartists; a number were Irish; almost all were young. For safety's sake they chose as their own candidate for the Legislative Council Robert Lowe, a nob, a lawyer who had come to the colony to make his fortune and then return home, and to whom the expediencies of politics now suggested a new political force in "the people".

The nomination was done modestly. This was the "first time the citizens of Sydney have ever dared to nominate a candidate of their own, and it has created a great deal of surprise and indignation that we should have the impudence to nominate one not introduced to us by our betters". There was confidence in the campaign. ("Let this be a commencement of a new era, in which the people shall ... be looked upon ... as a mighty and self-acting power.") And their victory was hailed as "the birthday of Australian democracy". "The glory of a new era in the political history of New South Wales is ours ... Our watchword is 'Onward to national freedom and happiness.' "

Other than the election to the Legislative Council of a man who, even if a nob, was the first to be successfully nominated by the unnobbish, the European turmoils of 1848 found little echo, beyond an intensifying of rhetoric. A newspaper could remind its readers that "while Europe is striking off the fetters which despotism has forged for the people" New South Wales labours under "a government more despotic, and more oppressive than any in the world"; but it was not until 1849 that the new radicalism enacted a drama that in matter was unique to the colonies, and in manner within the central tradition of

European street politics.

Transportation of convicts, suspended at the beginning of the decade, was to be resumed. A cargo of ticket-of-leave men was to be dumped in New South Wales. When the convict transport anchored at Sydney, guards with fixed bayonets stood behind the locked gates of Government House. Reserves of soldiers waited in the stables. Police hid in the kitchen. A "Great Protest Meeting" was held on the waterfront with the top of a horse omnibus as the speakers' platform. Between this and the second Great Protest Meeting the Superintendent of Convicts organized the unloading of some of the "exiles" and their dispatch up country, but almost every town in the colony had its protest meeting. There was a sense of crusade; it was an issue that overwhelmed all others and seemed to throw light on the colony's whole social condition, with a transcendant radicalism that illuminated many other issues. "Let us send across the Pacific our emphatic declaration that we will not be slaves . . . the time is not far distant when we shall assert our freedom not by words alone. As in America, oppression was the parent of independence, so shall it be in this colony." Some of this radicalism was laced with caution, and comparisons with America in 1776 were deplored as "erroneous". But in politics the colony was now doing something for itself.

The movement spread through all three eastern colonies and into South Australia. An Anti-transportation League was formed, with the flag of the Southern Cross—five stars set on a Blue Ensign—as its symbol of revulsion against the convict system. There were protest meetings in cities and towns, threats of separation from Britain, and a general letting loose of radicalism.

The British Colonial Secretary tried a last compromise—that a new penal colony be started in the north. Then the British Government changed and the British gave in: there were to be no more convicts. When the last transport arrived in Hobart, the town took a holiday to celebrate the end of its shame. Two years later its Legislative Council asked that the name of the colony be changed from Van Diemen's Land to Tasmania, since the old name was blackened with embarrassing memories.

It had not been nobs or squatters leading this radical movement but city merchants and professional men, with support from shopkeepers and artisans and other voices of "the people".

Now that the colonies were demanding the self-government already given to the Canadian colonies and to New Zealand, it was these new liberals who wanted to shape this future. The battle for self-government was fought and won in New South Wales, then extended to the others. It was won partly with nobbish leadership, but when the new constitution was debated the new liberals, speaking in the name of "the people", wanted a constitution that was amenable to them. The conservatives were opposed to "democratic and levelling influences". ("Who would stay while selfishness, ignorance and democracy held sway?") It was suggested that the upper house should be hereditary, to provide a "strong check to the arbitrary will of the multitude" and, since wisdom was believed to accompany the ownership of property, there was special concern for the "great interests" in the colony. But the new liberals won their victory: although the "great interests" were still to have a grip on the upper house, the lower house was to be elected on a wide franchise. Now that the itch to struggle had been ennobled by the participation of men who saw themselves as tribunes of "the people", the colonies, so weak in faith, had acquired a belief that it was through politics and decisions of governments that the human condition could move closer to perfection.

Part 2

THE AGE OF IMPROVEMENT
1851-1910

Part 2

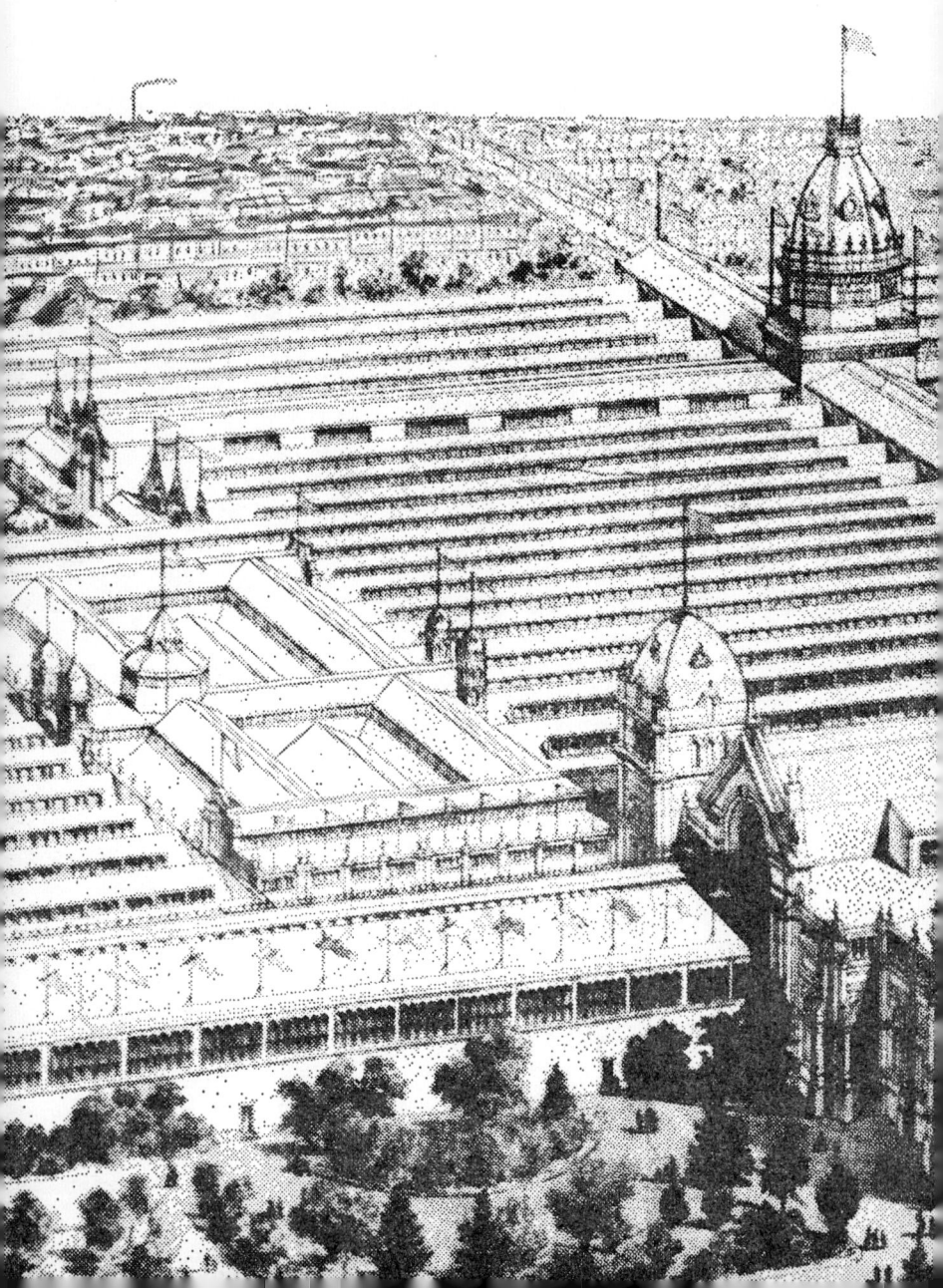

The Age of Improvement

1851—1910

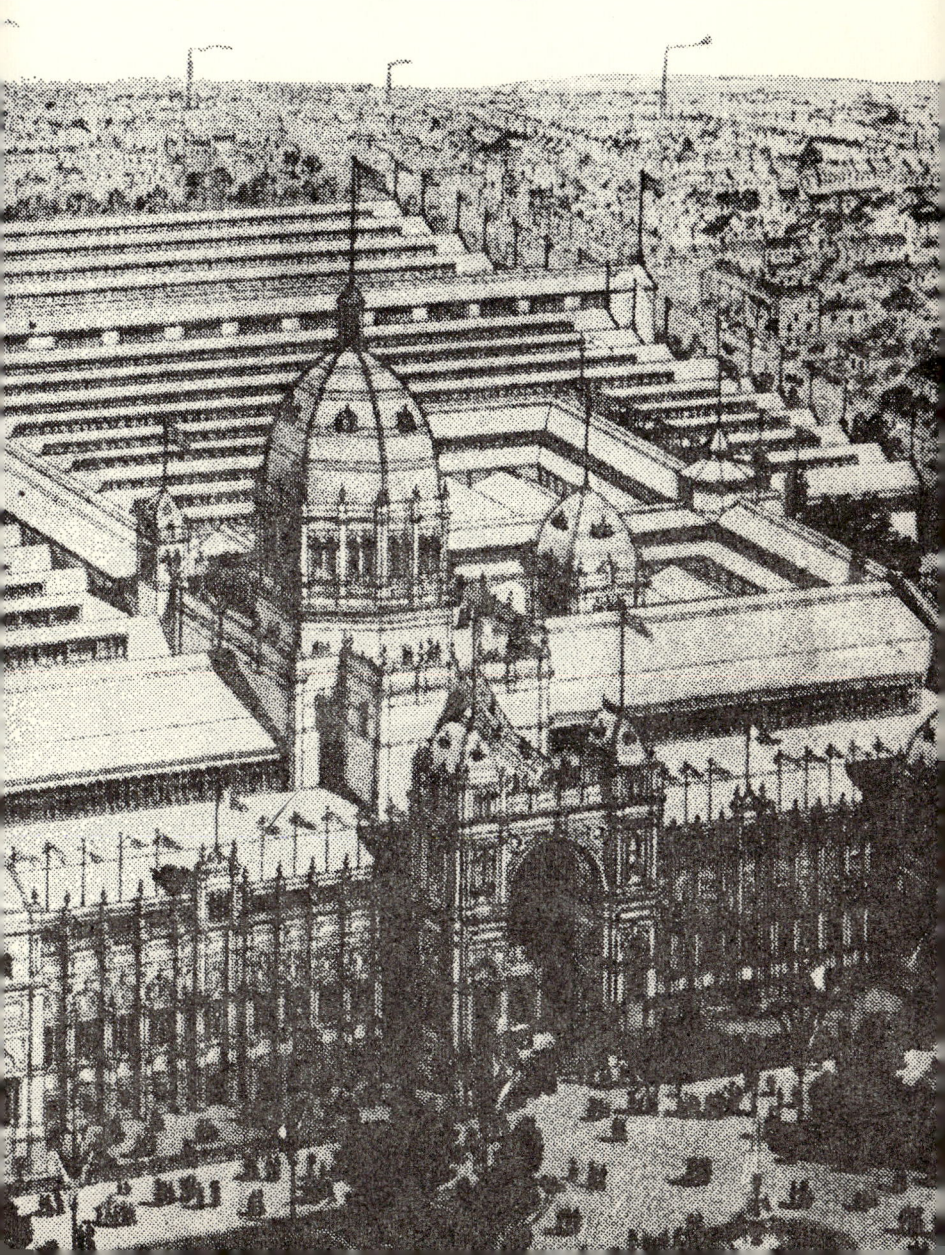

Chapter 6

AUSTRALIA UNLIMITED
1851-1885

The diggers

When Melbourne learnt that it was to be separated from Sydney the celebrations lasted five days. Hilltop fires and rockets, thanksgiving services and sporting events, a procession, a fancy dress ball and a Separation Anthem welcomed the birth of the new colony. Then it settled down to what seemed a predictable future in which the first step was that a Legislative Council would be elected in September 1851 and meet in November. But by November Victoria had reached such a state of gold fever that its governor asked London for military reinforcements.

Gold had already been found in the colonies, but for various reasons nothing had happened. But early in 1851 when a New South Wales prospector back from California turned a small gold discovery into a rush the government gave in. ("It would be madness to attempt to stop that which we have no physical force to put down.") Goldfields Commissioners were appointed and a system of licences improvised to cover expenses and to try to limit the number of gold diggers. There was a drift of men from Victoria into New South Wales—a bad start for a new colony; so rewards were offered for a Victorian strike. By July a few hundred men were at two Victorian diggings; by August, at what was soon to be Ballarat, the diggers began to strike it a bit richer; in September in one go 60 pounds of gold was discovered; by October

Ballarat had between 6,000 to 10,000 diggers. Then new finds at Castlemaine caused a rush of 10,000. In Melbourne "When are you off?" became a normal beginning of a conversation.

There was a run on the banks. Many businesses closed down. Ships were left unloaded. Work stopped on farms. Men turned their cash into tents, shovels, sieves, cradles, buckets, pickaxes and cooking pots and set off along the bullock tracks to camp on the diggings. The governor wrote: "Cottages are deserted, houses to let, business at a standstill and even schools are closed. In some of the suburbs not a man is left." By December 20,000 diggers were spread out across the midlands in what could seem hostile camps threatening Melbourne. When several thousand of the luckier ones invaded the capital to spend Christmas, drunken parties went on night and day, horses were shod with gold, cigars lit with $5 notes, champagne bottles used as skittles; prostitutes rode in carriages. To the pious, God's intentions seemed clear. Melbourne was being punished.

In the new year thousands of diggers came in small steamers from Van Diemen's Land and thousands more walked or rode overland or sailed in from South Australia. About half the men of these two colonies tried their luck in Victoria. Later in the year fortune-seekers from the British Isles floundered in, looking for quick riches and a first-class ticket home. The poet Tennyson said he would have gone if he hadn't been married and, depressed by their reception in England, the Raphaelites almost went as a group. Nearly 300 ships came to Port Phillip and by the end of 1852 Victoria's population had gone up in eighteen months from 77,000 to nearly 170,000. In the next year 900 ships came, bringing men from the United States, China and Germany as well as the British Isles. The population jumped to within a few thousand of New South Wales's total, and in the following year it was 40,000 more. Later in the decade the rushes became even bigger as up to 50,000 men would stampede to a valley, loot it and then rush somewhere else.

At the diggings at night with hundreds of fires shining outside the tents it looked as if an army had taken over the gullies. In some ways the gold rushes were like the kind of safe, minor military campaign for which a man would volunteer and remember with growing affection for the rest of his life; there were not many deaths; there was plenty of fresh air; and there were the excitements of failure or success, the bonds of exclusive comradeship, and the feeling of free choice that can come from an unpredictable event.

There were enough hardships and tediums to test manliness. Although some put up bark huts or slab huts and some even brought their wives, most lived in calico tents with only an outside fire for cooking, with boxes, chests, saplings, sacks or tree-trunks for furniture, and for meals mutton chops, damper and pannikinfuls of tea, all highly priced (even the price of water could be high), and only pipes of tobacco to make the food seem better once it was swallowed. In the winter there were colds, rheumatism and cramps, and in the summer eye infections and diarrhoea. Many were ruined. Gentlemen from England could go down in the world irretrievably. But these very trials added pride to the thought that the diggings were "a wonderful place to take the conceit out of men who expect much deference". It did not matter what a man had been before: what mattered was how he would react to the challenges of the diggings. In this sense they were a test of a man's ability to be his own master, but the group solaces (and demands) of comradeship could be more important, in particular how a man fitted in as one of the four to six partners who usually worked a claim. The term "mate", formerly an occupational term for a two-man partnership, was now extended to this slightly larger occupational group. In a wider solidarity a feeling of difference could come from being an "old hand" instead of a "new chum", or a white man rather than a Chinese; but above all the distinctiveness was in being a *digger*, whether American or Irish, Australian or Scot, English or German; and with moleskin or corduroy trousers, blue or red jersey, leather belt and knife, there was even a special uniform for it.

"Happy days . . . glorious freedom from all the restraints of home life" . . . The diggings gave a wonderful chance to have a good time . . . fiddles, banjoes, accordions . . . pipe bands, brass bands . . . and an improvised main street, much of it still in canvas, that might go on for two or three miles, with saloons, sly-grog booths, brothels, theatres, eating-houses, shooting galleries, boxing booths, bowling alleys, gambling dens. At night, lit by tallow lamps, with the hucksters shouting and so much canvas, it looked like a carnival. As ever, there were also strong tides of respectability, especially on the sabbath when the Methodist meetings boomed, the bands played politely as if the diggings were a park, and the diggers dressed in their Sunday best to make their Sunday visits. But good times were there to be had—given more excitement by the overwhelming fantasy that a man might make his fortune, if not from a lucky stricke, then at least from a two up game.

The larger diggings had a wooden barracks with the Union Jack above it, where the troops and the police were quartered and the log jail was guarded. "The traps", hastily recruited, many from "the very lowest class", some ex-convicts, had become the hated representatives of the incompetent and corrupt administration of the goldfields. The miner's licence, renewable monthly at £1 a time, became the diggers' symbol of grievance; for the traps it gave the opportunity for licence hunts, organized in surprise attacks, ambushes and encircling movements ("a good deal like a rat hunt").

Protests sometimes burst into disorder, but surprisingly it was at Ballarat, in 1854, that there was a brief set piece of rebellion—surprising because the Ballarat digger had been spoken of as "a man of capital, able to wait the result of five or six months' toil before he wins his prize" so that "he will always be a lover of order and good government". But when the owner of the Eureka Hotel at Ballarat was let off by a magistrates' court for a killing in which there was prima facie evidence against him, thousands of the small capitalists held a protest meeting. At the end of it some of them burned down the hotel.

A few diggers were now gripped with the feeling that "moral persuasion is all humbug, nothing convinces like a lick in the lug", but most followed the promptings of Improvement: a Ballarat Reform League was formed, in which the Chartists added to the special grievances of the miners some more general recipes for the general betterment of humanity. Oratory flourished. Deputations moved in and out of officials' rooms. A Royal Commission was set up.

It turned out it was to be a lick in the lug after all. The governor sent more troops. Stones were thrown as they marched through the diggings with fixed bayonets. A drummer boy was shot. There was a public burning of licences, then a retaliatory licence hunt at which the Riot Act was read. A few shots were exchanged. At the Eureka lead there was talk of rebellion: pit slabs were piled into breastworks and men began to drill. A thousand or so diggers gathered in the stockade, with the flag of the Southern Cross hoisted above them. ("We swear by the Southern Cross to stand by each other, and fight to defend our rights and liberties.") Two days later only 120 were still truly standing by each other (most of them asleep) when before sunrise 400 troops and police marched up to the stockade and fired. Ten minutes or so, and it was done. About thirty diggers were killed, a hundred taken prisoner. The flag of the Southern Cross came down.

The small capitalists were satisfied with the reforms that followed this event—replacement of the monthly miner's licence by an annual "miner's right", and the setting up of locally elected miners' courts in each mining district to make the district's local mining laws. The greatest disorders in the goldfields then came in occasional outbreaks of persecution by the diggers against the Chinese, whose numbers were moving up towards 10 per cent of the adult male population. Not very attracted to this remote place at the very edge of the Southern Ocean, the Chinese, like the early squatters and most of their fellow immigrant miners, hoped to get their loot and go back home. But to the others they were "a swarm of human locusts", and there were riots against them in both Victoria and New South Wales, with violence and burning.

Some diggers stayed on the goldfields for the rest of their lives, moving in the 1850s from one field to the next along a one-thousand-mile stretch of the Great Dividing Range in Victoria and New South Wales, then in the 1860s swarming off when gold was found in some of the roughest parts of New Zealand, and moving on again when there were reports of new strikes in one or other of the Australian colonies. Whenever there was unemployment in a colony its government would hope that a gold find might provide the answer. But perhaps as many as half the diggers gave up after a few weeks. If luck did not come at once, capital was needed and most of the rest found that after six months or so they lacked the money to go on.

Many who stayed on at fields like Ballarat worked for wages in the mining companies that were now forming, but the revolt of the "little capitalists" of Eureka became part of their view of themselves as wage-earning miners, and this view began to spread to the coal miners and other kinds of miners as an example of the kind of thing miners could do if they stuck together. So a dormant memory of this brief rebellion remained. Later it could acquire some new meaning. In the same way there remained the idea of "the Chinaman" as a threat. For a while colonial governments tried to restrict the entry of the Chinese, but by the 1860s, as the number of gold finds diminished, Chinese immigration dropped, and governments worried about other things. The idea of the Chinaman as a threat was still there, however, if also temporarily dormant. Another idea had come up—that of "the digger" himself, independent-minded but fraternal, above social pretension, a man who had stood a test. To have been a digger, even if only for a few months, gave a man a sense of being unique. Even if what they saw in themselves was much the same as what the successful Emancipists, Natives and Emigrants had already congratulated themselves on, the diggers could imagine they were a new kind of person. Overall, the colonies' population almost trebled within the decade, from 437,665 to 1,168,149, and some diggers felt that with them things had really started.

Apart from the economic boom, the gold rush's greatest significance was that it peopled Victoria, making it the biggest and most go-getting colony. In ten years its population rose from 77,000 to 540,000, more than half as big again as New South Wales, and holding nearly half the total of the Australian population. In those ten years, from being a district of New South Wales Victoria had become the most celebrated of the British colonies. It consisted predominantly of immigrants: of the 230,000 who came to Victoria from the other colonies only about one in ten stayed, but of the immigrants from other countries only about one in ten went home. They were to set much of the tone in Victoria for a generation, the generation in which Victoria was to be the most important of the colonies, seeing itself as setting the pace for the rest.

The New York of Australia

It was into the pockets of Melbourne tradesmen, saloon keepers, merchants, landlords, property speculators and builders that the diggers' money mostly went, and then it re-circulated amongst workmen as part of the general boom. While most diggers made at the best no more than a living wage, with perhaps three or four thousand finding more than £1,000 worth of gold and only a hundred or so making more than £10,000, publicans could build up fortunes of £520,000 in three years and those who had invested small savings in Melbourne land before the rush could sell out for a profit of up to £100,000.

Jobs came from new factories, extra demand for farm produce, new roads, new railways and above all from house-building. With the magic of confidence that released all this new prosperity Melbourne became the fastest-growing city in the world, with land prices to match. Ships were used as dormitories to sleep in. Then whole suburbs of canvas nailed over wooden frames went up. Flimsy weatherboard cottages were put together in a few days and let out at $1 per week per room. But even in 1861 a third of the population of Victoria was still living in tents and huts.

This onrush of a city's confidence was soon more attractive to immigrants than the lotteries of the diggings. They came with their wives, wanting to settle in a place with so many new opportunities. On the face of it, Melbourne was a goldrush town, even wilder than San Francisco: the theatres were packed, the hotels boomed, prostitutes provided relief services day and night. But it was not the diggers *qua* diggers who set the basic nature of Melbourne. Those who stayed on in the diggings were more concerned with their own affairs as little capitalists. It was the attitudes of those immigrants who were attracted not by the diggings, but by the opportunities of a money-making city.

They were somewhat better educated and had more money-making skills than the colonists of New South Wales; they were better at getting on in the world; they were more given to the practice of religion, Methodism and Presbyterianism in particular. And in their attitudes to their new country they were not prompted by Melbourne's earlier Native moods— its conflicts with the squatters, its fight for separation from New South Wales, its campaign against transportation. They took all that for granted. Their ambition was quick to rise above the improvisations and the squalor: they wanted to get on with the job of building a fine city in the south land, as modern as the mid-nineteenth century.

As early as 1853, in its first flush of confidence, Melbourne decided to have its own university. In the next year Australia's first Town Hall building was planned, a copy of Inigo Jones's Banqueting Hall at Whitehall, and it was decided to match it by building a splendid Public Library. Prestige buildings went up in half-finished streets, with sewage floating in front of them in huge open gutters. The new Parliament House was one of the boldest inspirations of Imperial Rome built anywhere in the nineteenth century. The unemployed marched past it with banners: "We want bread! Give us work!" The opera was "worthy of the English metropolis itself". The shops were "equal to the best in London". The new buildings for the gentlemen's club "would not disgrace St James' Street".

It took only till 1852 for one of its legislators to put in a claim for Melbourne as the "seat of Supreme Government", since it was clearly "the centre of Civilisation and Christianisation in the Eastern Archipelago". By 1859 one of its writers not only claimed that Victoria was "the New York State of Australia" and that Melbourne "would be the great central heart, regulating all the pulses of the Australian continent"; he also suggested that ". . . here, amidst the Austral-Asian and Austral-Indian group, compact in feeling and action . . . would be a fair scene to which you might shift the seat of empire."

The building boom led to building workers' gaining an eight-hour day in Melbourne, a reform still only a dream elsewhere in the world, but proclaimed at a public meeting on 11th April 1856 by the Mayor of Melbourne as such an obvious necessity that he offered a ten guineas prize for the best address on the subject. The eight-hour movement was slow to spread into other industries and other colonies, but a Trades Hall went up in Melbourne ("This hall is the first ever erected by working men") and the eight-hour day festival became the most important annual event in trades union life, promising that new future that, some felt, Victoria would be the first to offer, so that the workers would have the leisure to devote themselves to moral and intellectual Improvement.

There were other aspirations to Improvement. It was Methodism that had captured the biggest attendances at the diggings and by 1861 a third of those who went to Church in Victoria went to Methodist Chapels. The repressive side of evangelicalism had for half a century been unsuccessful in taming the colonies' wildness, but in Melbourne puritanism now enjoyed at least one victory: it took possession of Sunday. An Evangelical Alliance, open to all Protestant denominations, was formed in 1857, and it enthusiastically pursued Melbourne's salvation by controlling what it did on the sabbath, even if it could not yet control the exuberance of the other six days of the week. There were fanatical protests when Sunday trains ran on the newly built suburban railways, with decency's only triumph a restriction in timetables. When the Public Library was built it was shut on Sunday. So were the saloons, a change not imitated by the other colonies for more than a generation.

Amid the aspirations towards being both an Imperial city and a centre of Improvement was the clink of coin, the rustle of bank drafts, mortgages, ledgers. Melbourne was a hard, pushy place. In its get-rich-quick bustle, it was said, "a most unbounded spirit of avarice actuates all classes" . . . "to take care of number one is the guiding rule of action" . . . "he who displayed the greatest ingenuity in *taking in* his friend or his neighbour is called a smart fellow." Although it wanted shops equal to the best in London and clubs that would not disgrace St James' Street, for many years Melbourne was seen as the "American-style" city of the Australias. Sydney was believed to be "quieter, less assertive, more civilized", "a city of charm with an element of the ideal", with "an essential respectability" and "a respect for constituted authority, typical of an old-fashioned crown colony". Sydney's charm lay in its crumbling past: Melbourne, the "phenomenal city of Australia", was busy organizing its future. "There is a bustle and life about Melbourne which you altogether miss in Sydney" . . . "The Melbourne man is always on the look-out for business, the Sydney man waits for business to come to him." "Victorians of the upper classes . . . both in their defects and their excellences . . . approach nearer to the American than to the British type. And in this respect the Victorian is distinct from the colonist of New South Wales who retains more of the John-Bull attributes of the mother country than his younger and more energetic brother in the South."

The blast of the trumpet

As prosperity goes, the Australian and New Zealand colonies were for a while the most prosperous countries in the world. Export earnings from gold jumped ahead of export earnings from wool and were to stay ahead until about 1870. The colonies found new markets: Newcastle's export of coal rose from 71,000 tons to 368,000 tons. Of the two main export industries, wool-growing was large scale, capitalized, and employed relatively few people and mining was growing in scale; internally the passing stimulus of gold had brought a much bigger work force, a much bigger local market, and a confidence that made capital easy to get. British investors put money into the colonies—through finance houses and government loans—on a scale they had not thought of before. At times half a year's investment capital came from London speculators, and increased British demand in the 1870s helped cause a pastoral boom that brought wool ahead of minerals as the main export. Although, as the decades moved on, other countries were to catch up on Australasian prosperity, the rate of economic growth was double that of Britain and second only to that of the United States and Japan (with Sweden and Germany a slow third).

The most important single internal impetus to the colonies' economic growth was the housing rush, which took up about a quarter of all capital investment, private and government. Above all, national development meant the extension of the towns. The oscillations of the cycle of more immigrants-more houses-more immigrants more houses pumped life throughout the economy. The housing boom—a product of immigrant labour, immigrant demand, a revolution in rising suburban expectations, and the development of building societies—was as important a stimulant to the economy as the earlier rushes for wool and then for gold.

Population went up from nearly one and a half-million in 1860 to more than two and a quarter million in 1880, by when there were about 860,000 people in Victoria, 740,000 in New South Wales, 276,000 in South Australia, 211,000 in Queensland, 115,000 in Tasmania and 29,500 in Western Australia. Melbourne was a city of 282,000, Sydney of 224,000, Adelaide of 104,000. Immigrants accounted for almost half the total population increase. When the Northern District of New South Wales became a separate colony in 1859 (called "Queensland" as if "Victoria" was not homage enough to the distant monarch) this new colony of 668,000 square miles with only 25,000 Europeans in it was so anxious to catch up with the others that sometimes the recruiting to Australia of immigrants to work as navvies was left to public works contractors. Whenever there was unemployment there was agitation to end assisted immigration—sometimes successfully, but only until the next boom.

In the 1870s a "spirited policy of public works" sprang up in all the colonies, bigger than before, providing further stimulus. Often borrowing in London, colonial governments became such big spenders on public works that governments provided up to 40 per cent of total capital investment; wages went up; jobs were even easier to get. Now and again there was a panic: Queensland, most reckless of the spenders, had gone broke—for a while . . . until another loan from London came in, and there was a gold strike as well. But overall there was the feeling that Australia was unlimited with "no price too high to pay for national development." "What America has done, Australia can now do."

The colonies now bought almost 20 per cent of Britain's exports; in the 1850s shipbuilders in Britain and the United States had enjoyed a new boom because there were so many new ships to build to carry cargoes and immigrants to the Australian colonies. Driven by westerlies, clippers drove down from the Irish Sea into the Southern Ocean, bringing British immigrants and British manufactured goods. The colonies seemed as maritime as ever: crews were shanghaied in colonial ports; the flags of thirty shipping lines, many of them Australian, flapped over Sydney: Australian-owned steamers ran a busy coastal traffic, providing the main link between the coastal cities, and traded with Pacific Islands. (In Sydney there were dreams of a Sydney empire of plantations spread across the South Pacific.)

Because of high charges, steamship traffic with Britain developed slowly, even after the opening of the Suez Canal; steam cut the average passage of mail from 90 to 45 days, but even in the 1880s most cargoes still went by sail. As well as the coastal trade, steam had important effects on the connected river system of New South Wales, Victoria and South Australia where paddle steamers now ran, with plenty of trees on the river banks to chop down in passing and use for fuel. There were shoals and piles of driftwood and overhanging trees, and some rivers did not have enough water in them for nearly half the year—on the Darling a paddle steamer was occasionally marooned and had to wait for months for the water to come back—but the river trade offered cheaper freights than bullock wagons. With their quays and warehouses, river ports flourished on an inland water transport system that ran for more than 4,000 miles. One of them, Echuca, was Victoria's second largest port; with thirty-five steamers, seventy barges, a long wharf, and hydraulic cranes, it was "destined to become the Chicago of Australia". For those not near this system transport was usually by roads, with bullock wagons for freight and Cobb and Co's mail coaches for passengers (by 1870 offering 28,000 miles a week). The driest and most desolate regions were serviced by camel trains, bred from imported camels and run by imported Afghans.

Then railways became one of the most spirited of the public works, in the 1870s making up more than half of all government spending. At first railway construction had been slow, with only a few local lines. (The first line at Sydney was opened to a salute of twenty-one guns and the playing of the "New South Wales Railways Waltz".) Less than 200 miles of track were in use by 1859, most in Victoria. By 1875 there were little more than a thousand. By 1880 there were 4,000. Then the real boom began. Lengths of steel rail became an important import item in ships' cargoes.

Governments found themselves in the railway business by accident: private ownership had failed because the towns large enough to generate traffic were too far apart, and since most were ports they were more cheaply serviced by sea. But having set up Departments of Railways by chance, governments found good politics in them. Since railways were not run for profit but as a public service, freights could be kept low to subsidize farmers (in Victoria the extension of railways opened up new areas for wheat farming and the colony became a wheat exporter); railway construction work was sometimes started to provide extra jobs (a thousand or more navvies would arrive, bringing a canvas township complete with stores and saloons). Sometimes a railway line was extended to get political support. Some towns had their most prosperous period when they were at the head of a railway line.

Telegraph lines linked Sydney, Melbourne and Adelaide by 1858; a cable went under the sea to Hobart, and later Adelaide and Perth were linked. Meanwhile the telegraph line from London was moving across land and under water to the Dutch East Indies. Two thousand miles of wire were then strung along poles across uninhabited dry country between Adelaide and Darwin, with little stone fortresses every hundred miles for the relaying operators to work and live. In 1872 the cable from the Dutch East Indies reached Darwin, and through it the six colonies. Now trade information and decisions could pass directly between the colonies and London: brief news items could be telegrammed to the colonial newspapers (what the Kaiser was doing, the new policies of the Czar). The latest sporting results came at a cost of 10s. 4d. a word. In 1878 Melbourne installed its first telephone exchange: even Perth had one by 1887.

To all this was added a boom in city buildings. Use of the new passenger lifts spread quickly after a lift was installed in a Sydney store in 1881. Buildings went as high as six or seven stories; in 1885 a ten-storey building went up in Melbourne; city land values went up correspondingly. With lifts, the new "grand hotels" were being built, with several hundred rooms, and flourishes of marble and mosaics, mahogany and plate glass. New theatres went up, equally grand with red plush and gilt; town halls sprouted by the dozen, pushy and showy.

In Melbourne, Sydney and Brisbane, Intercolonial Exhibitions were held where machinery, stock, produce and manufactured goods, among the shrubs and flowers and paintings, expressed confidence in progress. In 1879 Sydney put on the colonies' first International Exhibition in a "crystal palace" of concrete and steel, built in the Botanic Gardens; the colony's first electrical plant was installed for this, to enable work to go on by night as well as during the day, and the colony's first steam tram ran on the opening day. The next year Melbourne replied with an International Exhibition: the building, a mixture of French and Italian styles, was topped with a dome higher than St Paul's. A cantata was written for its opening, hailing Victoria, Queen of the South.

"You are told constantly that colonial meat and colonial wine, colonial fruit and colonial flour, colonial horses and colonial sport, are better than any meat, wine, fruit, flour, horses or sport to be found elsewhere. And this habit springs from things national to things personal," said Anthony Trollope after his visit to the colonies in 1871. In Sydney ". . . it is asked . . . with bated breath, and with something of an apology, 'Of course you have been bothered out of your life about our harbour;—but it is pretty; don't you think so?' " But ". . . the blast of the trumpet as heard in Victoria is louder than all the blasts—and the Melbourne blast beats all the other blowing of that proud colony."

In this economic progress "Melbourne money and Melbourne brains" had led all the rest; but a pastoral boom in the 1870s helped New South Wales, and Queensland was galloping to catch up with South Australia; Western Australia stood almost still, and Tasmania was beginning to realize that it was not, after all, to become the Athens of the South. Overall there was the increasing feeling that ". . . free from the class and accumulated hindrances which act as drags upon the progress of other countries . . . we, having nothing to undo, can, if we will, make the last pages of their history the first of our own."

No class too poor to play

The colonists in the bigger towns were enjoying a profoundly satisfying victory, one gained in little more than a generation, and one that satisfied both the desire to feel the same and the yearning to feel different: they were beginning to beat the old country at its own games.

"There is no class too poor to play, as at home." Sport had been democratized, passing from the control of private patrons to that of clubs and associations, and the plentitude of playing areas, the good climate, increased leisure time and perhaps the sheer drive to be democratic on a question that mattered, had made sport "the colonial *carriere ouverte aux talents*". Before any European or North American country had generated a wide range of new mass outdoor entertainments for the working classes, ordinary Australians had become "the most sporting country in the world".

Up to 80,000 would attend the Melbourne Cup; the crowds ready to watch rowing, sculling, footracing or swimming were so great that promoters could offer prizes big enough to attract international champions. As soon as a new diversion was invented in England—cycling, modern tennis—it would be imitated as quickly as a Benthamite political principle. The one Australian-invented game—"Victorian Rules" football—was so popular that Melbourne began to divide into football club rivalries with some of the intensity of Romans divided between the racing clubs of the Circus Maximus.

When an Australian sculler met the undisputed champion of England on the River Thames and won by four lengths, Sydney rejoiced as if it had won a great battle. After an Australian team went to London and beat the M.C.C. team captained by Dr W. G. Grace, cricket began to give a sense of national role: "As Napoleon's soldiers remembered that they carried a marshal's *baton* in their knapsacks, so the young Australians all remember that they have a chance of becoming successors of that illustrious band of heroes who have recently conquered the mother country. . . . Not to be interested in cricket amounts almost to a social crime."

The usual delights of city life were still available. Theatres, menageries and circuses, nightly free concerts in inns, public rejoicings (street decorations, fireworks, processions, banquets), photographic studios, skittle alleys, waxworks, phrenological museums, billiard saloons, gambling, prostitutes (one of the bars in a Melbourne theatre was called "the saddling paddock"), drinking (licences were easy to get and hotels were open till midnight). Successful entrepreneurs had built up chains of theatres, with local companies supplemented by touring companies from Britain; there were theatres in the larger country towns as well as in the capital cities; in one year in Melbourne two Shakespeare seasons were on at the same time. Brass bands and choral societies were forming in towns and suburbs (the aspiration of every choral society was a full performance of Handel's *Messiah*); visitors found it curious that even members of the working class owned pianos.

No-cards-on-Sunday was an almost universal rule (although there was a division between those who played tunes other than hymns on the piano on the sabbath and those who did not) and Melbourne still kept one of the world's strictest Sundays, but it was said of Sydney's Sunday that it was ". . . rapidly becoming Continental. Public galleries are open; concerts are given; there are endless trips and picnics about the harbour and to pleasure resorts; boating, sailing in all sorts of yachts": the kind of activity that prompted the English visitor J. A. Froude to remark, "It is hard to quarrel with men who only wish to be innocently happy."

The ordinary people were winning another profoundly satisfying victory. The paddocks near the big towns were being divided with rectangular grids of streets, and being marked into allotments, back to back, which went under the auctioneer's hammer in thousands at land sale carnivals that offered free travel and free lunches (with boosters pushing the prices up). By the 1880s, as the new suburbs spread along the new railway lines, it was said that "the overflow of bricks and mortar has spread like a lava flow".

Terraces and attached houses were becoming "universally disliked", although not so effectively as to prevent speculators cramming thousands of them into the inner suburbs for rent-payers. There had been a unique strengthening and sophistication of the building societies, and an extension of general mortgage systems; along with the South Australian invention of the Torrens Title, which stripped land purchase of its feudal past, these made possible the democratization of suburbia in ways less primitive than those Jevons had seen in the 1850s.

The new suburban houses were single storey, detached, usually with three-foot boundaries between one house and the next, and in Queensland with elevated floors. In memory of the past, verandas remained in front, although with the development of Gothic styles one of the two front rooms tended to push itself forward flush with what was left of the veranda. A hall led straight through the centre; the back veranda had a kitchen at one end, and a bathroom at the other. Exotic flowers—geraniums, hollyhocks, roses—grew in neat beds in the front garden (a display area otherwise not used); vegetables and fruit-trees were in the backyard. Houses were painted black or brown; florid cast-iron decoration took the eye away from inadequacies of design. The furniture was made up of "the frowsy carpets and heavy solid chairs of England's cold and foggy climate"; but Yankee ingenuity was also there, in the new ice chests, vegetable cutters, jelly strainers, egg beaters and the other novelties displayed at the Exhibitions. The sewing-machine revolutionized dressmaking. The lawnmower revolutionized gardening. Of the general impression of these new suburbs it was said: "The houses are all as like one another as peas in a pod—four-roomed squares or six-roomed oblongs built of red brick, with every detail exactly the same."

By 1880, about 57 per cent of the people in Victoria and New South Wales lived in towns (even if some of them were very small). An unusually low proportion worked on farms—less than a third, compared with about 50 per cent in commerce, manufacturing, transport, construction, government and the professions. Manufacturing had risen rapidly from a very low proportion to providing more than a quarter of the colonies' wealth, and in the reverse of what had happened in the new industrial towns of Europe, industrialization did not create towns; the towns, having assembled people for government and commerce, created industrialization.

There was said to be a confidence of manner in the towns. "A man feels himself a unit in the community, a somebody." To some this showed a dangerous democratic levelling, to others "a greater sense of self-respect and responsibility". Even the sons and daughters of the well-to-do were noted for their openness of manner: the girls were seen mostly as of the "jolly" type, piano strummers, able to cook and make their own dresses, outward-going, if dissolving into nothingness with marriage; the boys were a "caution", school-hating, sport-loving, cheeky, disrespectful. Although, in the manner of the age, almost one in ten of the work force were domestics (many of them Irish), there were fewer servants in private houses than in most other countries. A householder on £1,000 a year might have to make do with one maid of all work. There was usually a labour shortage, and an employee could afford to display a certain amount of spirit. In the 1860s particularly, there were times of unemployment—processions would march, deputations would form, soup kitchens would become busier—but in Sydney and Melbourne unemployment could mean as little as 1,500 men out of work. In Queensland when the 1860s financial crash led to a group of unemployed railway navvies marching on Brisbane, the police were given guns, the civil servants batons, and a reserve force of citizens was armed with rosettes; all the shops and banks closed and the

Riot Act was taken out; but only 135 navvies turned up. Some stones were thrown, there were a few arrests, then the navvies were headed off and given something to eat.

It continued to surprise visitors that working men should be able to afford to eat so much meat, three meals of it a day, roast or boiled, hot or cold, served in hunks, washed down by tea, often with potatoes the only vegetable. The deprivations of history were being revenged: the working man seemed determined to cram meat into himself to make up for what his predecessors had lacked. As the eight-hour day spread, and the idea of a half-day off on Saturday was accepted, the colonists' success at cricket was explained as due to the fact that they had more time to practise.

Chapter 7

ALMOST EVERYONE A LIBERAL
1855-1885

The liberals

When the colonies were given self-government in the 1850s the new legislators were predominantly "Emigrants": in the first Victorian Parliament "Emigrants" outnumbered "Natives" by fourteen to one. They set up as exact a copy as they could of the British Parliament: lower houses played the House of Commons; upper houses played the House of Lords; governors played the monarch; and members of Parliament decided whether governments rose or fell, so that the government was "responsible" to parliament, in the British fashion. Speakers wore wigs; maces were put on tables; before moving on to what he really thought, a member would address his fellows as "honourable members": soldiers were "honourable and gallant", lawyers were "honourable and learned"; the upper house was "another place". "Having imported their whole constitution and law books holus bolus from England," said the visitor R.E.N. Twopeny, "the legislative equipment of the young Australian corresponds pretty nearly to the tall hats and patent leather boots which fond mothers provided for the aspiring colonists. An exogenous growth has prevented originality of ideas, for which the most part has been supplied by English thinking."

For a while there was concern among conservatives whether

the new politicians could work this venerable system. Sneered at as "the wealthy lower orders", these merchants, lawyers, journalists, publicans and traders risen to liberal leadership in the anti-convict agitation were sufficiently un-nobbish for the question to be raised of whether "the sudden uprising of persons of subordinate rank to a level with the best society of the place" might mean mis-government, even tyranny. There were complaints about vulgar abuse in debates, about drunkedness, corruption and favouritism; but governors had earlier complained of the vulgar abuse of the squatter-dominated Legislative Councils, and there had been a great deal of corruption when government departments had been run by gentlemen officials from England who were themselves appointed by favouritism.

Just as they took old ways from England, the new liberals also tried to put into effect as quickly as they could the new ideas of England, most of them not yet even tried in the mother country. In a quick series of liberal amendments to its constitution South Australia showed the way, instituting adult male suffrage for enrolled voters, the secret ballot, triennial parliaments and a one-man-one-vote rule that gave Adelaide two-thirds of the seats. The dreams of liberal England were now realized in South Australia. It had "the only thoroughly Benthamite constitution in the world". John Stuart Mill began sending letters to colonial acquaintances telling them how to be liberal.

When Victoria and New South Wales followed South Australia, the three colonies were amongst the most democratic societies in existence so far as liberal concepts of democracy went. No sooner was Queensland established than it also set the same modern liberal constitution. This liberalism had flaws and inequalities, but it was of the very latest pattern.

The new liberals were all Improvers; they professed belief in "the people", in land reform, in education, in the capacity of human nature to do good. Their power did not depend on radical support: some of the radicals who had earlier supported them joined them as liberals; most of the rest went into decline. Some radical phrases continued, but for a generation republicanism almost disappeared. (Separation from Britain was not as familiar an idea as payment of M.Ps.) What appealed to them was any policy of Improvement already urged in Britain, and they put many of these policies into practice "long before they had emerged from the region of theory in their native land". With the general change in mood, with the scepticism of the Age of Authority gone, and with the new economic buoyancy, even conservatives became optimists. The future suggested that "advancing with rapid wing's stride", Australia, "the country of true liberty", with "no poverty . . . to distress it", would "build on the wrecks of the Past", and become "the shelter of Freedom and boast of the world. . . ."

As part of their secular faith, one by one the colonial governments withdrew assistance to the churches. Then they made an assault on church schools. Catholics feared that secular schools were "the seed plots of future immorality, infidelity and lawlessness"; Protestants proclaimed that the Bible should remain the basis of all teaching and Anglicans that everything should go back to the proper state it had been in when the colony began, with the Church of England in command of religion. But governments withdrew their grants to church schools and instituted State systems of education that were supposed to be "free, compulsory and secular", and to provide a sense of creedless unity. ("Let our children be sent to the same schools irrespective of creed and let them be brought up in the creed of kindliness which will make them forget that other creeds divide them.")

In the interests of unity it was even demanded that God should be a Victorian. A member of the Victorian parliament said in 1872: "It should be our constant aim to render our churches less English or Genevese, less Irish or Roman, and more Victorian . . . purer and more patriotic faiths." Another said: "In a couple of generations, through the missionary influence of the State schools, a new body of State doctrine and theology will grow up and the cultural and intellectual Victorians of the future will discreetly worship in common at the shrine of one neutral tinted deity, sanctioned by the State department." By this means would be created "a united community, the first germ of a nation".

To help this process, readers in Victorian schools were partly re-written to cut out religious divisiveness. Such changes were made as replacing the words "the great reformer John Wycliffe" with the words "the celebrated John Wycliffe", or replacing an article called "Paul in Athens" by an article called "Wonders in the Cotton Manufacture". Even English history was suspect, because of its potential religious divisiveness.

Although the State schools outside Victoria had religious instruction, it was of a pale and neutral kind. The official school ethic was one of respectability; the principal rationale was to achieve social cohesion. The idea continued of a sense of common identity fostered by the culture of the mechanics' institutes and schools of arts, "the Palladiums of our Nationality . . . making us conscious of our brotherhood".

There were, however, technical flaws in the prevailing liberalism. For English-speaking countries an unusually centralized system of government, with unusual powers, had formed in the capital city of each colony. These governments engaged in land reform; they directly ran the railways and other public utilities; they played an important part in the control of other essential services, and in their "spirited policy of public works" and in other ways provided a larger portion of capital investment than a government did in any other country except Japan. But these were matters that were simply accepted without being talked about, so that there were no theories about what was original in colonial policies: the self-congratulation was saved for what was derived from Britain.

The main exception was whether governments should adopt protective tariffs, a matter over which there was endless dispute. Victorian governments had made up for a lack of revenue by instituting customs duties and then decided that this would mean, as in the United States or Prussia, a programme of protection for "infant industries"; fighting against the depredations of the squatters and the merchants of Collins Street they would preserve young industrial goodness from attack and rear it to a manhood of independence and prosperity. In New South Wales, where governments had enough revenue from land sales not to need extra revenue from tariffs, free trade could seem the natural state of mankind, the free play of the market part of progressive destiny and protection a perversion of the natural order. J. S. Mill was quoted on both sides.

David Syme, owner of the Melbourne *Age*, and the most famous propagandist for protection, wrote a book which was translated into German and given an American edition because of its assault on the pure liberalism of English political economy. Arguing that "free competition" tended towards monopoly, that trade practices could in any case be fraudulent and could prompt State control and that the ethical element in economic conduct could not be ignored, he attacked the defence of the free market by English political economists as a rationalization into universal principles of a special interest that suited British manufacturers.

In this clash between two conflicting ideas of the role of government in Improvement were some of the shapes of later and more general political battles, but for the moment it was confined to protection. In some other matters colonial governments were even less active than in England. No colony passed a factory act until 1873, and by 1885 Victoria was the only colony with anything approaching a modern, for then, attitude to factory legislation. The dangers of machinery, the employment of children, overcrowding, bad ventilation and insanitary conditions, were largely unchecked, and the "sweating system" was the kind of scandal a journalist could make a reputation out of. Standards were behind those of Western Europe because most factories were too small to generate adequate pressure for reform. In the same way, although even by the standards of the age there was poverty, particularly in Sydney and Melbourne—families crowded into single rooms, hovels crowded around filthy courts and alleys, pavement waifs, daughters sold into prostitution—there was no public policy about it: paupers were left to the Benevolent Societies, which colonial governments then subsidized. Pauperdom was assumed to need no other consideration, since it was believed to be merely a temporary phenomenon.

Overall, there was less talk of revolution than in the radical days of the anti-transportation movement of the late 1840s and early 1850s. A section of the First International was set up in 1872, but its connections were more with utopian socialism, J. S. Mill liberalism, Swedenborgism, and a spiritualist cult called "Harmonialism", than with Karl Marx. It lasted a few months, part of a general itching for Improvement also manifest in groups such as the Spinster Land Association of South Australia, the Eclectic Association of Victoria, the Sunday Free Discussion Society, the Victorian Co-operative Association and the Melbourne Spiritualist and Free Thought Association, all of which were seeking to restore mankind to what was seen as its natural goodness.

In the towns some unions were becoming stronger, first the builders' and building materials' workers, then the iron workers and allied trades, with the coalminers displaying the greatest militancy: in Newcastle in 1861 the wives of striking miners picketed and fought "scab" labour and 40 police were sent up from Sydney. But it was also the Newcastle Miners' lodges that agreed with the pit-owners in 1873 to take over from England the new idea of arbitration in industrial disputes, and also adopt a scale of wages related to profits. The agreement was celebrated by a procession of 4,000 with their own brass bands, and for seven years disputes were settled by reference to an arbitration committee of four "disinterested persons" and an umpire. Various Trades Halls and Trades and Labor Councils ("the Senates of the working class") began to form. In 1879 the first intercolonial trades union congress was held.

Perhaps there was more antagonism against the Chinese than against employers. From the 1870s unionists in the capital cities began to agitate against what they saw as a threat from the Chinamen. Most of the Chinese grew vegetables or tobacco, or were greengrocers or servants, and the only industry with any numbers of them was the furniture trade; but they were seen as a threat to meat three times a day, and when the most powerful Australian shipping line proposed to meet competition on the Chinese run by employing Chinese sailors, the threat seemed realized. With the support of the Sydney Trades and Labour Council, the shipping unions went on strike; unions in Victoria, Queensland and South Australia sent money in support; coalminers' unions refused to cut coal for the shipping company. There was disorder and violence, and the strike lasted many weeks. The resultant ill-feeling later caused an inter-colonial conference to consider what the colonies could do to save themselves from the imminent danger from the Chinaman.

But while Chinamen might tremble, the well-to-do could sleep safely in their beds. "The pauperdom of England has grown at a rate scarcely less rapid than her wealth, and both have reached colossal proportions . . . the social condition of this colony is, thank Heaven!, widely different. Here we have no 'dangerous class'. The number of paupers bears an insignificant proportion to the men of the community. Every Australian citizen is interested in defending his just rights of property, and the smallest freeholder will as earnestly maintain those rights as the large capitalist who has invested tens of thousands in the soil."

Within the general political agreement that everything was going to Improve there were no divisions into a true party system, although party names were sometimes used. With almost everyone professing to be a liberal, parliamentary life became a ballet of intricate groupings and re-groupings, with some independents thrown in to make weight (or rock the boat). South Australia averaged a new government a year, New South Wales and Victoria a new government every sixteen months.

At the basis of a group was a core of loyalists. "My dear old Chief," wrote one of them to Henry Parkes, his faction leader, "Are you not my chief? I am the only one of the present team who was with you in '72 when you for the first time took your proper place as Prime Minister—first and foremost—facile princeps—and unless you sit on my right hand on Monday I shall be miserable." But more gritty matters could also attract loyalty—expectations of office, hatred of other leaders, and new, if sometimes temporary, adherents might be gained by specific promises.

No sense of general ideology bound a faction together, although sometimes a particular principle might be a cohesive force. There were no party organizations, although when a coalition of factions was in office the cabinet system usually combined the ministers in loyalty to each other. A group seeking a share in office would try to increase its numbers by expediencies, and when the mating of two groups seemed near there would be a hunt for independents to bless the union with enough numbers to give legitimate birth to a government. The groups and independents making up the opposition would then seek out the weaknesses of a governing coalition and try to shake it to pieces.

The number of voters in each constituency was small, and as there were no party machines, and for most elections no defined issues, "appropriate attention to the needs of the district", whatever they were, might help swing a seat, unless it was a time when special principle (trade, education) might do the trick. Since there was no choice of parties, it could make sense for an elector to vote for a candidate on the basis of purely local issues or one particular "national" issue. Candidates were chosen in an extreme form of democracy where what settled their elections might be disparate local considerations, or one general issue.

Although there were no true parties, political leaders might patch together primitive and highly secret personal political machines, dealing with local men, who might seek reward in promises of local public works, or jobs for local boys. Relations between a leader and his local man were kept private from the others, so that no consistent pattern emerged publicly from a series of separate bilateral obligations. A local man might suggest that a certain candidate was likely to pledge himself, or that another candidate, who looked like a winner, might give limited support on specific conditions: he might also deal with local conspiratorial groups, of which the most common were the Orange Lodges and the Catholic Church. The most talented of all the New South Wales faction leaders, Parkes was for a season able to get support from both the Orange Lodge *and* the Catholics, because the Catholic conspirators were secretly delivering the Catholic vote.

"The curse of the Australian politics is that . . . there are no parties in the strict sense of the term, but merely cliques or groups," wrote one governor. But the result was not an apathetic electorate, it was an electorate that was more interested in *issues*—sometimes vehemently so—than in *politics*. The world could still appear to divide into forces of light and forces of darkness but it did so not on party lines. However it seemed wrong that while so much English aspiration seemed to have been achieved, the colonies could not imitate England by dividing themselves into a party system. Observers sought signs of infant parties with the eagerness of a boy searching his face for the first pimples of adolescence.

The war on the squatters

It had been a culture shock that the colonies should resemble a great sheep walk without a "numerous, industrious and virtuous agricultural population", but once representative government challenged the squatters' political power things could be made more like home. There were dreams of how "the deserted interior was to present a beautiful scene", a thousand farmhouses with flourishing English gardens along each creek, if the monopoly of "the squatting lords with their serfs" could be overthrown. Yankee notions of land reform were popular, and the new liberal politicians took up the cry of "unlock the lands".

Their opponents saw this as a collapse of civilization. ("In a few years we should see white savages, clothed in sheep skins, straying over the land with their wretched flocks.") But the new politicians were city men, with support from country towns and what was left of the anti-squatter landowners, and their whole political impetus was against the squatters: if a colony were to be one great sheep walk, what place was in it for them?

In the 1860s they declared war on the squatters with a series of Land Acts, first in New South Wales, then in the other colonies, that gave a right of selection for lots of up to several hundred acres on the squatters' leasehold runs, with five shillings an acre down and easy terms. When a district was about to be declared open for selection, selectors would gather and at midnight rush off and peg their claims; within a few weeks hundreds of their wooden huts would be up, and there would be the sounds and smells of clearing and burning off. Within one week of the first Victorian Land Act, 900,000 acres were selected.

Dreams of a rugged, independent yeomanry seemed about to come true. But defects in the Land Acts meant that a squatter could use fraudulence, sometimes backed by bribes, to extend his stake. He could "pick the eyes out" of his own run, snapping up the best bits by faking a land use that did not exist and by using others as dummies. At other times he might be the victim of a land shark who got control of some of the most important parts of a run and then blackmailed him into paying a high price to get them back. To these illegalities were sometimes added violence, arson and theft. Two hostile groups were warring over the same territory.

Even worse, most selectors were misled by their belief that "anyone can be a farmer". Even established farmers could be up to a hundred years behind English practice; many "cockatoo farmers" knew nothing at all about farming. With no knowledge of soils or seeds or rotation of crops, hostile even to the use of manure, and with no capital, the "cockies" happily acquired too much land. Even if they had been experienced they would have found it difficult to set themselves up and tide themselves over with no money. Lacking anything tangible to offer the banks, the cockies borrowed from moneylenders at up to $27\frac{1}{2}$ per cent, and paid up to 50 per cent extra to merchants who gave them credit. (Some managed to get their own back by getting money twice over on the same security.) They sold out or were sold up—to the squatters, to the moneylenders who built up big holdings by foreclosing on debtors, and sometimes to the "boss cockies", who, by accumulating other selections, were able to put together holdings big enough to carry sheep and make a living.

Little help came from governments. No credit arrangements were made, no Departments of Agriculture were set up. Governments subsidized local pastoral and agricultural societies to spread knowledge, but this failed. Above all, the fault came from a misunderstanding of the land itself; the best use for large parts of it was as grazing land, organized in big economic units using only a small amount of labour. The lack of a huge class of semi-subsistence peasants was the greatest single reason for the colonies' extraordinary prosperity; if land reform had met its own ideals that prosperity would have lessened.

More often than not, the result of so much enthusiasm was failure. After twenty years of free selection in New South Wales, only 550,000 of 39 million acres sold were under crop and fewer than one in eight of the 190,000 selectors remained on the land. In Victoria, of 15 million acres sold only 1,500,000 were under crop, and half of the best land in the colony was in the hands of the squatters. Though they were patched and re-patched to cover loopholes, the greatest single effect of Land Acts intended to help the little man was to pass land into the hands of the big man. The cockie, living in a bark humpy with a beaten earth floor, with sugar-bags for a bed and packing cases for furniture, was becoming one of the colonies' stock figures of fun.

Paradoxically, there was continuing improvement in agricultural techniques. In South Australia, where a quarter of the breadwinners were farmers, the biggest burst of technological innovation known to the colonies began; inventions in agricultural machinery were to lead to the "stump jump" plough, the "mullenizer" (a log roller that cleared tough scrub), and a complete harvester, which stripped, winnowed and bagged in one process; South Australians also worked out "dry farming" techniques of working the soil into a good tilth, conserving nitrates and moisture for the next crop. When this sense of innovation spread to Victoria, dry farming, along with new implements and the spread of the railways, caused a rush of wheat farmers inland.

But most cockies didn't know anything about these novelties. In New South Wales selection worked only when it opened up market gardens and dairy farms (for "cow cockies"). In all the colonies success came only to the more experienced farmers— the families of the older "dungaree settlers", the "boss cockies", or others with holdings big enough for mixed farming. The cockies' role had been to clear the scrub, break up the virgin soil, and then hand it over to those who knew how to use it.

The squatters were now putting their business on a better basis. Ring-barking trees could double stock: pastures were improved; earthen dams were built; windmills were used for underground water. New types of merino sheep were imported; more care was taken in breeding; stock horses were improved; the kelpie, a new smooth-haired, prick-eared sheep dog, emerged; the preparation of the clip for the market became less primitive. Shearing was done by contract teams. In the 1860s the city institution of the pastoral house developed, providing long-term finance, large-scale wool assignment, and other services. Clearing rivers for paddle steamers opened up large parts of New South Wales to pastoral expansion; then railways moved into the sheep districts. By 1880 ten years of experiment in methods of refrigeration began to open markets in England for colonial meat.

Perhaps most important of all was a technological change that began in Victoria in the 1850s, then spread through New South Wales in the 1860s and reached Queensland in the 1870s: this was the discovery by the squatters of the use of the fence. Shepherds were no longer needed; sheep could run free over the big fenced "paddocks", with a few boundary-riders to keep an eye on them. The saving in wages soon repaid the cost of fencing; it was then found that with these healthier conditions more lambs lived, sheep and wool were in better condition, and more sheep could be run on a property.

Buying out the cockies had made many squatters freeholders, but the cost of this, along with the cost of improvements, had put many into the hands of the banks and mortgage houses, and this meant a loss of some personal initiative. But they were now living better than before. The wooden "head station" had become a substantial homestead (and the whole property was now known as the "station"): the richest (100,000 head of sheep or more) might run to a butler and a professional male cook, and those who could afford it bought a house in the city and sent their children to the Rugby-type corporate schools where they learnt nothing about sheep or cattle stations and little about anything else--except something of the manners of an English gentleman, which some of them wore with special arrogance.

Stations of any size were run by a sterotyped but economic hierarchy of manager, overseer, bookkeeper, stockmen, boundary-riders and jackaroos that left many station owners with not enough to do; some of the richest contrived some smartness in living, but most lived like a working man grown rich—chops for breakfast, cold joint for lunch, hot joint for dinner, washed down with tea. Their most regular household pleasure was to enjoy tobacco and brandy and water after dinner on a wide veranda made comfortable with lounging chairs, table and sofas. In town they might spend most of their time in their clubs, waiting for the gas to go on so that the gambling and drinking could begin.

Wool did not contribute a huge part of the national income, nor did it provide a great proportion of employment—less and less, in fact, as management became more efficient. But after 1870 it was the most valuable single export, and the prosperity of the pastoral industry encouraged further growth in the city ports. The squatters saw the cities as their towns, and the bigger stations themselves provided small townships of their own. The squatters' main community service was their part in the hospitality system, now institutionalized so that a traveller who was a gentleman, or could pass himself off as one, gave his name and was put up in the homestead, and travellers who were not gentlemen went to the kitchen for their rations and were put up in a hut. In this the squatters most served the rural character who had most emphatically dropped out of orthodox society—the "swaggie", who passed from station to station doing odd jobs for his rations, walking with billy in one hand, waterbag in the other, with a swag across his back, with blanket, clothes, soap, towel, flour, tea and sugar wrapped up inside his tent, and providing sufficient sense of threat to get the little he wanted.

English visitors were disappointed in the squatters' failure to provide a landed class with a sense of social responsibility beyond feeding the swaggies. Perhaps, they decided, "by the fourth generation there will be a true aristocracy". One favourable omen was that although the younger generation gambled more than their fathers, they drank less.

The original owners of the land—now called the "blackfellows"—gave little trouble in the long-settled areas; from the capital cities they seemed a faraway problem. Although they were a nuisance in the quick expansion across North Queensland, a strong reliance on the Native Police fragmented and destroyed their society as successfully as it had earlier been destroyed in the southern colonies. "No," said a witness in a Brisbane inquiry, "I don't think they can understand anything else except shooting them." Ideas for protectorates and missions had languished: of the forty-two small reserves in South Australia, thirty-five had been leased to Europeans. With the growth of social Darwinism it seemed clear enough that the problem would soon be solved by the extinction of an inferior race. For humanitarians there were Trollope's comforting words: "Of the Australian black man we may certainly say that he has to go. That he could perish without unnecessary suffering should be the aim of all who are concerned in the matter."

The perils of the liberals

In their shiny frock-coats and ill-brushed hats and with their heavy gold watch-chains and diamond rings, many of the business men of the cities, along with the professional men they might meet at their clubs, were members of parliament, sometimes providing some of the underpinnings of liberalism. The Victorian Parliament became a kind of businessman's and land speculator's club, with chances for quick killings.

These new men upset many of the traditions of "society" with its court-like emphasis on government officials. Now the highest officials were "not infrequently the least esteemed socially", although what was left of the "ancient nobility" was respected, the Church of England still had some social *eclat*, and the black-hat cliques most favoured at Government House continued to see themselves as an inner circle. The new men tried to keep up English manners (if sometimes disturbing English visitors by their drunkenness and swearing); but it was wealth not position that established importance, although the line was drawn to exclude retail traders.

The richest of the city rich were still mainly merchants and financiers. Most manufacturing concerns were small with primitive production processes; many were in country towns. The most solid forms of business, even more in Sydney than in Melbourne, remained what they had been in the beginning: importing English goods to sell to the colonists, exporting colonial products, arranging credit within the colony, and putting money into speculations on the side. A couple of dozen men in Melbourne and another couple of dozen in Sydney between them shared the directorships of most of the main business institutions of each colony, and about four times that number were important minor figures. Interests interlocked: the directors of the main pastoral house were also directors of some of the main insurance companies, banks, mortgage companies, mining companies, shipping lines, island trading companies, newspaper companies, gaslight companies, shipyards, flour mills, iron foundries, sugar refineries and breweries.

Set up in large suburban estates, hidden by trees from their neighbours, with aggressively ostentatious houses, complete with banqueting halls, ballrooms, coats of arms and four-poster beds, to assure themselves of their significance, some of these central figures in the colonial economies, along with the squatters, provided much of the opposition to some of the Improvements of their lesser business colleagues and others in the lower houses in the colonial parliaments. Their spheres of interest were in the upper houses, the Legislative Councils, maintained at the time of constitution-forming in the 1850s, with members who were either nominees, or elected on a restricted property franchise, said to represent "the interests" as against "the masses".

At that time of constitution-building one of the governors

had written home: "There is an essentially democratic spirit which activates the large mass of the community: and it is with the view to check the development of this spirit and of preventing its coming into operation that I would suggest the formation of an Upper House." The upper houses did this job well. Proving to be more vigorous in their assertion of rights than the House of Lords, they emasculated or threw out Bill after Bill. Parliamentary crisis between the two houses—with appeals sometimes to the Privy Council, sometimes to the people—became as normal to colonial politics as the faction system. By these disruptions the upper houses, although not representing "the people", began to weary some of the energy of the liberals and to stale their appetite for Improvement.

There were other frustrations. God was not only a Victorian. He was also an Irishman. Catholics were being urged "to build up in Australia an Irish Church that in the coming time will rival in sanctity and learning the unforgotten glories of the ancient Church of Ireland". Like the churches in the United States and Canada, the Australian Catholic Church had become a dependency of the Archbishop of Dublin: not one appointment was made to the Australian dioceses without reference to him; not one recommendation by the English-born Archbishop of Sydney was accepted. As the Irish bishops, Irish priests and Irish nuns took over, they provided a sense of folk as well as of faith, and even their faith was expected to follow Irish devotional practices and Irish Church discipline. They were scandalized by the statement of the first Archbishop that a mixed marriage was better than none at all, and hastened to make their church insulated and exclusive.

Catholics began to appear more credible as "aliens, enemies of the English crown, of English laws"; the counter-bigotries of the Orange Lodges took on new strength in secret organizations designed to exclude Catholics from positions of power or influence. In 1867—a year in which there was regular news of violence in Britain—an Irishman fired a pistol at the first English prince to visit New South Wales, and the colonial parliament became demented in its fear that the Irish were forming a secret society to overthrow Queen Victoria in New South Wales.

God was also becoming an Italian. Pope-worship became an alternative to Queen worship, and when the Vatican Council debated the infallibility of the Pope not one Australian bishop opposed the idea. Pius IX's attack on liberalism in his Syllabus of Errors seemed so strange in a society based on what the Pope saw as "the principal errors of the age" that initially even Catholics did not respond to it; but by the late 1870s "liberal" was being given Pius's meaning, and as well as episcopal assaults on the godless conspiracies of freemasonry there were forays against materialism, progress, modern civilization, and other matters that to many colonists seemed to give existence a great deal of its meaning. Catholics began to seem more peculiar.

As the State systems of education were fabricated, the Catholics built their ramparts higher and fired off bigger guns. "A system of national training from which Christianity is banished is a system of practical paganism, which leads to the corruption of morals and loss of faith, to national effeminacy and to national dishonour." The Australian Catholic Church began to establish an independent comprehensive system of education parallel to the State schools. There had been no plans for such a system (more than half the Catholic children were attending State schools), but the bishops felt forced towards it because the State system was being set up just as the Australian Church had found that Rome's anathema against liberalism might after all be applied to Australia. Nuns and brothers were recruited (some from Ireland, some from Australia) and to the commitments of faith were added an increasing commitment to raffles, jumble sales, fetes and socials, as a second education system was improvised. When the Archbishop, in a pastoral letter, thundered against the errors of secular education 20 per cent of the Catholic families with children in State schools took them away in one week.

Even the State schools were proving disappointing. They paid lip service to the new Swiss educational principles of developing a child's personality; but they also imitated the English system of elementary education, which, apart from those of Southern Italy, Portugal and Spain, was the worst in Europe. Officials might claim that the intellectual and moral development of the individual child would release his will to goodness, but when the English system of "payment by results" was copied in the 1860s, Her Majesty's Inspectors, instead of helping teachers, became examiners who would descend on a school, set the children a test, and mark the results into one of ten grades on which depended the teacher's level of payment. By the 1880s most of the inspectors were overworked bureaucrats playing a routine part in an established system. Some of the old ideals were still given formal expression: "object lessons" meant to encourage a child's sense of the concrete and his natural curiosity were continued, but now they were learnt out of books.

The system developed one characteristic—a high degree of centralization—that was more French than English. The local school boards had failed and, following their failure, to the standardizing effect of the inspectors' examinations was added the detailed control of each colony's schools from its capital city. Instructions went out on the exact material to be taught, often with reference to page numbers in set textbooks; teachers filled in forms to assure the department that they were all the same.

With so much government activity, departments proliferated. A Department of Land and Works might be formed from the old Surveyor-General's Department, then it might split into two separate departments. The new Department of Lands might then split into three more separate departments, of Mines, Lands and Forests, while the new Department of Works might split into two separate departments of Works and Railways. The colonial civil services were increasing at rates of up to four times the general rate of increase of the population.

Since the patronage system still applied, the power of appointments to the civil service was one of the delights of office, and sometimes an essential part of the process of gaining local political support. Each minister could run his department according to his own ideas of how conditions, promotion and salaries should be regulated. If money had to be saved, salaries could be cut, or there could be dismissals of some of the large numbers of temporaries and supernumeraries. However, there were opportunities for greater flexibility than in more rigid bureaucratic systems: if one man were no good at his job it was possible to leave him in the function in which he most assisted administration, that of doing practically nothing, and appoint someone else to do the work; for a minister who had an eye for talent, promotion of it was possible.

It was a time when new theories were developing in the

industrializing countries about what kind of education government officials should receive. There was no such concern in Australia. Lacking the educated elites of the European countries, and lacking the deeply ingrained belief in education of the United States, the Australian colonies saw little connection between educational institutions and work in the departments. The rate of administrative activity was high. The concern about who should do the administering was low.

Ostensibly Victoria imitated the new British system in 1862 by setting up civil service examinations, and Queensland and South Australia imitated Victoria; but New South Wales did nothing at all; and in the other colonies an escape clause that "persons of known ability" could be appointed to the civil service as well as those who passed examinations was so flagrantly abused that in Victoria, twenty years after selection by examination was instituted, nine times more had been admitted on "known ability" than by examination. There were agitations for more orderly methods—but they were mainly on questions of fairness, predictability and precedent. And when in 1883 Victoria ended patronage by setting up a Public Service Board to control the civil service, it was the question of fairness that prevailed: it is true that entry, except for specialists, was to be exclusively by competitive examination, but educational standards were low (they had to be), and there was no inducement for the entry of the better educated.

Throughout the colonies little direct relation was seen between education and usefulness. A continuing discussion in England about how "both the masters and foremen of foreign countries are more scientifically educated than ours" meant a continuing discussion in the colonies on technical education. But the results proved as whimsical as in England. At a time when in the United States, following the example of the new German Technische Hochschule, there was a proliferation of technical schools, there was not one technical school in the Australian colonies, apart from several mining schools in Victoria. There were evening classes at the Mechanics' Institutes, and later a technical college was set up in Melbourne and then one in Sydney, but they were mainly devoted to spare time classes in subjects like languages, arithmetic or political economy. Only a few classes were devoted to subjects like mechanics or mechanical drawing, and there was a blank refusal to provide any straightforward trade training. Following aristocratic, pre-industrial English attitudes, there was an emphasis on "mental culture": if practical subjects were to be taught, it was to be theoretically, so that the principles underlying a craft might be studied, but not the craft itself. "Schools of design" were favoured—degenerating into little more than drawing schools—but not instruction in the use of what had been designed. In the United States there were many agricultural colleges, but it was not until the mid-1880s that agricultural colleges began in the Australian colonies (and then there were only two, one in South Australia, one in Victoria). Education seemed to have as little to do with prosperity as it had with the government departments.

As State universities proliferated in the United States and the faith of Americans in education reacted to the demands of a new age, the old emphasis on "classical" curricula was destroyed and replaced by a broader, elective and more democratic system. But in so far as the Australian colonies provided university education (by 1885 Sydney, Melbourne and Adelaide had small universities) there was still a considerable concern with classical studies. There were three professional schools at Melbourne University, but Sydney did not get its first two until 1883 and 1884: in both universities Greek, Latin and mathematics were compulsory. The universities were ". . . too timid to boldly make themselves samples of the modern education theory; they have limited their appeal to the exhausted Anglo-Australian tradition." In 1880 there were only 263 undergraduates in Melbourne, and in Sydney after nearly thirty years of existence there were only 76, and the staff had been reduced to six.

At a time when State high schools were appearing everywhere in the United States, the Australian colonies had none. Some New South Wales elementary schools were developing "grammar classes"; the other colonies had no State secondary education; in England there was no state system of secondary education; so it was also to be in the Australian colonies. There were a number of private schools, but in these, according to Francis Adams, a follower of Matthew Arnold, "A good three-quarters of the knowledge acquired by an average boy" was "of no subsequent use whatever to him, either in the culture of himself or in the prosecution of his business or trade."

By the 1880s those of these schools that had survived were turning into little Rugbys (although with very few boarders), increasingly devoted to the theory that the important aim of Australian education was to mould boys' characters into the ideal of an English gentleman. The prefect system was introduced ("If boys could be gradually schooled into subordination to the intellectual and moral leaders among them, the habits of obedience thereby created would be of immense benefit themselves.") and to it was added the "hearty comradeship" of the house system, school colours, school uniforms, cadet corps, and organized team games (which at once took on more vigorously than had been imagined possible in England). The result was that "the moral tone . . . in some cases almost rises to that of a second-rate public school at home".

Before the 1880s, such fee-charging secondary schools as there were in the colonies had been influenced by the academies and city high schools of Scotland and by the private and dissenting academies of England, so that a wide variety of courses was offered. But now courses were being narrowed into "dead, dry intellectual knowledge". At a time when even in England the old "classical curriculum" of Greek, Latin and mathematics was being weakened and broadened, in the Australian colonies it was now being given emphasis.

"So far as I am aware," said Adams, "there is not a single colonial politician who seems to realise that if the education of the People, the rulers of the future, is of vital importance to us all, the education of the Middle—or, as we should say now, the Upper Class, the rulers of the present—is of importance at least quite as vital." The liberals had not worked out a way of educating the people who were going to run the place.

Chapter 8

LOOKING FOR AUSTRALIA
1870-1885

Members of the Empire

It was not surprising that education should be so imitative: among the age groups with power, and in the towns which were the centres of initiative, immigrants still outnumbered the native-born. It is possible that at the top cities had become *more* British than they were before the gold rushes when the ideas of the Emancipist and of the Native had some life in them. National anthems were written less frequently, until the habit seemed to die; people from Britain dominated the little Rugbys, the universities, the churches and the professions; in "an infant community" English ideas of accent, manners and deportment were taken as best; knighthoods and other honours came from "home"; the dominant town cliques of loyal Anglo-Australian clubmen, judges, barristers, rich squatters, professors and merchants were mostly English-born, and the others imitated the British. The novelist who did best out of Australian themes was Henry Kingsley, a visiting Englishman, who portrayed Australia as a sunny, wide-open society of landed gentlemen where an Englishman could enjoy a little adventure, make a fortune, and go back to England to spend it.

When General Gordon was trapped in Khartoum, hopes and anger swept the Australian cities as fiercely as they did in London, and with his death in February 1885 there was an hysterical impulse for revenge, given material substance by a decision to send a military contingent from New South Wales to the Sudan. "As members of the Empire we are defending ourselves and all most dear to us just as much in Egypt as if the common enemy menaces us in this Colony. The Queen's enemies are ours wherever they are." "While we have a gun, a ship or a shilling, England shall never want assistance." Volunteers marched through the streets to the tune of "The girl I left behind me"; hotel balconies budded into red, white and blue for mayors' patriotic addresses; after thirteeen days drill, when the volunteers marched to their ships it was under banners reading, "For England, Home and Gordon".

Beyond guarding a railway line near Suakim the colonial troops took part in only a few village skirmishes, but they earned their Commander a C.B. and their Premier a K.C.M.G. In the rhetoric of blood and sacrifice the disgrace of Botany Bay had been washed out in the waters of the Nile. One Victorian patriot said that Australia had now been "precipitated . . . from a geographical expression to a nation".

It was mainly when England lagged behind the colonies' version of the imperial dream that it was most likely to be criticized. From the late 1870s colonial governments, disturbed by French activity in the New Hebrides, and by the extension of German trading from Samoa to New Britain and New Ireland, urged British annexation of these areas. In 1883 the Premier of Queensland decided to settle the issue: he ordered the magistrate at Thursday Island to run up the Union Jack and claim New Guinea as a British possession. When the British government disowned this action there were protest meetings, and at the end of the year a convention met with delegates from the Australian, New Zealand and Fiji colonies. The next year when Bismark, as part of a complicated world double game, sent a German warship to North New Guinea to hoist the German flag, Britain gave in, and proclaimed a protectorate of what was left of New Guinea. The three eastern colonies said they would pay some of the costs. The colonies now had a share in a colony.

The gum-suckers

Amid all these imperial concerns, carried on mainly by the British-born, the locally born Australian could be seen as a kind of insolent native who did not make way for you on the streets. "The Australian boy is a slim, dark-eyed, olive-complexioned young rascal, fond of Cavendish, cricket, chuckpenny, and systemically insolent to servant girls, policemen and new chums . . . . His face is soft, bloomless and pasty . . . . He can fight like an Irishman or a Bashi-Bazook; otherwise he is orientally indolent, and will swear with a quiet gusto if you push against him in the street, or request him politely to move on." But fortunately the natives still kept their place: "Such a young gum-sucker must not be confounded with the ordinary middle class Englishmen who form the majority of the professional and businessmen one comes into contact with in the present day. The native Australian element is still altogether in the minority in everyday life, and the majority of adults are English-born colonists."

The idea of the Australian as a town tough found its most convincing practical expression in the "larrikins" who, in bell-bottom trousers, broad-brimmed slouch hats and high-heeled fancy boots, provided enough nuisance and at times enough vandalism to be compared with the b'hoys of New York, the hoodlums of San Francisco and the blueskins of Boston. But there was also a certain respect in the towns for the wildness of the larrikins. If some successful man confessed that he had been "a bit of a larrikin" when he was young, his audience might praise him for it; he had followed the colonial style. It was what there was to offer against English manners.

To the larrikin was added the bushranger. In his earliest forms he had been made a hero for the benefit of convict resentment and Native sullenness. When Victoria saw a revival of bushrangers during the gold rushes in the 1850s they were still mainly ex-convicts, but when New South Wales had its turn in the 1860s, the new generation of bushrangers were mainly failed or struggling selectors. Sympathy for them broadened. Settlers gave them some support, passing on information of police movements by the "bush telegraph", and in the towns their acts were glamorized in songs and pamphlets, and their forms immortalized in waxworks. Even respectable people despised the police, very few of whom were native-born; their drunkedness, brutality and incompetence made it credible that some bushrangers had been hounded into crime by police persecution; bushrangers were almost a national institution; 15,000 signed a petition to reprieve one bushrangers' gang;

and when after eight years of peace from bushrangers the Kelly gang had its two years run some saw them as national heroes.

Although there were some commercially successful Australian-written melodramas in the theatre, there was little reflection of Australian life. Of the few locally written satirical comedies, one was banned by the Victorian Premier because it lampooned him, and another about the families of a squatter knight and an upstart ironfounder, lasted only five nights. The Press put on a more impressive performance: some daily newspapers achieved high provincial standard, and at last there were a number of successful weekly and monthly journals. These included weekly news magazines produced by the daily newspaper companies and quite original in form, with a strong Australian emphasis. Most capital cities had imitations of London *Punch*, the best-lasting of which, Melbourne *Punch*, achieved a distinctively metropolitan wit, being joined in the 1880s as a magazine of metropolitan vision by the Sydney *Bulletin*.

Cartoonists and illustrators saw Australia as mostly metropolitan, but some painters found the freedom of the open air and the relaxed ways of drovers and stockmen distinctively Australian; some discovered a familiar sense of adventure in gold diggers and bushrangers, or in droughts and bushfires. One began to paint Australians as men of sardonic humour, and a careless contempt for authority. With the great excitement caused by attempts to cross the continent, the deaths of explorers became a subject for painters. Some found friendly landscapes, others a sullen despair in the "melancholy gum" and the "frowning hills". Even the animals could seem grotesque or ghostly in "that wild dreamland termed the bush".

Work songs, boasting songs, bushranger songs and funny songs had become popular in the bush, accompanied by concertinas, accordions, Jew's-harps, gumleaves, or a piano brought to a property on a bullock dray. Their Irish, English and United States derivation and the printed concert music form of most of them had shaped their nature, but they were felt to be of a particular kind that belonged to the bush, and they did not catch on so well in the cities, where the bush could seem a dull place without cricket teams or brass bands. These songs were generally cheerful—if hardship were described it was usually with dry humour—but when their subject matter did take on in the cities, its style became more melancholy.

Adam Lindsay Gordon, the agent of this change, was an English expatriate, a daring rider who tried his luck in the bush, and saw himself as a second Byron. Not much of his verse had an Australian setting (and that was little regarded by him) but it gave the colonies their first idea that they were a people with a poet. In 1870, on the day after his latest volume, *Bush Ballads and Galloping Rhymes* came out, depressed by his lack of recognition and his inability to pay the printer's bill, Gordon shot himself dead. The book was an instant success. His work seized "a place in the heart and mind" of the people, in the cities as well as the bush, although not among Anglo-Australian cultivated circles. His extraordinary popular appeal came partly from the way he described sport and violent action, but part of it also seemed to come from his scepticism about life's journey, which he saw as almost meaningless except for helping the weak, and from his stoic message of living uncomplainingly and being ready to die game. "No one has sung our modern woes more healthily," said Francis Adams.

Ten years later Henry Kendall, a poet who had suffered a breakdown from alcoholism, won a newspaper prize on the subject of the forthcoming International Exhibition in Sydney (with one of his worst poems). His next book made money and he enjoyed celebrity for two years before he died. He had taken metaphors from the inland to express his own unhappiness and frustrations, and metaphors from the coastal scenery to express his longings, so that from him as well as Gordon the townspeople of Australia were able to begin to commemorate themselves as a people of rural virtue and thus, by seeking to identify their condition, to conceal it.

The pride of the colonies

In New Zealand, despite a central government, the six provincial governments had largely followed their own ways; the sea was so much their chief highway that news sometimes passed from north island to south by means of journeys to and from Australia. In the 1860s the south island was jolted from a population of 50,000 to 159,000 as Australian diggers swarmed across the Tasman in the gold rushes; in the north the frontier sporadically became a battlefield between whites and Maoris, with the whites finally breaking the Maoris' grip on the land. In the 1870s a boom equal to that of the Australian colonies—and partly an extension of it—was accompanied by the abolition of the provincial governments, with some of their power going to local authorities and the rest to the central government.

The 450,000 white New Zealanders had achieved a form of common government, but the 2,300,000 white Australians were passing through a period of disintegration. Each blasting its own trumpet, each fighting the others by trade restrictions, shipping regulations and freight rates, each competing for British capital and immigrants, the colonies had refused co-operation, apart from occasional intercolonial conferences. When the British withdrew their military garrison in 1870, leaving only naval protection, an intercolonial conference decided to re-establish units of militia, but whatever pride was served by bodies such as the Victoria Volunteer Yeomanry or the South Australian Troop of Mounted Rifles, it was the pride of each separate colony. Few businesses except financial houses and shipping lines operated in more than one colony; many businessmen and politicians had not set foot in another colony. Even the railways were of different gauges.

Overriding all other discords was the rivalry between Sydney and Melbourne. In Sydney Victorians seemed "a people to be distrusted" and Melbourne "the city of stewpans and stockbrokers". In a kind of retrospective irredentism, Victorians laid claim to part of New South Wales, wishing to spread to at least this part of the backward-looking colony some of Victoria's "moral, conscious power". Even the taste in entertainment of the two cities was seen as different: "The play that succeeds in Melbourne rarely succeeds in Sydney, and vice versa."

From being the second largest colony Tasmania was now second smallest, and from a sense of its own importance it had passed to a fear of Melbourne's power. South Australia aloofly took pride in a mastery of agriculture that would have pleased

Virgil, and Adelaide was so firm in its respectability that it had no larrikins. Western Australia remained remote and resentful, small and failed: the transportation of convicts had ceased, but there were hardly any free immigrants.

A new kind of Australia seemed to be developing in the tropics and sub-tropics of Queensland. The great holdings of semi-arid steppes of the cattle kings of the west reached dimensions not previously imagined. For a while there were fears that the Chinese, brought by gold, might take Queensland over; in one remote field the 17,000 Chinese outnumbered the whites several times over and there was talk that the 100,000 Chinese on the U.S. west coast might come to Queensland if they were expelled from the U.S. But it was when sugar plantations spread along the hot coast that the greatest difference emerged. It had seemed self-evident that white men could not work in such enervating heat, so black men ("kanakas") were brought in by traders, bought or kidnapped from Fiji and other South Pacific Islands, and used, or abused, as indentured labour. In Brisbane both conscience and economic expediency denounced this as slavery. A doctors' report to the government in 1879 announced that death rates on some plantations from overwork, malnutrition, bad water, lack of medical attention and general neglect were as high as 10 per cent.

Would the north break away from the rest of Queensland? If it did, there were fears that other new colonies might form along the north coast of Australia, setting up planter-slave communities in what might prove a tragic parallel with the Southern States of America.

Chapter 9

THE NORMAL MARCH OF PROGRESS

1885-1910

The fall of Melbourne

More confident than ever, "Marvellous Melbourne" was now sprawling across a hundred square miles as municipal councils tried to outboost each other and land and mortgage companies constructed edifices of hope on new heights of credit. Melbourne was seen by its most hopeful boosters as the centre of an area which in fifty years time, Australia's population by then being bigger than Britain's, would be ready to take over the government of India. But although it had seemed an important part of the purpose of life that rich men should become richer by buying and selling land, the banks suddenly put up their interest rates, and then cut their overdrafts. New financial institutions had to be improvised: for a season the boom became more frenzied, but now there were more houses for sale than money to buy them. Prices fell. The market collapsed. Immigration ceased.

This failure was part of a more general disaster. Farm prices had fallen by as much as 50 per cent, and when a financial crash in Argentina had frightened world speculators British investors had begun pulling their money out of Melbourne. The government added to the panic by stopping public works. There were runs on the savings banks. A couple of dozen land finance companies failed. Then in 1893 the whole Melbourne financial system fell into pieces. In January one bank suspended payment, in April another; within a month eleven more. The Victorian Premier declared a week's bank holiday. His only comfort was the statement, "We are all floundering". Melbourne had lost 50,000 population; houses stood empty; unemployment grew. Processions, mass meetings, deputations, armed police, and soup kitchens, testified to the crisis. God's hand had struck at Melbourne's wickedness. The Presbyterians declared a day of public humiliation and prayer.

Through a bank of which he was a director, the Premier had lent himself and his associates nearly £750,000; he retired to London as Agent-General. The Speaker was arrested, but government delays helped him get off. Another M.P. announced debts of £1,500,000, on which he paid a halfpenny in the pound; when he died in London in 1907 his estate was worth £250,000. Enough came out in the courts and in Press exposures to reveal that cliques of those belonging to "a worldly Presbyterianism" had falsified balance sheets, paid dividends out of capital, manipulated the share markets, given each other unsecured credit and, by their control of banks and other financial institutions, helped themselves to other people's money. A former Solicitor-General declared them "an aristocracy of criminals".

A general crisis had seized all the eastern colonies. As confidence vanished, with fallen farm prices and withdrawn British funds, the previous banquet of unproductive investment left no sustenance. Throughout there was the kind of unemployment and distress not known since the early 1840s, but it was in Melbourne that the crisis was most serious. Melbourne was not again to seem the clearly dominant city in the land of the Improvers.

South Australia's depression had begun in the late 1880s when drought and grasshoppers had proved false the South Australian slogan that "rain follows the plough". A reckless run into the dry interior turned into a sad retreat. But this disaster was faced with more coolness than in Victoria, and by 1893, the year of financial collapse in Melbourne, a new government, uniting both liberal and radical elements, was to institute women's franchise, a State bank, factory inspection, progressive land and income taxes, death duties, and other measures that were to make South Australia briefly one of the most progressive places in the world. By the end of the century

Adelaide was to seem like a German *Residenzstraat*, the neat capital of a little principality, "with its park and gardens, its little court societies and its general air of laying itself out to enjoy quietly a comfortable life", but devoted to the well-mannered pursuit of democracy. In population and economic activities, however, it had been outraced by the cruder vigours of Queensland, with only 357,000 people to Queensland's 493,000.

While the others were suffering their worst economic disaster, Western Australia rushed into its golden age. Given self-government in 1890, several years later it saw two of the biggest gold rushes in the colonies' history. New wheatlands attracted many of South Australia's failed farmers, and in the north there was a spread of cattle stations and a development of the pearling industry. Perth's population increased tenfold, the colony's population jumped from 48,000 to 179,000 bringing it ahead of Tasmania. In 1890 Western Australia had the smallest public debt of the colonies; by 1900 its growth was so great that, proportionate to population, it had a debt twice as high as that of any other.

New South Wales also knew scandals during the depression: companies failed; a Mines Minister was jailed; the building industry collapsed; there was much unemployment. But New South Wales had not been so taken by surprise as Victoria. When the financial crisis came, instead of announcing a policy of "floundering" the government helped tide financial institutions over.

By 1900 all the colonies had staggered out of the depression, but assisted immigration was still abandoned and private investors and banks were still cautious. New South Wales passed Victoria in population; by 1900 it had 1,360,000 to Victoria's 1,196,000; and although, with 496,000, Melbourne was still ahead of Sydney, it was by only 15,000 people; in the decade Sydney's population had risen by 100,000, Melbourne's only by 6,000. A Sydney magazine said that Victoria, "tainting the Continent with its foulness", should be declared an infected province.

The commonplace rich

By 1910 Australians had made new records in prosperity and

all the capital cities were again bidding against each other for immigrants. More than a quarter of a million were to arrive in the next four years. The normal march of economic progress appeared to have resumed. But to visitors, used to the idea that prosperity should seem to be deserved, it could seem economic progress without intelligent leadership either in country or city.

In the country some saw the squatters as almost "extinct", after a devastation of the sheep industry. As the trees had been felled across the more arid stretches of wilderness and sheep nibbled away the grass, the natural cover of the earth had been removed so that at times of drought the sun dried the top soil into a powder; when the westerlies blew they lifted this powder up and blew it away as dust. By the 1890s there was a new source of devastation: imported rabbits. Rabbits had become a pest in Victoria in the 1860s; by the 1880s the governments of the four eastern colonies were building hundreds of miles of fencing to stop them spreading, but the rabbits were crossing New South Wales at the rate of about seventy miles a year, and by the 1890s they had reached the coast of Western Australia. All the fences were built too late. When the rainfall was low the rabbits would not only eat the grass but also kill the edible shrubs that were a standby for sheep in bad times. In this way most of the west of New South Wales was eroded. In some areas of better rainfall there was a different plague. Prickly pear, originally introduced as a pot plant, and then used as a hedge, had infested 10 million acres by 1900 and was spreading in a way that seemed uncontrollable. These scourges came together in the eight years of the Great Drought which culminated in the "Sahara year" of 1902. Accompanied by a big drop in world prices for wool, the Great Drought led many outback squatters to walk off their properties. It was cheaper to give up. In 1891 there had been 106 million sheep in Australia; in 1902 there were 54 million.

However, during the drought some squatters had done well out of the disasters of others. (From failures of other squatters' mortgage repayments, one cattle man built up control of nine million acres.) There were still enough squatters left to be both hated and held in awe for their wealth and for the isolation they maintained both from the country areas where they lorded it and the cities where they took most of their diversions. Prospering on their overdrafts, devoted to "wealth, senseless leisure, or the stupid adoration of titles and royalty", the only civic duties they accepted were to maintain a black-hat Anglophilia in their clubs and Government House attendances, and to be patrons of the race courses. They saw the maintenance of racing stables as their particular public service, and race meetings as the important ritual of the State. For some the culmination of both Anglophilia and horse-racing was to join "the rich racing set in England", and for most of them the proper division of society was between those who went to the Members' Stand, those in the Paddock, those who used the Leger, and those who could afford only the Flat.

In the towns there was a rise in manufacturing. With so much money wasted on unsuitable pastoral expansion or ridiculously high prices for city properties, there was such a gap in investment in manufacturing that after the depression it was one of the main places where money could go. Even if factories were still small, the use of electric power rapidly expanded, and the number of factories and factory workers was to double, with New South Wales now moving faster than Victoria, and both colonies together controlling about three-quarters of manufacturing activity.

The biggest of the manufacturers now joined the older merchants and financiers in command of the cities. They were "the common-place rich", and their citadels were the gentlemen's clubs where men would relax over dominoes and cigars for so long after a lunch of soup, joint, sweets, cheese and salad that one observer regarded the atmosphere as more mediterranean than Northern European. Except for "an intransigeant opposition based on the defence of their profits", they were little concerned with public affairs, and even less with the intellect. Like the squatters, they had not learnt to clothe their self-interest in even a pretence of acquired culture or social responsibility. "Aggressive in manners and blatant in dress", with ". . . neither homeliness nor splendour; only bad taste and cold indifference . . . *money-making* and *racing* seem their only concern." The racing sets had become so important that even Government Houses had to bend to their ways.

No system of education, except an imitation of the English, had been found for the children of those who through wealth controlled many of the colonies' affairs. To learn the assured arrogance of lucky birth, but none of the techniques of business, the children of the rich and the well-to-do went to the now proliferating colonial Rugbys: even the Catholics and Methodists set them up. There was no provision for a useful education; the emphasis was on honour. After learning their manners, the squatters' children went back to the land; many of the brighter children of the rich or the well-to-do went into medicine or law; the others went into their families' businesses.

In business their theory of management was English: that only a gentleman could command. It was said in 1910 of the education of the colonial Rugbys: "It breeds a certain kind of man—a man who can rise to the top, who can face difficulties, who can lead others, who can manage affairs successfully; a man who may be neither smart nor doctrinaire nor scientific nor original, but in whose hands any piece of business is safe which entails the management of men." That seemed all that was necessary.

Given the self-assurance of gentlemanliness, even the technical training of wage earners seemed unnecessary. While the practice of technical education had previously been perfunctory, even derisory, and often non-existent, there had at least been a lot of talk about it. Even the talk had now subsided. Neither manufacturers nor trades unions were interested; students from the government schools were not usually sufficiently educated to follow technical courses; there were not enough good instructors; there were no classes in the higher levels of trades. The supply of skilled workers declined. In 1910 the Associated Chambers of Manufactures of Australia demanded large scale immigration to fill the gap.

An exemplar to the old lands

It was not to the commonplace rich but to their own governments that the colonies looked for progress. And here, despite the opposition of the Legislative Councils, change was so remarkable that a few social scientists from other countries came to Australia and New Zealand to write books about them. "Australasia has not contributed much to social philosophy, but she has come infinitely further than any other country in the practical field . . . Western Europe is richer in doctrines, Australasia in realities," said one of them.

State action had come in a series of improvising reactions to difficulties for which imported political ideologies, except un-Anglo-Saxon ones, were of little use, but no distinctive theory developed to sustain it. "Australian politics concerned themselves with day-to-day affairs. . . . The poverty of the theoretical basis . . . is astonishing to those used to the polemics of Europe." Phrases such as "State socialism" and "colonial socialism" were sometimes used, but *etatisme* seemed un-British and no phrase caught on that could enable people to imagine what their style of government was. "Colonial governmentalism", a phrase invented by a New Zealand politician, was a useful description, but not a cry to stir men's hearts.

Nevertheless many of Europe's progressive aspirations had been achieved in Australia and New Zealand. Labour laws were seen as "not matched elsewhere in their number, boldness and stringency": compulsory arbitration in industrial disputes was unique; factory acts had become more extensive; early closing in shops had been instituted everywhere except Tasmania; several colonies had adapted English workers' compensation legislation; New Zealand and New South Wales were two of the first countries in the world to set up government unemployment bureaux; wage boards were concerned with maintaining minimum living standards; graduated income and land taxes and death duties introduced a mild redistribution of income. When New South Wales imitated New Zealand and legislated for old-age pensions in 1901 the only other place with a non-contributory scheme was Denmark. (The German contributory scheme was seen as not suitable for "a free country like New South Wales" and "impossible of accomplishment in Anglo-Saxon countries".) New South Wales introduced a non-contributory invalid pensions scheme in 1908, the first place in the world to do so. The divorce laws of New South Wales, Victoria and New Zealand were amongst the most advanced in the world; payment of members of parliament and women's suffrage were introduced ahead of most other places. Governments were the main landlords, with intricate rules for land administration, land reform and subsidizing of farmers; some saw the tariff as the basis of all human progress. Governments owned the railways, controlled central education systems, pursued active policies of immigration, and ran homes for neglected children and the aged and infirm.

The "petty suburban proprietor . . . who sat on his veranda on sunny Sunday mornings, smoking, and discussing all these things with his fellow workmen" even hoped for a peaceful end to industrial disputes. His small, iron-framed, time-payment piano attested to his respectability, and it was hard for him not to see some order in existence. A Royal Commission had said: "It is frankly admitted that a great many disputes originate in ignorance, in mutual misunderstandings, in unfounded suspicions, in exaggerated claims, and that very much is gained if all these disturbing accessories can be got rid of, and the controversy can be narrowed to its simple issues." New South Wales, later followed by the others, took over the New Zealand system of compulsory arbitration by quasi-legal bodies in industrial disputes. By taking ignorance, mutual misunderstanding, unfounded suspicions and exaggerated claims into court rooms it was believed that they would disappear.

"Australia," said a trades union newspaper, "has ever been an exemplar to the old lands . . . it has steadily forged ahead, initiating and perfecting, experimenting and legislating, on new lines."

Every worker a gentleman ?

In the new century, after a Polynesian boy had gone body surfing at Manly beach in Sydney, surfing developed so rapidly that property values in some beach suburbs trebled. As the habit spread around other parts of the 12,000 miles of coastline, shooting the breakers became "an institution as important to Australia as standing armies, established churches, music halls and sturdy beggars are in older civilisations". Almost as important as the ability to surf was the need to acquire a suntan: on the beach "the white man represents the pariah class, despised by all". After a portable reel rescue line had been invented at Bondi and a military-style rescue and resuscitation drill developed, surf life-saving clubs were formed and the life-savers became ". . . the Samurais, the oligarchs, the elite . . . a gladiator class, envied by all the men, adored by all the women."

The "near-nakedness" of the beach was seen as a reshuffle of values, with the new elite those who were best at browning their bodies and shooting the breakers. In this the beach was simply part of the larger democracy of sport: most of Australia's heroes were the great champions of swimming, tennis, cycling, boxing, footracing, football and, above all, cricket, a game followed so keenly that when there was a Test Match in England crowds stood outside the newspaper offices at night waiting for each cable that gave progress reports on the day's play.

The democracy of the beach and of sport (part of "a genuine Democracy, the people really wanting what it wishes to get") was one of the causes of the self-congratualtion on how fortunate manual workers were assumed to be in Australia. It was estimated that one out of every four male adults was the possessor of some property, compared with about one in eleven in Great Britain. Said the *Sydney Morning Herald*: "The distribution of wealth is not paralleled in any other part of the world."

Except for the 1890s depression (and even then, for those who kept their jobs, real wages rose) the chronic scarcity of labour had given manual workers both status and prosperity. By 1900 the demand for labour was as high as ever and of a total population of nearly three and three-quarter million only 30,000 were out of work. Two-thirds of trades had gained the eight-hour day. In the rhetoric of some trades unions both capital and labour were assumed to be marching together towards a common good. The union movement was commended by the Catholic Archbishop of Sydney. In other countries the Australian trades unions were seen as among the world's most advanced.

The provision of lower-priced "workmen's tickets" on the trains encouraged manual workers to move farther away from the city. At the evening rush hour workers crowded into buses, trams and trains, homing to their suburbs. The central parts of the cities were becoming more respectable; there were moves to ban barmaids. While vaudeville and musical comedies such as *Floradora* or *The Merry Widow* flourished and *cinematographie* became a craze, serious drama descended into little theatres. The cities were becoming quieter at night.

With the new diversification of the suburbs manual workers might now never set eyes on the houses of the rich, nor gain entry to the more expensive of the white collar suburbs; but there were mixed suburbs, office workers, small business men and manual workers all together, (families might sometimes contain examples of all three) as well as suburbs in which manual workers predominated.

When a new railway station was built and nearby estates were subdivided at prices manual workers could pay, a shopping street would form along the railway line; footpaths would be cleared, gas and water pipes laid, schools and churches built; a telephone exchange installed, a volunteer fire brigade and a volunteer ambulance started; a new municipal council incorporated. Schools of Arts went up (no longer "palladiums of nationality", but lending libraries for light books with billiard rooms and halls for hire) and the municipal councils quickly founded sports ovals and bowling greens; there were many public tennis courts and even a number of suburban race courses. There were beaches to go to and, as *cinematographie* spread, there was a "Saturday night at the flicks".

The old gregariousness was gone: hotel licences in the new suburbs were restricted, and hotels had ceased to be places of assembly; observers noticed the growing "puritanical reserve" of many of the suburbanite manual workers—their sabbitarianism, their abstention from alcohol, their polite avoidance of certain subjects or words in conversation. "Barebrick habitations . . . unrelieved by trees or grass . . . shrivel up every poor little instinct and aspiration towards natural purity and beauty." It was strange to visitors that a manual worker should be "a petty surburban proprietor", and repellent that it could seem that "the people are . . . all of them gambling profit-makers, keen on realising the Individualist ideas of the lower middle class of 1840-70".

The novelty of this new sense of achievement became so great that a French visitor said: "If the forward march, for the working class, consists of attaining the exact level of the bourgeoisie, the manual worker of Australia has raised himself as high as possible. He has, in effect, placed himself in the category of the 'respectable people' and has assured himself of the prestige of outward appearance, so useful everywhere, but more powerful in British Countries than in the rest of the world.

The Australian worker has become a 'gentleman'. He dresses himself after his work, he is housed, and he behaves like a person of good society . . . . More and more one can observe the external difference between the worker and the bourgeois diminishing except during working hours."

Every farmer a yeoman ?

In the U.S., Canada and the Australian colonies, at roughly the same time, new techniques and expanded world markets gave wheat farmers relatively sudden ideas of their own importance. In the Australian colonies the wheat farmer had already been honoured in South Australia as a rational agriculturist compared with the squatter-depredator: rash expansion and subsequent disaster dulled some of his brightness, but now he came into his own in Victoria when the rush into the mallee, backed by railways and new farming techniques, made Victoria the main wheat colony. Then from 1894 to 1899 New South Wales doubled its wheat production. It doubled it again in the next decade. By 1911 its wheat crops were roughly ten times as big as those of 1891. New South Wales was now the leading wheat producer. The railways had opened up virgin farmland and now, after so many sardonic failures, Governor Phillip's dream had been resolved: New South Wales could grow wheat.

In the biggest wheat-growing areas new towns grew up or if towns were already there they were made pay honour to wheat. Wheat trains joined other symbols of prosperity as they rolled on to the city ports. Wheat farmers saw themselves as sturdy pioneers, an idea unusual in Australia, where the squatters had been dismissed as greedy gamblers, and although the idea was often derided they began to imagine that they might provide the most admirable characteristics of a nation whose goodness was otherwise being sucked dry by the evils of the cities and the excesses of the wealthiest squatters. They began to organize in dissident, sometimes radical, groups and to plan new political parties, in which some of the smaller graziers also showed interest. Even some of the dairy farmers, the despised "cow cockies", now began to claim respect as, like the wheat industry, dairying was modernized. They too became interested in new political parties.

Further honour was given to small farmers when the problem of lack of water began to be amended by technology. Water was pumped into irrigation canals that could turn one unprofitable sheep station into a cultivated area providing a living for 3,000 settlers. Soon there seemed no limit to "the triumphant march of water . . . bringing life to the grass and flower, to the loaded tree. . . . No price is too high for the promise of such progress."

The desire to establish a class of "virtuous and industrious" small farmers was now so strong that utopianism during the depression about the virtues of rural life prompted the three eastern colonies to pass laws enabling autonomous co-operative communities to be set up, with the right to govern themselves. One of man's old dreams—the right of self-organization in small units of common wealth—had now been enacted by Australian laws, but very few village communes were formed. (The most famous of them, "New Australia", was set up not in Australia but in Paraguay, where several shiploads of utopian Australians emigrated to found "a community where all labour in common for the common good". It was a disaster.)

Governments turned to buying success: "free selection" had failed; more costly schemes of land reform were developed, given the name of "closer settlement", and government money was put behind them. Governments bought large estates to subdivide and sell off on easy terms as small holdings; large estates were taxed; government banks were instructed to give cheap credit for improvements. Holdings were often too small to be economic, but governments were now prepared to subsidize them: if "closer settlers" defaulted, their indebtedness was often cancelled. Backed by government research and government agricultural colleges and by government sponsorship of cheap land, of irrigation, of trade and of pest control, and by the readiness of government Departments of Railways to cut freight rates or even run lines at a loss, there was at last produced the long-awaited independent Australian yeomanry.

With self-respect for both "yeoman farmer" and "petty suburban proprietor", the improvement of the human condition by government legislation, control of conflict by rational arbitration, and the ability to be prosperous without thinking about it, dreams seemed to be moving towards realization. But it was now the "modern age". Other dreams were around.

Chapter 10

THE MODERN AGE
1885-1910 *(cont'd)*

The rise of the professionals

"Box-like . . . gigantic . . . hideous . . . grotesque . . . gruesome . . . ugly . . . monumental without being sublime." The new city buildings, towering up ten or even twelve stories brought protests; limits were soon placed on their height. There were other signs of the "modern age": the Marconi Company set up two broadcasting stations in 1905 for communicating across the Bass Strait; horseless carriages passed the stage of seeming an expensive public nuisance, and by 1910 there were 5,000 of them; a flying-machine built on a Victorian sheep station flew twenty feet above the ground for 200 yards at 25 miles an hour; in 1912 Australia was to see its first air race.

In this new age with its new demands, the colonial Rugbys, although offering no training, except in arrogance, for the "management of men", nevertheless had to show some concern for the "smart" or "scientific", or even the "original", because of the uses that had been found for the universities after they had been forced to abandon their dreams of providing a classical education for Australian gentlemen. Since no one else, apart from the Schools of Mines, had provided technical and professional schools, the universities had stepped in, with considerable efficiency. Now there was expansion.

One reason for this expansion was the renewed boom in farming. The development of wheat farming had not come merely from railways and new markets. The establishment of Departments of Agriculture had led to a scientific approach. There were careful experiments in breeding new strains; the importance of superphosphate was discovered; machinery continued to improve; agricultural colleges were founded. With science, technology and education now showing the way, yields per acre almost quadrupled. It was the same with dairying. Australia had imported butter from New Zealand, but cold chambers on ships made chilled Australian butter available to British markets, and refrigeration and the spread of the railways increased markets at home. Swedish cream separators appeared in Australian dairies, co-operative butter factories were set up, pasteurization was introduced. From 1900 to 1910 the amount of machinery on dairy farms doubled. In the twenty-five years after 1890 the production of butter quadrupled. Refrigeration had also provided an opportunity for an alternative industry to wool-growing. Freezing works had been set up at the city ports and refrigerating machines in the holds of the fast mail steamers. With New South Wales mutton and Queensland beef on the British market, sometimes at a quarter of the price of British meat, one-ninth of export income came from frozen or chilled foods.

Specialists were needed for the new Agriculture Departments. Veterinary science and agricultural science schools were established at the universities, and these and other demands led to an extension of science departments. To meet new demands in technique university engineering schools expanded, an expansion made greater by the development of manufacturing and a considerable growth in discoveries of new mineral fields. In New South Wales the opening of new coalfields beyond Newcastle meant almost a doubling of coal production; the Western Australian gold fields boomed; in 1893 the Mt Lyell Copper Co. in Tasmania proclaimed itself owner of the world's richest copper mine. Silver and lead were discovered at Broken Hill and Broken Hill Proprietary made nearly £1,152,000 profit in one year. It set up a lead smelting works at Port Pirie in South Australia and after developing the "flotation" process to separate zinc from zinc sulphide re-worked the dumps of the Broken Hill mines to extract another $30-million worth of minerals. To find a use for the sulphur extracted from zinc separation, it built a sulphuric acid plant, began producing superphosphates, and, having acquired two mountains of iron ore in South Australia, decided in 1910 to go into the steel business at Newcastle. By this time in some fields Australians were among the world's leaders in metallurgical skill.

As well as the expansion of the university schools that followed the expansion of farming and minerals, schools of architecture, economics and education were founded to meet other demands. Original research was done in geology, biology and anthropology. Most practitioners of the older professions of medicine and law were now Australian, so there was expansion of those schools as well. The medical schools began to produce highly competent graduates, a few of whom produced original research. The New South Wales Government set up a Bureau of Microbiology; an Institute of Tropical Medicine was established at Townsville. Dentistry and pharmacy schools were instituted.

By 1910 little more than a quarter of university students were studying Arts; the biggest single schools were in Medicine. Useful at last, the universities were largely training schools for specialists, producing new kinds of people claiming professional status—engineers, scientists, dentists, economists, architects, agricultural scientists, veterinary scientists. Without them Australia's prosperity would not have existed.

The Arts faculties were still given the highest honour in lists of precedence and academic processions but, palely derivative of British institutions, they provided neither a meaningful cultural background nor a useful general education for those who were to exercise the generalist arts of administration in business or government.

"Colonial governmentalism" was not sustained by a reservoir of talent. Scorned by the rich and the well-to-do, the government bureaucracies reflected the ". . . muddling on, with a high standard of honour and a low standard of efficiency [that] is the dominant note of Australian public life." Recruiting policies showed no concern for attracting talent; there was no recruitment of people with higher levels of education, and attempts to relate advancement to tests of ability were defeated by concern for the "decent duffers" who might otherwise miss their promotions. Everybody had to start at the bottom, and after that the slow climb through the hierarchy usually depended on seniority. Heads of departments tended to be elderly men of a kind found only in the lower divisions of the civil service of other countries. In an annual report one Public Service Board wondered if something more might be needed; it raised the question of "the desirability of introducing to the Government Services young men who had secured a full university training". The idea was not mentioned again.

In the higher reaches of business the standards were still those of the black hats. Australia's prosperity was sustained by derivation, specialist professionalism, and administrative improvisation; it lacked some of the innovations of the countries that were now taking the lead from Great Britain.

The rise of the employees

While most new "professionals" had come to the university specialist schools from the colonial Rugbys, there were new if lesser kinds of respectable jobs for those whose parents could not afford to send them to these schools. As "office life" developed as an idea, with cash registers and telephones adding to its pace, typewriters bringing female typists, and expansion producing bigger organizations, the idea of "the employee" began to emerge. Bright boys looked for clerical jobs in the pastoral houses, the shipping and trading firms, the friendly societies and insurance offices, or the department stores. Others settled for becoming salesmen. At the same time the civil service in each colony had been reformed (and renamed "the public service" to show that it was different). Offering permanence of tenure, pensions and guaranteed incremental rises in salary, and with low standard entrance examinations, it offered the sons of the not-so-well-off a safe respectability as "government officers", and became, it was said, "an attractive haven of mediocrity". The railways departments, Australia's biggest employers of labour, their now independent Commissioners treated like lords in their ornate offices and lavish special trains, offered clerical jobs and "officers' " postings; so did the other semi-independent government-owned business undertakings now being formed. For some, entry into respectability was to be a teacher for one of the education departments; for others, to have become a bank clerk was to have arrived.

Suburbs began to diversify. The rich had already moved out of town to group together in new bastions of richness, their former houses becoming lodging-houses or being knocked down and replaced by shops or offices. Now some "employees" and "government officers", together with small businessmen, gathered in new suburbs that they saw as better than those where manual workers predominated. In these new suburbs a new vogue produced a romantic profusion of the Queen Anne style in which the flourishing redness of bare brick was a confident assertion of taste and respectability. Joined in this purpose, the newly introduced terracotta Marseilles tiles were shown off to the uttermost in contorted roofs; even the iron roofs of weatherboard houses were painted red to imitate them. Leadlight windows and flowery decorations (gumnuts, sheep, kangaroos) of a debased Art Nouveau then added further romantic novelties. Wire baskets of ferns hung on verandas; "sleep-outs" were added; a superficial "naturalness" was now becoming the style.

To choose who should wear a white collar, there were Public Service examinations, Institute of Bankers examinations, Teachers Admission examinations. But there were no government high schools to prepare students for them. By the beginning of the new century, the United States had 7,200 State high schools; Australia had only five, all in New South Wales. There were arrangements here and there for minor forms of secondary education but, tied to imitations of the English system, the government education departments, a Victorian Royal Commission reported, "had been quite stationary". Not even government teachers were properly educated. Under the "pupil teacher" system 14-year-olds were apprenticed to headmasters; they would do a full day's teaching and after hours pick up a little more education; most received no further training.

Prompted by the need to provide an education system for the new "employees" and "government officers", Royal Commissions were set up and then revealed the hollowness of the education department's optimistic annual reports; officials were sent to Europe and the United States and after they returned with their reports the education departments set up high schools and junior high schools in each capital city. They were considered an expensive item, restricted to "those fitted by intelligence"; there were not many of them and their curricula were quickly shaped to fit the entrance requirements of the universities, although most of those who went to them could not afford to go to the universities. Those who could not attain the high schools were channelled off for a few years into commercial, technical, agricultural or domestic science schools, as befitted their mental station or the financial situation of their parents.

A minimum standard of secondary education had been improvised to meet the demands of a new society, with new ways of making a living. But to many of those employees or government officers who woke each morning in their brick cottages, fastened white collars around their necks with studs, and went off in trains or trams to office desks, carrying their lunches in attache cases, the new standard meant little more than a ration of clerk's virtue.

The New Imperialism

With huge new systems of self-justifying belief, the great powers of Europe had expressed their modernity by moving into the age of the New Imperialism and this now became a motivating factor in the Australian colonies as had earlier the Age of Improvement. Each of what were considered the four main world civilizations—Slav, Teutonic, Latin and Anglo-Saxon—was seen by its followers as uniquely able (because of its God-given power) to save humanity by spreading Christian ideals and an equitable world order. University teachers, writers and journalists preached the good news of this messianic force; propaganda organizations, monuments and exhibitions gave testament to it. Its cult of service demanded hard, dutiful work so that an elect nation could take up the civilizing burden; its cult of power justified possession as nine points of God's law; its pride in itself was evident in everything from grandiose buildings to strutting about in uniforms; its cult of the heroic made saints of contemporary colonial conquerors and ransacked history for supporting tales of adventure and derring-do; its cult of blood saw war as "a link in God's world", a cleansing "bath of steel", regenerating national character. In the shadows of glory there was gloom: if there were waverings all might be lost. Old hatreds between nations swelled into fears for the whole world. Writers made reputations by discovering "the American peril", "the yellow peril", "the black peril", "the Cossack invasion", "the Zionist conspiracy".

The British exceeded the others both in the heights of their boasting and the depths of their gloom. Arrogant ideas that went back to the seventeenth century were adapted as part of the new imperial propaganda but at the same time there were greater fears of decline: Britain's industrial power was being challenged; Ireland was threatening unity; rival imperialisms were beginning to confront British supremacy in the cult of naval power. When Victoria celebrated her diamond jubilee in 1897 it was said that "no sovereign since the fall of Rome could muster subjects from so many and such distant countries all over the world", but it was also the occasion of Kipling's "Recessional": the far flung battle lines might waver, then disappear. Dreams of a Greater Britain were revived, in which "colonial imperialism based on a confident nationalism" would come to the aid of the mother country, to make it seem safer and bigger in a federal world structure based on the certainties of "the British race".

In Australia, mainly in Victoria, the Imperial Federation League had enjoyed a season ten years before. Its strongest advocates were well-to-do businessmen, squatters, officers of the colonial militia, Church of England bishops, professors—in short the clubbable men, the Government House sets. It had propounded as Australia's true inspiration the sanctity of the Royal Family and of the British aristocracy, the destiny of the Anglo-Saxons, the power of the Royal Navy, the bonds of blood, trade and sentiment, and the excitements of knighthoods, orders, medals, flags and promotions on the field. The *Australian Naval and Military Gazette* had been renamed *Young Australia* and had issued regular calls to a duty that could only have been satisfied by the union of 500 million people, most of them not Anglo-Saxons. There were no branches of the Imperial Federation League in New South Wales, and elsewhere only a limited number of people supported it; but as the movement disintegrated its individual excesses spread, so that imperialistic rhetoric became an essential part of Australian public life in the 1890s, sometimes its dominating part.

Melbourne put up statues to both General Gordon and the eight-hour day; trade union banquets began with the loyal toast. "The fleets of a great empire are ready to assist us," said a Premier of Queensland. "The British tie gives us a standing in the world," said a Premier of New South Wales, "which is illumined by all the glory of the fatherland, and which carries in its very fibre the heroic greatness of our race." The Rev. W. H. Fitchett, headmaster of the Methodist Ladies' College in Victoria, author of such works as *Deeds that Won the Empire*, with 750,000 copies of his books sold, became one of the Empire's best-sellers. A regular school examination question was: "How would you answer a boy from a foreign country if he were to ask you why you are proud to belong to the British Empire?" In 1905 Empire Day was instituted as a holy day for schools, with stirring imperial oratory, flapping of Union Jacks, marches, imperial songs, brass bands and free bags of boiled lollies. (But the British were keeping a sceptical eye on colonial imperialism. "The only good way of dealing with the local authorities is to firmly refuse to permit them to have any say as to the disposition or management of the squadron," the English admiral commanding the Australian naval station wrote to the First Lord of the Admiralty in London. "They understand firmness: they do not understand concession, which they always take to be weakness.")

A dual loyalty was taught in the government schools; there was a narrow "patriotism which is concerned solely with the country in which we live", but there was also "that wider patriotism which embraces the whole empire". At least a quarter of the songs taught in schools were on British patriotic themes. To teach Australians "pride of race" it was necessary to go back to Wulf the Saxon Boy Who Helped to Make England, then learn the other exemplary tales of "the great men of our race". Britain, "the leading nation in the world", Mother Country of an Empire on which the sun never set, having put her own house in order after the Civil War, "sought and found a great work ready to her hand which she alone could accomplish": the bringing of civilization to the "inferior races", who were "only children". She was able to accomplish this great work through the expression of the British Christian virtues of which the Victoria Cross became a profound symbol.

In an Empire built on the adventures and noble deeds of a race of clean-living heroes, the "race" had reached its finest hour in General Gordon, "the Christian soldier".

The Catholic schools learnt their history differently, with martyrs instead of heroes, and if heroism was taught it was more that of St Thomas More against the "cruel tyrant Henry VIII" or of Mary Queen of Scots against Elizabeth. When the Boer War presented an opportunity for Australians to enter the great adventure of empire-building, Cardinal Moran was one of the few public men who questioned the idea of volunteers "expected to go to every place where a British war might happen to be carried on".

After 16,175 Australian men and 16,314 Australian horses had served in the Boer War, Australia felt it had entered history: six men won V.Cs. Memorials went up, and South African Soldiers Associations were established to retain the memories of comradeship. In "a war to uphold the British prestige all over the world", Australia had undertaken a responsibility that "would develop national self-respect, and the respect of the authorities in London".

The syndicalists

Another modern trend—the revelations of revolutionary socialism, the nineteenth-century version of Christian millenarianism—had now come to Australia, if only to the chosen few: there would be a great turning over of things; the just would be raised up, the wicked would be cast down; socialism would descend upon earth and there would be eternal improvement.

Its form was not that of political revolution but of revolutionary syndicalism, its origin was not Britain or Europe, but the United States. Most socialist literature in Australia at the time was printed in Chicago—and after an earlier period in which several groups, making up perhaps 2,000 people in all, had debated the form of man's earthly liberation so passionately that their main struggles were with each other, International

Workers of the World clubs began to form: they brought from the secular revivalism, jailings, bashings and lynchings of industrial disputes in the United States the syndicalist belief that the apocalypse that would herald the arrival of socialism was the general strike. While waiting faithfully in Newcastle for this event, the duty of man was to disrupt things as best he could. There were bitter quarrels within the I.W.W. clubs as to how this disruption should occur, and between the I.W.W. clubs and the rest of the union movement as to whether it should occur at all. There was a great deal more debate than action, but in some unions, the miners' in particular, these new promptings produced an intensity of concern that went beyond immediate material advantage.

It was the coalminers, in 1888, who, without meaning to, precipitated a new kind of strike, one which the newspapers presented as a national crisis and one in which the government intervened, and this new kind of strike made some of the rhetoric of the syndicalists seem more credible. The newspapers sent special reporters to the coalfields and the government an artillery unit with seventy men, seven officers and a field gun. Sixteen strike leaders were arrested. When the miners tried another strike in 1896 their failure was again abject. Another ten years passed before they recovered the conditions of 1888; then in 1909, when they called a general coal strike, one of the most bitter known, the government came out singlemindedly against them, even passing specific laws to jail them. Miners were led off in handcuffs, their leader chained in leg-irons. (But at the next elections this action helped defeat the government. The new government released the miners.)

Rather than a syndicalist revolution, the preoccupations of most union leaders were a "living wage", a universal eight-hour day (with a Saturday half-holiday), and preference to unionists. But the new techniques of government intervention against union action had led even some of the more peaceful unions into disaster, most notably in the maritime strike of 1890 which involved a range of unions in the three eastern colonies. In each capital city special constables of militia took arms; in Newcastle the mines were shut down and guarded by troops; in Melbourne an officer ordered "Fire low and lay them out" (the order was not followed); in Sydney 36 mounted troopers charged a crowd of 10,000 protesters; in Queensland Parliament passed a severe Peace Preservation Act to give itself more power. After two months of sensation, the strikes collapsed, and so did some of the smaller unions. When the shearers struck in 1891 in Queensland, they formed into camps of as many as a thousand and did military drill under the Eureka flag. In camps near by there were government artillery, militia and armed police. There was talk of revolution and civil war. A new attitude developed: strikers were declared "a closely knit band of criminals", "a force of armed bandits".

It remained generally true that, "The word socialism, which appeals to many European reformers by its philosophic and general nature, repels and disturbs Australian workers by its very comprehensiveness. One of them, whom I asked to summarize his programme, replied: *My programme? Ten Bob a Day.*" But a sense of belonging to a "working class", different from the rest of society, became characteristic of many individual wage-earners, and in some suburbs and towns it approached a group ethos. Despite talk of the "petty suburban proprietor", not all—not even most—city manual workers owned their own houses. While by 1910 about half the houses in Australia were owned by their occupiers, a ratio that was probably at that time the highest in the world, in the capital cities only a little more than a third of houses were occupier-owned. In the cities most manual workers still crowded into the old inner zones of rented houses, now dilapidated and out of fashion. Part of the rinds of the inner cities of Melbourne and Sydney were now decaying: the slapped-up terraces, inadequately drained, rat-infested, damp, unhealthy, shored up against their ruin, crumbled into slums. Those who lived in the slums were seen by the suburbs as roughnecks, but by themselves as the only true Australians, working class and proud of it.

The strongest sense of a beleaguered working class, self-defined, suspicious and sometimes heroic in style, existed in those partly closed communities in which most householders shared a common occupation. Of these the mining communities —especially in the coalfields north and south of Sydney, and at Broken Hill—were the most clearly delineated. It was amongst them that there was the strongest continuing trades union militancy. They re-interpreted what was now the Eureka Legend to make it seem part of "the working class struggle".

The coming of the parties

By the 1890s something approaching party politics was emerging as various groups would find themselves concerned with the same rallies, manifestoes, lobby groups and debating clubs: with one party formed, enough of their scattered opponents would coalesce to form another. In some colonies the reason for existence of the parties was a conflict on tariff policy; in others it was a matter of a "continuous ministry party" versus those who could not achieve office; there were other divisions. As this system spread the words frequently used, in imitation of the English political vocabulary, were "Liberal" and "Conservative".

When another English name was added—that of "Labour" —a three-party system emerged. The trades unions had been putting individual representatives into parliament, with local Labour Electoral Leagues running candidates financed mainly by union levies, and with the onset of the party system the Labour Leagues joined together. In 1891, with a solid voting base in the new working class suburbs and miners' settlements, the N.S.W. Labour Electoral Leagues won thirty-five seats; in 1893 the Australian Labour Federation in Queensland won fifteen seats, and the United Labour Party in South Australia eight. In several cases union leaders came out of jail and went almost directly into parliament. In December 1899 there was, in Queensland, the "first Labour Government in the world"—a six-day ministry that survived for only four hours in parliament but had enjoyed the chance of having a quick look at the government files.

Each Labour Party followed different relations with the liberal forces of Improvement. As the official opposition, the Queensland party was the first to go close to displacing middle-class liberalism. The New South Wales party acted as a "corner party" prepared to bargain with governments. The Victorian party was a junior supporter of the Liberals; in South Australia relations were so friendly that a joint Labour-Liberal coalition held office for four years; in Western Australia, although in a minority in parliament, the Labour Party held office for a year without distinctive policies; in New Zealand the Liberal Party held such a monopoly of the spirit of colonial governmentalism that the Labour Party was absorbed into it.

These Labour Parties were unique in that they did not grow out of socialist organizations but were the exclusive creation of the trades unions. Socialist organizations formed *after* the Labour parties. The most that many Labour men knew of socialism was from American popularizations, in particular Laurence Granlund's *Co-operative Commonwealth*, which tried to digest Continental socialism in a form "Anglo-Saxon in its dislike to all extravagances": it defined socialism as "the extension of the functions of government". The American Edward Bellamy's utopian novel *Looking Backward* was perhaps the widest influence, so that the book that could mean most in the Labour Parties was one that dreamed of the co-operation and love that might prevail by the year 2,000. Labour's fostering of love and co-operation by the extension of colonial governmentalism was sometimes challenged in its idealism by the single-tax simplicities of the American Henry George. "The two great schools of economic thought," said one Labour leader, "are the single tax and the socialist schools." The dreaminess of Labour idealism was matched by an eclectism that came both from the prevailing liberal mood and from the desire to attract political support from small farmers and small business men.

By 1897 a plan calling for socialization was nailed into the N.S.W. Labour platform, mainly because of the work of a group of young socialists; but the strong opposition of Cardinal Moran, Archbishop of Sydney, helped break it. Later it was pulled out. Just as unique as the trades union origin of the Labour parties was the way they were becoming a vehicle for Catholic integration. Although a significant fraction of Catholics were still Irish-born and the Irish still dominated among the bishops and priests, Cardinal Moran, although Irish-born himself, wished Catholics to share an Australian patriotism. In the centenary year of 1888 he had managed to have all six colonial governors at a ceremony marking the beginning of the completion of St Mary's Cathedral; he had urged the formation of an Irish Rifle Corps in the colonial militia; when Pope Leo XIII had issued his encyclical *rerum novarum* on workers' rights in 1891 the Cardinal had given a public lecture on its significance, sitting beside representatives of all the political parties. He had declared the various organizations of Improvement, from friendly societies to trades unions, free of Continental liberalism and socialism, and he had extended the same benefaction to all political parties. But in the new century integration came to mean in particular a movement into the Labor Party (which now spelt itself without the "u", to show its modernity). Through their usually low place on the economic scale, Catholics were joining Labor parties anyway; to this was added the impulse that came from attempts by minority militant Protestant and Loyal Orange Lodge factions to use the other parties against Catholics. The Catholic newspapers urged Catholics to support the Labor parties and by 1910 as many as half the members of these parties in eastern Australia may have been Catholics.

Despite Labor's moderation in action and despite its Catholic support, the rhetoric of some Labor leaders ("socialism in our time") and the kind of resolutions passed at conferences of the Labor parties ("war on the wealthy") provided enough material for the political leader George Reid to raise for a while the cry of the "socialist tiger" and rename his party the "Anti-Socialist Party"; but this was not as effective in discrediting the Labor Party as the appeals to anti-Catholic prejudices that his party was also promoting. However the Employers' Federation began to support candidates "who openly expressed a determination to protect the rights of private enterprise and oppose socialistic legislation".

The words "Labour" and "Monopoly" were much used; the world seemed more complex, with new threats occurring in what politics were supposed to be about. Among the Liberals, still commanding the political centre and most of the political power, some opposed Labour more than they opposed Monopoly; others opposed Monopoly, but argued that Monopoly should be broken up, whereas the Labor Party believed that it should be taken over by the State. It was an argument without conclusion, since Monopoly was neither broken up nor taken over (nor, for that matter, greatly existed), but it was a diversion that was beginning to replace the earlier political divisions between Free Trade and Protection. It was pursued with equal passion.

The result was that the centre—the very basis of Improvement—began to disperse, and with it the new three-party system. With Labor more evidently in the field, and more tightly organized, the maintenance of the Liberals as popular radical parties of Improvement was becoming impossible. From 1907 there was a tendency for the two non-Labor parties to "fuse" into a group that for old times sake called itself the "Liberal Party". A generation of political enemies had united as one party, opposed to Labor. Now there were to be two parties. Founded on a non-party system, sustained during a three-party system, with a pervading concern for progress as its sustaining power, the Australian Age of Improvement had now reached a new, and perhaps terminal, situation.

Chapter 11

THEORIES ABOUT WHO THEY WERE

1885-1910 *(cont'd)*

The other side of the range

Now that a majority of adults were native-born, Australians were again beginning to have theories about who they were. The most significant national sentiment was the simple belief that Australia was best. Best at sport. Best at scenery and animals. Banquets were held at which it was boasted that all the food and drink were Australian. Distinctive Australian clothing styles were detected. In praising Australian social reform patriotism knew no limit: "It is here in Australia that human society will develop itself, and that the yet unanswered riddles of the sphinx will be finally solved."

But beyond being *best*, what were they? The usual sources for national definition were not very helpful. For their high moments politicians now preferred the language of the new imperialism and for workaday speeches they stayed with the language of Improvement. Even the optimism of Improvement did not seem to have touched the few historians who had emerged: they had no theories of Australian uniqueness. Such intellectual leadership as there was came from the Press which provided "almost entirely for the conscious culture of the whole Antipodean community", and served what at that time may have been the highest rate of newspaper readership in the world. Most Press proprietors were themselves journalists and, liberals or radicals almost to a man, they were usually concerned with Australian-ness only to the extent that it moved towards their liberal ideals.

Perhaps the best-performed attempt at self-description was provided by a form of Impressionism that came from a series of painting camps and spread its influence: its very spontaneity and unpretentiousness seemed to suit its subjects. One of its special talents was to catch the colours of Australia, in pursuit of what one Sydney writer described as Verlaine's "cult of faded things"—"delicate purples, delicious greys and dull, dreary olives and ochres" in contrast to "English ideals of glaring green, or staring red and orange". This Impressionism was wide-ranging in subject—looking to both city and countryside—and as the most substantial body of good work at that time it provided an artistic acceptance of Australian life at a level not previously achieved.

The uniqueness that dismayed many commentators was that Australia seemed to have become the world's most town-dwelling society. With Sydney, Melbourne and Adelaide containing about half the population of the areas they governed these three cities seemed "huge cancers whose ramifications of disease spread far into national life". With a lack of knowledge of economics that would have done justice to Cicero, from whom he seemed to have got his ideas, one Sydney writer saw the city-dwellers as ". . . non-productive inhabitants . . . carried on the back of some struggling farmer or miner or stock-raiser." "The civilization in the Australian cities is not new," said another, "but an old, hoary-headed, decrepit European civilization, which appears half the world over to be tottering to its grave. Any stranger can see in Sydney the luxury and refinement and vice of the old world gnawing at the heart of the new." To one, the only hope was that "the Anglo-Saxon devotion to sport and athletics" might save Australia from the effects of its towniness.

Out of this grew the habit for writers and cartoonists to make the larrikin the symbol of city life. Ballads and short stories were written about him, he was put into plays and vaudeville and drawn in cartoons, and when Australians made moving pictures, he appeared in those. At times he was a symbol of violence and low life; at other times he was softened as a comic character, even a sentimentalist. He was being turned into one version of a "typical Australian".

Apart from the larrikin, writers chose to find little that was distinctively Australian in metropolitan life. They turned to the bush. "It is not in our cities and townships that the Australian attains pure consciousness of his nationality." "The one powerful and unique national type produced in Australia is . . . the Bushman." As part of a more general movement throughout the English-speaking world in which the work of men like Kipling, Service and Bret Harte became best-sellers, ballads were developed as a commercial art form and most were about the bush. The ballads of the Sydney journalist A.B. Paterson sold better than any Australian books had sold in the colonies before. They put forward a heroic and adventurous view of Australia that seemed more exciting than city life: Australians were tall, lean, suntanned, self-reliant yet comradely, tough yet sentimental. Just as Americans were imagining themselves as cowboys, Australians were beginning to dream of themselves as bushmen.

The Sydney magazine *The Bulletin* was quick to do well out of this new commercial fashion: it took up the new vogue and became its chief vehicle, combining bush ballads with bush short stories, the short story being another commercial art form of the time. Usually stylized into melodrama or farce with surprise endings, and kept very short because *The Bulletin* didn't have much room, its artificially contrived bush short stories helped sales. The new painters also began to be most admired for their treatment of the bush: in their big paintings they came to concentrate on country landscapes, rural pursuits, and heroes from the past, such as bushrangers. They usually made their humans laconic, in the bush manner. The first full-length feature movie made in Australia was on the Kelly gang. Even in the schools it was now possible to discover Australia: its history was the story of its "heroic explorers"; its distinctiveness lay in the peculiarities of the plants and animals of the bush.

There were other modes. A school called "the nationalists" delebrated their Australian-ness in late Victorian verse: fashionably, pretty poetry was written; as evidence of their cosmopolitanism, both a poet and a painter peopled Australian landscapes with fauns and satyrs; a university poet discovered French symbolism. But the concentration on either larrikins or bush workers was the principal characteristic of *The Bulletin*, and *The Bulletin*, although its appeal was limited to a minority, was the only publication with a national sale and the "one really talented and original outcome of the Australian Press". For better or worse, it was distinctive, and at least the short stories it published by Henry Lawson reached high quality as, in a concentration of genius, Lawson turned to advantage the extraordinary limitations of *The Bulletin* style of writing.

It was in these stories, and in other writing, that theories of Australian-ness were developed, attempting to cast up images of a national type found on the other side of the range. The outback Australian was seen as sardonic, stoic, sceptical, laconically brave. "Sullen and sombre-souled" (characteristics blamed both on the climate and on excessive tea-drinking), he held so deeply to his freedom that if faced by patronage he might simply not recognize it although, "biliously and satanically proud", if he saw it for what it was he would take violent offence. He could enterprisingly make something out of nothing; he was recklessly generous and a compulsive gambler: he might "grinningly throw away his life for a trifle".

For those who were radical, to the cult of the bushman a new history had to be added. The Eureka incident seemed to provide it. Just as Englishmen had struggled for their freedom against Charles I (as taught in schools), so Australia had "set her teeth in the face of the British lion" at Eureka. It seemed an affront to the spirit of the age that so much of Australia's freedom and prosperity had not been earned by the shedding of blood; the diggers' blood was used retrospectively for that purpose. The Eureka Stockade, it was declared, "led to government by the people". For most, the convicts seemed so remotely improbable that memory of them was suppressed; but a few turned the convicts into radicals, re-inventing them as sturdy Scottish crofters, Irish rebels, English Chartists and "offenders against the brutal game laws"—"the best of stock for the breeding of a new nation".

The social philosophy of bush society—its sense of mateship ("Socialism is being mates"), its demand for equality, its irreverence for values other than its own—was turned by some of the new cultural nationalists into a unique prescription for a new society. This was something that Australia could show to the world, a new sense of brotherhood and equality. It was still a submerged attitude, alien to the kind of leaders in politics and journalism who preferred the Australian version of Improvement, and distasteful to the Anglophile imperialists, but it received confident expression in some of the trades unions and it seemed to find some echo in the hearts of many other Australians. This submerged feeling was probably the strongest form of nationalism that Australians had, even if it was a nationalism that lived as a minority movement in its own country.

Now the petty suburban proprietor smoking on his veranda on a Sunday morning could take some pride in belonging to the land of the wattle and the kangaroo—both of which he might not regularly see except in art-nouveau suburban household decorations—and entertaining himself with the works of those who saw him either as slum larrikin or laconic bushman.

Nevertheless, there could often be something of the image of the bushman and the larrikin in him, even if his sardonic temperament was expressed in the trades unions or at the surfing beaches rather than in the bush or the slums. It came out most clearly in an openness of manner that demanded at least the forms of equality even when denied the substance. "This is a true republic," said Francis Adams, "the truest, as I take it, in the world. In England the average man feels that he is an inferior. In America that he is a superior; in Australia he feels that he is an equal." However it might be challenged, an Australian carried his sense of equality in his heart.

Australia for the Australians

When there were none of Britain's colonial wars to send expeditions to, sport seemed the most important instrument of Australian foreign policy. Australian swimmers won world fame in England, and Australian cyclists became track stars in the United States; to the international cricket matches were added international football matches; the world heavyweight championship fought in Sydney in 1908 brought a gate that was a world record; Australia won the Davis Cup in 1908 and retained it till 1912. Perhaps it was true that "the only names of Australians at all familiar to the general run of

Englishman are those of cricketers, rowers and prize fighters", but ordinary Australians would not have seen anything wrong with that. When expeditions were sent to the Antarctic this was an extension of the idea of a touring team; after the Australian opera singer Nellie Melba made her world reputation she was greeted on her returns with the enthusiasm due to a sporting event.

From 1888, the anniversary of Phillip's landing was celebrated as a national holiday; a few more anthems, including "Advance Australia Fair", were written; Henry Parkes announced that he was going to re-name New South Wales "Australia"; but there was little expression of political nationalism in its most significant form: the desire to cast off the bonds of Empire and establish an Australian republic. The more usual attitude was self-congratulatory on the moral advantages of belonging to the British Empire. It was only within this context that outspokenness in relations with Britain was applauded: this was a matter of the Australians and the English being British together. When the Victorian political leader Alfred Deakin spoke up in London at an Imperial Conference he became a national hero: on his return he was greeted by addresses of congratulation at every train stop between Adelaide and Melbourne. He was hailed as the first of the native-born to perform at the centre of the world; but it may have been more his criticism of British government policy than the applause these criticisms generated in London that made his journey a success to Australian voters.

On this occasion, as on others, dissatisfaction with Britain was politically expressed as a concern lest "when our domestic policy runs counter to England's imperial policy, Australian interests will go to the wall". The English were seen as too concerned with their own affairs in dealing with Asiatic powers, and their policy in the South-west Pacific seemed perfidious. Moderates wanted the British to keep the other world powers out of the South-west Pacific; enthusiasts wanted the British to take over whatever islands were left, holding them for Australia's later acquisition. Famous as a liberal spokesman, Deakin said: "We intend to be masters of the Pacific by and by."

But although politicians and Press were usually pro-British and sometimes slavishly so, there was a wide undercurrent of contempt for the Old Country, particularly among the town manual workers and in the bush: Britain could seem a snobbish society of title worship, class distinctions and privilege, of oppressive injustice to the poor, of dowdy, "dust-covered customs", a stagnant nation compared with liberal, confident and progressive Australia, where "the intellect of the people is freer, stronger and more original than in the age-old states of Europe".

This undercurrent broke only rarely to the surface. A Republican Union, made up of "the debating-society, hard-reading crowd", had formed in 1887 in Sydney in opposition to the Imperial Federation League; in the same year republicans had twice defeated attempts in Sydney Town Hall to pass a loyal resolution congratulating Queen Victoria on her jubilee—the resolution was passed at the third meeting only after its opponents were excluded; in 1888, when the Republican Union was replaced by the Republican League, branches were extended to Melbourne and Adelaide; there were calls to Australia to achieve greatness by following the United States. But republicanism was taken up by hardly any politicians or trades unionists; in the Press *The Bulletin* was its only significant supporter, and its republicanism was one of the most important reasons for that magazine's widespread unpopularity.

Where influential Australians seemed most ready to assert Australian independence was in its whiteness. "Australia for the Australians—the cheap Chinaman, the cheap nigger and the cheap European pauper to be absolutely excluded" was an idea accepted and proclaimed by politicians, Press and trades union leaders alike. A Labor writer noted for his utopianism could say that he would rather see his daughter "dead in her coffin than kissing [a black man] on the mouth or nursing a little coffee-coloured brat that she was mother to". A Chinese could be lampooned in the Press as "Ah Filth"—"not morally, physically or intellectually fit to sit down in the same continent with Europeans". Along with the arbitration system, old-age pensions and so forth, one of the tokens of Australian progress was that "never before in any known period" had there been a continent of "a people almost wholly of the one race and one language". A cultivated literary critic, A. G. Stephens of *The Bulletin*, could write: "Next in importance to the preservation of national life is the preservation of the race, the purification of the national blood . . . living on the border of

Asia, we are always exposed to the danger of Asiatic incursions, and it is certain that the establishment of Asiatic settlements, or of a European breed, will tend to degrade and destroy the whole breed." Common sense (a mixture of opposition to cheap labour and of British racism) suggested that the almost complete exclusion of non-Anglo-Saxons was one of the greatest achievements in "a land that is Freedom's from shore to shore".

There were a few who thought otherwise. One wrote: "England has become what she is by a fusion of races. Australia will become great by a fusion and mingling of races . . . East and West will join hands. The unequalled metaphysical power of the Hindoo, the unswerving steadiness of the Chinese, the singular artistic faculty of the Japanese, will be joined by the idealism of the French, the philosophy of the German and the practical sagacity of the Anglo-Saxon." But to most influential Australians such a statement would seem as demented as an attack on the early closing of shops.

Chapter 12

BIRTH OF A NATION
1885-1910 (cont'd)

Coming together

"Whilst Victoria during the last thirty years had produced a host of able public men, New South Wales has brought to the front few men above the intellectual standard of the parish vestry men," said David Syme. "Amongst Victorians there were hundreds of thousands of the very scum and filth of the criminality and rascality of all mankind," replied a New South Wales knight. Old enmities continued. Borne up by their own ebullience in the 1880s, Victorians often urged union of the colonies; but New South Wales, with the belief that it was the only true Australia, didn't care. Then in 1889 Henry Parkes, perhaps because it was the only policy left to suit his political advantage, perhaps because he was old and afraid that fame might still escape him, made a speech in a town near the border of New South Wales and Queensland calling for "a great national government for all Australia". For political reasons unable to ignore this call, the next year the governments of all the colonies sent representatives to Melbourne and for seven days they discussed what to do about it. Out of this, in the following year, came a National Convention of delegations from the Australian colonies and New Zealand. After meeting for thirty-eight days in Sydney they decided to found a Commonwealth of Australia; there were some doubts as to whether "Commonwealth" was not too revolutionary a word, but translations back into the Latin were reassuring.

The new Commonwealth would need a new constitution: one was drafted in ten days. The determination of existing governments not to vote themselves out of existence, regional economic interests, and the example of North America, all demanded a federal system. The envies of all the colonies demanded that the federal government be weak, with only certain defined powers, and that all other powers should remain with the colonies. The fears of the smaller colonies demanded that the federal upper house represent each colony equally, the smallest having as many representatives as the largest. The example of the United States suggested that the lower house be called the House of Representatives, the upper house the Senate, and that the colonies be known as States; but, apart from its federal nature, the new nation was to be governed more or less as government was understood in London. For a day or so the question was raised of a separation of executive and legislature; the idea was too strange to consider.

The Convention debated the first draft of the constitution. Then the drafting sub-committee of four went off in a government steam yacht and after two days came back with the final draft. The Victorian and South Australian parliaments adopted it with no enthusiasm; none of the other colonies considered it. The idea of federation seemed important mainly to politicians, and they had lost interest.

In 1894 another New South Wales Premier, also finding political advantage in the idea of federation, suggested a conference of colonial Premiers. A year later the Premiers met and agreed to submit Bills for elections to another National Convention. New Zealand had lost interest and two more years passed before four of the Australian colonies got around to agreeing to hold the elections. Another year passed before the elections were held. Absorbed in its own concern about a possible split between north and south, Queensland abstained; in Western Australia the old order was trying to preserve itself against the new men on the goldfields, so rather than risk an election its Parliament appointed delegates. In New South Wales the decision of Cardinal Moran to stand for the Convention created such bitter interest that a Protestant ticket was returned; but in the other three colonies only half the usual number of voters turned out. Newspapers attacked this apparent indifference.

Nevertheless the cause of federation was now clothed by

slightly more than the interests of a small group of prominent colonial politicians. Federation Leagues formed, taking liveliest shape in border districts where intercolonial tariffs were a most obvious nuisance; there were agitated references to the need for common policies on defence and immigration; some economic interests believed they would gain from federation; others attacked it because they saw themselves as losing. A diffuse rhetoric developed . . . common bonds being sealed . . . a new century approaching . . . an appropriate time to come of age. One politician said: "We shall create a glorious nation and meat will be cheaper."

The elected delegates to the National Convention met for 32 days in Adelaide, for 22 days in Sydney, then for another 55 days in Melbourne, making enough speeches to fill 5,000 pages. Differences between large and small colonies, between protectionists and free traders, between Victoria and New South Wales and between liberals, radicals and conservatives came together in a set of compromises which the drafting committee finally turned into a revised and somewhat more liberal constitution. The following year it was to be presented in a referendum to the voters of the four colonies that had accepted the idea of federation. (Western Australia had joined Queensland in staying out.)

Apart from sealing bonds and coming of age, appeals for support were mainly to economic self-interest: outback voters saw federation as an attack on metropolitan interest, some city interests saw a great new tide of profitable commerce. Opposition also came from economic self-interest in groups who saw their economic advantages threatened; they were joined by many of the Labor Leagues, who opposed what they saw as a conservative constitution and by a few conservatives who feared what they saw as a dangerously democratic constitution. The Press was divided. Clerics intervened. Brass bands and campaign songs were added to the oratory of public meetings. This all aroused sufficient interest for the proportion of voters to rise to nearly half of those eligible.

New South Wales did not register the required majority. In 1899 there was another conference of Premiers: New South Wales was given somewhat better terms and agreed to a second referendum; this time Queensland joined in. A majority voted Yes and at the last moment the Western Australian government was forced into union by secessionist threats from its new goldfields. There was to be a new nation, brought into being by 42.91 per cent of all electors.

Early on New Year's Day in 1901, when the official proclamation of a Commonwealth of Australia was to be made, between half a million and three-quarters of a million people came into the city that had grown on the site Governor Phillip had chosen as a penal colony 113 years before. Some had New Year's Eve hangovers, but the proportion of hangovers was less than among the thousand or so who had stood among the red gums at the beginning of this whole enterprise to listen to the three volleys of musket fire and the governor's proclamation that convicts found in the women's tents at night would be shot.

Almost thirty committees had met to plan the celebration. Triumphal arches—including one made of coal, one of wool, and one of wheat—attested to material gain. Of the banners that stretched across the poles and wires of the new electric tram system some looked forward ("One people one destiny"), some back ("The crimson thread of kinship"). In the five-miles-long procession there was much that proclaimed the New Imperialism; detachments of Imperial forces—Life Guards, Hussars, Sikhs, Gurkhas—marched along with the colonial troops. There was also much that proclaimed the old Improvement: no other new nation had given such a part of its celebratory procession to trades unions and friendly societies; even the eight-hour day banner was paraded, borne aloft behind the Railway Band. But there was little that proclaimed the new minority dreams of nationalism—except perhaps the shearers marching at the head of the trades union part of the procession and the thirty bush-workers riding on horses behind them, sustaining a belief in rural virtue beneath the wires of the city's electric trams. Colonial governmentalism was celebrated in the dozens of carriages of top-hatted dignitaries. Old religious divisions were celebrated by the absence of the Catholics from the procession. Snubbed by a Protestant-controlled management committee on whether a Catholic cardinal should take precedence over an Anglican archbishop, the Catholics had withdrawn, although in a compromise the procession stopped outside St Mary's Cathedral to hear 4,000 Catholic children sing "God save the Queen" and a specially composed Federal hymn. Thirty thousand designs had been entered in the contest for an Australian flag: the winning design—white stars on a blue ensign—was curiously similar to the flag of the Anti-Transportation League of fifty years before that had sometimes accompanied radical threats of a republican nationhood. But convicts and republics were both forgotten. It was an English earl who was sworn in as Governor-General. The guns thundered. There were fireworks, dinners, picnics.

Four months later an English royal prince in an English admiral's uniform stood on the flower-decorated dais of the Exhibition Building in Melbourne and proclaimed the opening of the first national parliament. At the concert that night Madame Melba sang a hymn to Australia and one English visitor noted that the new Cabinet Ministers had forgotten to bow when they passed the prince.

By this time the society of the brown Australians had been destroyed everywhere except in a few areas where white Australians had not yet seized land to make money out of it. Although still "black-fellows" to most, in official language they had become "Aborigines", a coolly scientific-sounding name, as if, like the platypus or the koala bear, they were one of the country's zoological freaks. A new pattern for their treatment was being set. Pioneered by Queensland, and adopted by the two other States where numbers were still significant, it provided for descendants of the first Australians to be drafted into reserves or into institutions, at the will of "protectors", most of whom were policemen. They could be forced to stay on the reserves if not lawfully employed: they could be lawfully employed only by permission of the "protectors". There were no provisions for appeal. A race that was assumed to be dying was, as far as possible, being got out of sight.

The new protection

The first Australian Federal Cabinet met on the afternoon of the Commonwealth's proclamation—between the procession and the fireworks—in a room lent by the Government of New

South Wales. It had been put together arbitrarily (until there was an election) with at least one leading politician from each colony, to set up the few new government departments. Those chosen as ministers happened, in varying degrees, to be protectionists. Through this accident, the Cabinet decided it also led a political party, but there were no national party programmes or national party organizations: each State fought the first federal election according to its ordinary political groupings and the parliament it elected was a collection of regional parties, making sense back in the States, but having to be forced into new coherence in the Commonwealth Parliament. The names they used were "Protectionist", "Free Trade" and "Labour", but the meaning given to these names could differ from one State to the other.

With no party having an absolute majority, those calling themselves the Protectionist Party became the government, those calling themselves the Free Trade Party became the opposition, and those brought together by the Labor Leagues sat in the corner giving general hints of support for the government. Although the apparent division was on the issue of protection, this issue was not significantly debated for some years, and then in new terms. In fact, in its three years' existence practically nothing significant came out of the first parliament, and in the elections that were to follow almost half the voters showed their lack of interest by not voting.

There was no national capital; with no agreement about where to build the new capital, the Federal Parliament was housed in Victoria's Parliament House: there was not much agreement about the new government's functions, beyond taking over the colonies' customs houses, post offices, and some odds and ends—some expected it to do little more than this. It was recognized that each of the States should be represented in cabinet, and that no policy could discriminate against one of the States. Although there was an "External Affairs Department", it was accepted that foreign policy was imperial, and the prerogative of the government in London. Australian foreign policy consisted of Australia making representations to London—through the Governor-General. Irish brogues, Scottish burrs and English dialects were common among the new federal members: of the six most significant men in the Labor Party four had been born in the British Isles. In defence of the name "Commonwealth" some had even argued that the word was apt to the new federation's position as it suggested something less than complete sovereignty. Australia had now gained a seventh government, but whether the world had gained another nation was not clear.

Something had to demonstrate why all this trouble had been taken. The gesture was found in the proclamation of the White Australia policy. Apart from the continued use in Queensland of indentured black islanders (a problem disposed of with only a little difficulty by trading a sugar bounty for their exclusion), there was no urgent objective reason for making this first parliament's only important Act a measure restricting immigration—at about 30,000, the Chinese were little more than one per cent of Australia's population—but it was a measure acceptable to practically everyone, and a subject on which newly elected parliamentarians could attempt to outdo each other in oratorical assertions of national manhood and national character.

With no other expression of common idealism available, Australian nationhood was confirmed in the self-evident truth that social and economic progress lay in racial purity. Students, tourists and businessmen from India and Japan were to be allowed into Australia for up to five years, but so far as permanent settlement was concerned, all "the tinted races" were to be excluded. The only political division was whether to restrict immigration with the maximum offensiveness, or with some form of politeness; the British urged politeness, and partly out of regard for British feeling the restriction chosen was that any immigrant could be set a dictation test "in a prescribed language". The Labor Party had wanted a direct prohibition of "any person who is an aboriginal native of Asia or Africa".

The second parliament began a period of six years of party confusion, with six different governments forming from various combinations of support between the parties. It was described as a parliament of "the three elevens" until the protectionists split into two groups, making four elevens. But political confusion had been no enemy of the previous Improvement, nor was it in these six years; parties seemed to struggle with each other for the right to carry out much the same policy. Much of it was Alfred Deakin's policy. It was almost as if he had invented the whole thing and without him they wouldn't know what to do. He could be confident that even in the periods in which he was not Prime Minister his policies would continue.

Colonial governmentalism was at last given a clothing of ideology; it was a method of "employing the machinery of the State to cope with the very great injustices which at present beset our social system". It was George Reid, the leader of the more conservative of the four parties, who said: "Even in the field of social economics, Australia can win victories and set examples which will teach the rest of the world." A national political style was developing, one of some economic justice and of State mediation to end conflict. Perhaps, some thought, this was what it was to be an Australian.

The Commonwealth adopted from New South Wales models for compulsory arbitration in industrial disputes and old-age and invalid pensions. The Victorian system of tariff protection became Commonwealth policy; there were experiments with trust-busting and antidumping legislation. A Commonwealth Literary Fund was set up to give pensions to old authors. Deakin sponsored an entirely novel policy of "New Protection", in which manufacturers would be protected from foreign competition only if they paid "fair and reasonable" wages and working conditions. When in 1907 the Arbitration Court decided that a basic wage should be set to meet "the normal needs of the average employee regarded as a human being in a civilized community" a great human ideal seemed at last to be satisfied.

The New Protection was disallowed by the newly established High Court, but it remained a distinctively Australian ideal for the rest of the decade—the first distinctively expressed ideology to have come from the complexities of Australian politics. At last Australia could feel that it had a political approach of its own. Its meaning widened beyond economic justice to a general approach of safeguarding Australians from the evils of the world. They were to be safeguarded from poverty and distress, they were to be safeguarded from internal tension, they were to be safeguarded from the competition of imported goods made by "the underpaid labour, the serf labour, the prison labour of foreign lands where less happy conditions prevail" and, by the White Australia policy, they were to be safeguarded from racial discord and sweated labour.

They were also to be safeguarded from military threats in

the world outside Australia where now, to possible dangers from France, Germany or Russia, there was added what was beginning to seem a threat from Japan. The Japanese victory in the Russo-Japanese War was at first seen as "the inspiration of nationalist enthusiasm in a just cause" (New South Wales had not built a fort in Sydney Harbour to protect itself from the Russian Pacific Squadron for nothing), but later it was feared that "the yellow man has taught the white man a lesson that Australians can neglect only at their peril". The Labor Party fought the 1906 election in terms of the yellow peril, but even more to the point was the British naval scare: Would German rearmament rival the Royal Navy? Subscription lists were started in newspapers to buy Britain a dreadnought. While Canada, South Africa and New Zealand ("One sea, one Empire, one Navy") remained content with things as they were, Australia ruffled the British by successfully demanding a navy of its own: a great national ideal was to be fulfilled when in 1913 the battlecruiser *Australia* and the light cruisers *Sydney* and *Melbourne* sailed into Sydney Harbour.

Australia was equally seeking novelty in its policy for land defence. By the middle of the decade the idea that there should be a compulsorily raised citizen army was prevailing: National Defence Leagues were formed, and by 1908 the Labor Party had adopted compulsory military training as official policy. Only a few conservatives opposed this apparently progressive idea. With a combined system of school cadet corps and compulsory militia training for young men, Australia became the first English-speaking country to introduce conscription in peacetime. The event was hailed as showing Australia as in the van of progress. "A citizen soldiery inspired by patriotism", "the boldest stride yet taken in any English-speaking country towards national land defence", seemed to reject old world militarism in favour of democratic progress. By this and other means the prevailing fashions in Australian nationalism had wedded themselves by 1910 to the dominant moods of the New Imperialism.

Part 3

THE AGE OF IMPERIALISM
1910-1970

Part 3

The Age of Imperialism

1910—1970

Chapter 13

BLOOD SACRIFICE
1910-1919

In the schools a new hope was beginning to test its strength. The tyranny of the inspectors had been replaced by the lesser tyranny of external examinations; teachers' colleges were being established; kindergarten methods were spreading in infants' schools; compulsory school attendance was at last becoming effective. Syllabuses had been revised according to new attitudes which were part of a shift in emphasis occurring in many parts of the world: education was seen to have a moral aim in which it was hoped that the new types of teaching in literature, history and science might overcome some of the failure of men to live according to their ideals.

In politics some hoped that Australia would be the first country to be controlled by a party of the "working class". By 1910 there was a Federal Labor Government in Melbourne and State Labor Governments in Sydney and Adelaide; in 1911 Labor came to office in Perth; in 1914 in Tasmania; in 1915 in Brisbane. The spirit of colonial governmentalism prospered in plans to set up State brickworks, State sawmills, State iron foundries, State metal quarries, State concrete works, State butchers' shops, State bakeries, State coalmines, State banks. The old political liberalism took new life in plans to abolish the Legislative Councils and State governors, and to give greater influence to the people by the referendum. The old Improvement took greater meaning with plans for extending pensions, nationalizing health services, formulating new industrial laws, reforming education, breaking up large estates. A world-wide competition was announced for a plan for the new national capital to be built at Canberra. The winning plan, submitted by an American, Burley Griffin, proposed to serve Australian self-definition by making Canberra a kind of super-Versailles in the modern style of a follower of Frank Lloyd Wright.

But in the States, Legislative Councils were intractably opposed to comparatively minor reforms, not to mention their own abolition; in the Commonwealth the constitution blocked many Labor policies and two referendums held to amend it were defeated—not least because State Labor Parties were jealous of their own rights. Many of Labor's programmes were not carried out. And the previous general agreement on progress and reform was departing. Bound by the demands of political debate to establish their difference from Labor, the Liberal Parties declared themselves anti-socialist, and as they began to move towards what was now being described as "the Right" there were more signs of the importance in their counsels of Employers' Federations and other such groups; in the new political debate Labor policies were unmasked as hiding "a bureaucratic tyranny".

Within the Labor Party there were strains from penetration by the Catholics and from the struggle for control by the trades unions. Tensions were developing between the parliamentarians and the oligarchic State Labor machines which insisted that they had the only true revelation of the needs of the mass of the people. In New South Wales an "Industrial Section" was formed to run a union ticket—settled by private ballotting between the unions beforehand—to obtain complete control of the New South Wales Government Executive.

Hoping to regain State aid for their schools, the Catholic bishops had accepted government inspection. To this end, secular and religious subjects were separated, a division in government schools that had previously prompted Catholic attack; but nothing was gained. Catholics now saw themselves as "fighting in a corner", threatened not only by secular education but by the evils of freemasonry ("a huge tumour growing upon the life and blood of the whole country"), mixed marriages, corrupting reading matter, divorce laws and the "race suicide" of birth control. "No wonder," said Dr Kelly, new Archbishop of Sydney, "injustice is rampant, perjury superabundant, and murder not infrequent." Catholics turned to blackmail. A Catholic Federation was formed in

Victoria, later spreading to other States, with a membership of 100,000 within two years. It tried to build up electoral registration of Catholics, sent questionnaires to election candidates, encouraged Catholics to join the Labour Party, and then threatened to withdraw its support. The Victorian Labour Party called its bluff and denounced it. After expulsions and walkouts, a Catholic Workers' Association was formed aiming at more organized penetration. "The work before the Catholic Laborites is to capture the labor machine," said the Melbourne Catholic newspaper, the *Advocate*.

When it was adopted, the policy of compulsory military training of males over fourteen had seemed to meet the wishes of almost everyone, yet of the 40,000 boys eligible in its second year of practice only 17,000 had registered. The Commonwealth began prosecuting defaulters—at an average rate of more than 250 per week for more than two years. Altogether 27,749 prosecutions were launched, 5,732 of them resulting in the locking up of lads in military establishments or civil prisons. When a boy at Broken Hill was imprisoned for a fortnight with a bread and water diet the miners gave him a medal. An anti-conscriptionist Australian Freedom League formed, gathering 55,000 members.

However, when news came in 1914 of a new crisis in Europe, Australians were almost unanimous in their desire to be part of it. Labour and Liberal leaders tried to outdo each other in offering Australia's last man and last shilling. In the streets crowds sang traditional Australian songs such as "Rule Britannia", "Soldiers of the King", and "Sons of the Sea", and Archbishop Kelly said "Whether our schools are treated fairly or not, we will do our duty." In a challenge even more exciting than a cricket test, or the Boer War, Australia would send off an Australian Imperial Force of 20,000 men. A new song was written—"Australia Will Be There".

Volunteers were measured for size and assessed for health. The biggest and healthiest were chosen and collected at emergency camps in race courses. They were clothed in uniforms of pure Australian wool, shaded by slouch hats bearing a badge of the rising sun, given overseas pay of 6s. a day (which, said King George V, was too much for a soldier), then sent through the streets so that everyone could have a look at them. In October off they went in 28 transports, along with 10 transports of New Zealanders, in the biggest military expedition ever to have sailed across the world, many times larger than the expedition that had founded New South Wales. They were not expected to be away for long. It was ordered that they were to have meat three times a day.

Rumours of spies began to spread; there were stories of lights flashing signals out to sea, of hostile aeroplanes and submarines. Other expeditions for the Australian Imperial Force were recruited—apparently the war was going to last longer than expected. They completed their training in Egypt, at a tented camp near the Pyramids, to which the first expedition had been unexpectedly diverted because training camps in England were already over full. The word "Anzac" was used to describe the Australian and New Zealand troops.

On 29th April the Prime Minister made a brief announcement that on the previous Sunday Australians had landed on the Gallipoli peninsular. That was all that was announced except for a message of congratulation from the Colonial Secretary. The next day congratulations came from the First Lord of the Admiralty and King George. What were the congratulations about? On 3rd May the first of the long lists of casualties was released, but there were still no details of what had caused them.

Then on 8th May a dispatch from an English war correspondent was published describing the Anzacs' landing in terms so full of praise that they touched deep into Australians' longings and uncertainties and brought forward at once the belief that from this sacrifice of its youth Australia had been tested as a nation and had proved its worth. On the day of the dispatch the Melbourne *Argus* announced that Australia had "in one moment stepped into the world wide arena in the full stature of great manhood". This brave, bloody adventure had given Australia "a place among the nations". "On the anvil of Gallipoli was hammered out the fabric of what is destined to be our most enduring national tradition." The Anzacs had made "a new Australia". Nationhood had come too easily; now the gladiators and martyrs were to die to make it real.

The Anzacs fought on mainly in mine tunnels and by sniping in the less than three square miles of dust and furze they had seized from the Turks after a second great attack had failed in August, leaving the bodies of Turk and Anzac, four or five deep, embraced in death. Flies shat the bacteria of dysentery and diarrhoea into their food; water was scarce; they clothed themselves in bits of uniforms, wearing what they liked, many half-naked like convicts who had gambled away their clothes. They rested in the gullies that fell down from behind the trenches and sometimes only half a mile from the centre of the front line, with shrapnel bursting above them; they swam from the beach they had named after themselves. Squashed together in common distress, they had found in each other as much brotherhood as men are ever likely to find. Life showed them two meanings: common fellowship and readiness for death. English literary men admired their brown bodies and turned them into classical heroes, but what they most admired in themselves was that they had "learned to accept a lost throw courageously". The failures on the sardonic frontiers of Australia had produced a style that matched this desperate occasion. From the honour and bravery of this failed adventure Australians began to find simple shadows of themselves, telling them what they thought they were, or what they ought to be. The experience went so deep that there were ceremonies in all States marking the first anniversary of "Anzac Day" in 1916, and in London it was celebrated in Westminster Abbey by King George and Queen Mary.

The Anzacs had left as silently as they had arrived, creeping away with guile; the Turks knew they had gone only on 20th December, when an attack found the Anzac's trenches empty, with nothing between Turk and sea except half a mile's walk. With the Anzacs temporarily out of the casualty lists, the Labor Party Prime Minister, "Billy" Hughes, now had his season, showing that Australia could be there. On a visit to Britain he joined the "Wake Up England" campaign with such stentorian vigour that German newspapers attacked and French newspapers praised him. Australians read reports of the fuss he was kicking up in the Old Country with such amazed pride that on his return he was greeted by enormous mobs at Perth and Adelaide shouting "Hullo, Billy", and on the train trip from Adelaide to Melbourne crowds gathered at every station to praise him with songs. His speeches were compared with those of Demosthenes; a scholar translated one of them into Greek and published it in the journal of the Melbourne Classical Association.

It was again the turn of the Anzacs to die to help the birth of the nation. At first when they were shipped to the Western

Front the going seemed quiet and things well-organized, far removed from the debilitating improvisations of Gallipoli. But an argument was going on at British G.H.Q. that would soon throw a division of Anzacs into a disastrous night's battle. It seemed obvious enough to the British generals that a feinting attack south of Lille would be a clever move . . . fingers pointed on maps at a bump in the line near Fromelles beside which was lettered "sugar loaf salient" . . . one general thought this was the place to attack . . . others didn't . . . then they let him have the 5th Australian Division to test his hypothesis.

The Anzacs went over the top late one afternoon to fight their way through to the third line of German trenches. Scattered parties broke out, leaving butchered comrades, but there was no "third line"—only muddy ditches. In the dark they tried to dig the third line, but the Germans were behind them, attacking. Ammunition was running out. All they could do was to charge through the Germans back to their old trenches. By breakfast time the next morning the Division had lost 5,533 men. It was to remain out of action for several months.

Three other Australian divisions were now fighting. With 100,000 British casualties already from the first two stages of his plan to "roll up" the German line on the Somme, General Haig was now organizing "a third great blow". More fingers pointed; the name of the 1st Australian Division was lettered in on the map opposite the village of Pozières. The village was already mere mounds of rubble and shreds of trees, the dead fruit of British corpses hanging on barbed-wire, when the Australians attacked it and seized its mud. When the Germans realized that it was the only success achieved in the third great blow, they concentrated their artillery on it, obliterating even the mounds of rubble. The 1st Division lost 5,285 men. When the 2nd Division relieved it they were ordered to throw themselves at a crest that was drawn on the maps. They seized it at night and lost 6,846 men. By the time the 4th Division had relieved the 3rd, British pencils were again pointing at some lettering on the maps. The 4th Division charged to this new stretch of mud and lost 4,649 men. One after the other, the three divisions were patched up and sent back to the attack. They fought for seven weeks—19 attacks, 16 at night. On one mile of this disastrous crest they lost 23,000 men.

In Australia there was a heightened sense of being, with

pride in the "Aussies" part in the inexplicable drama being fought in Europe and terror that such distant events could pull so many sons, husbands and lovers away from their homes and turn them into "the boys" at the front. Ceremonies of sacrifice were now established for the making of an Aussie: one of "the boys" would come home one night and blurt out his decision to enlist; he would have a "send-off" with piano-playing, songs and dancing; after he went off in his ship a photograph of him in his uniform would go up on a drawing-room table decorated with his regimental colours, a modest altar of hope. If he were gassed, or his flesh torn by steel, his next of kin would be told by telegram. If he were killed, they sent a clergyman.

The New Imperialism was proclaimed, with its gloomy satisfaction in blood-letting ("As gold is tried by fire so nations are punished by suffering"), but the war was also the greatest of the Australian sporting events; the Aussies were not only better fighters than the "poms" but bigger, cleaner and more handsome, and all the military failures were the fault of stuck-up British generals. The Aussies stuck by their mates, their sardonic wit sustaining them in facing death; on leave they were larrikins; on duty they were disciplined only when it mattered, showing remarkable initiative and readiness to "give it a go". And they were not only game but democratic, a people's army that, to the disgust of the British generals, did not even shoot its deserters.

But the democracy of Australians was now about to be tested in an extraordinary manner, and at home Universal Service Leagues were already demanding conscription; so was Archbishop Kelly; and when the British provided figures of necessary reinforcements (later found to be "enormously in excess of the need") the Labor Government put the matter to a national referendum, perhaps the first occasion in history when, at the height of a war, a people was asked to vote on the extent of its own sacrifice. Even the soldiers were to vote, as division by division, they returned to their rest areas behind the slaughter-yards.

The proponents of conscription knew that they would win by a big majority. True, there had been agitation against universal military service before the war, but had not two of the most publicized bread-and-water martyrs of that period been among the early volunteers in wartime? Posters went up that showed "the hun", in his spiked helmet, executing Australians in their own backyards. But to many Australians the danger was not as direct as that; it was not self-interest that made them support the war but a simple stubborn decision to support it. Even for many of the soldiers the fact that they had volunteered seemed to add satisfaction to the disasters that surrounded them; it was their own decision that they had subjected themselves to. A large number of them were to vote against conscription.

These were merely moods without political organization or stimulus—until the distrust of the Labor Party machines for Labor parliamentarians found in conscription an exciting and important cause for a showdown. The Labor machines became the principal organizational opposition to the Labor Government, and they were to bring with them a majority of the party's votes. But not all of them. A significant number of Labor voters still supported conscription, enough to carry it into effect. Perhaps the Catholic vote would defeat it. Having already found his voice in his quarrels with the Labor Party, and stirred by the British treatment of the Irish after the Easter Rebellion, Archbishop Mannix of Melbourne addressed "No" meetings of up to 100,000. But he did not carry with him a decisive number of Catholic votes.

The campaign exploded with excess. In Sydney, where five big city fires were believed to have been caused by I.W.W. arsonists, twelve members of the I.W.W. were framed and jailed. There were speculations about which way Jesus Christ would have voted. Even more sacred matters were involved: orators of the "Yes" campaign denounced "shirkers" as men who had blacklegged by stealing soldiers' jobs, while from the "No" platforms came counter-accusations that conscriptionists were conspiring to defeat the White Australian policy by filling soldiers' jobs with cheap imported labour.

The greed of the farmers became an issue. They had quickly learnt that it was their patriotic duty to make money out of the war. A Central Wool Committee had been formed to buy the wool clip at high prices; Britain was buying all the meat the farmers could produce, and the pressure on the government to force Australian wheat on to the British market was so great that Hughes bought fifteen ships despite British threats to requisition them back, and started a Commonwealth shipping line to transport it. Now, at a time of good seasons and high demand, here was a referendum threatening to conscript farm labour. It was by the switch in farming votes that the referendum was lost.

But the defeat of the referendum was seen not as a protest against the war, but as an affirmation that the war was to be fought in the Australian manner. "Fight for freedom's cause in freedom's way" was a principal "No" slogan. When the Labor Party split after the referendum (losing office in the Commonwealth, New South Wales and South Australia) the "Nationalist Parties" that were formed out of a combination of the Labor conscriptionists and the Liberal Parties proclaimed themselves the "win-the-war party" and, since the Federal Nationalists looked the more warlike of the two parties, they got back with a bigger majority in the election that followed the referendum. Nation-making demanded more blood.

After the butchery of Pozières the Aussies had spent a gloomy autumn. Absence without leave increased: men began to disappear just before a battle. Heavy rains brought mud so thick that it might take up to ten hours with five or six relays of stretcher-bearers to bring the wounded back to casualty clearing stations. Some wounded asked to be shot. Haig's attempt to "roll up" the German line petered out in mere reflex actions, and as winter came the Aussies became as concerned with mud and lice, rain and frostbite as with the bullets, bombs, shells and phosgene gas of the "hun".

The new year brought cold bright weather, with mud and water frozen hard and covered white with snow. The Anzacs were now working out a new name for themselves—"the Diggers". At Bullecourt the Diggers lay on snow-covered banks waiting for tanks that did not arrive . . . they charged barbed wire that the artillery had only half cut . . . their sense of irony increased. By May the first 16 mutinies broke out in the French army; the Russians were already in revolt. The Diggers were again thrown forward at Bullecourt, seizing and holding a narrow foothold deep in German ground, tactically useless, but their contribution to keeping attention from the French. Bullecourt cost them 10,000 casualties.

Now Haig had a new strategy—the "step by step" approach in which, with a proper co-ordination of infantry and artillery, one bit of land would be seized and consolidated, then there would be an advance on another. The new great blow would come from the battered Belgian town of Ypres; the morale of the Germans would collapse; the cavalry would charge through gaps in the line; the Germans would be driven from the

Belgian coast. But it rained for days before the offensive, turning the battlefield back to mud. The new strategy demanded dry weather. The offensive started in the wet.

When the weather again grew fine the Diggers found that the new strategy worked. Two of their divisions attacked side by side, in a single line, following a great barrage. Advance for half a mile. Pause for half an hour. Advance 500 yards. Pause for two hours. Another 200 yards. The plan worked perfectly: there were 5,000 casualties. It worked again: 5,500 casualties. In October four Anzac divisions fought side by side in a single line, to seize a ridge: 8,200 casualties. Then the rain came back. Diggers pushed forward in divisions, but only fragments of them reached objectives, then they fell back. In five weeks five divisions suffered 38,000 casualties.

As winter came again, after 55,000 casualties, despite reinforcements and the return of patched up men, the Diggers were 18,000 short. At home recruiting became more and more frenetic. In posters God was asked to "bless dear Daddy who is fighting the hun and send him HELP"; In Melbourne the Anglican bishops declared that "the forces of the Allies are being used of God to vindicate the rights of the weak". Forty-two German place names were changed; In South Australia Homburg became Haig; in New South Wales German Creek became Empire Vale; in Victoria Mount Bismarck became Mount Kitchener. Modern novelties were used: recruiting handbills wrapped around parcels, recruiting films, recruiting slogans hanging from box kites. Racing and boxing were restricted, and in four of the States hotels closed at six o'clock. Recruiting drives were held in the cities every day, with brass bands and long lines of speakers. At dances wounded soldiers appealed for volunteers; there were recruiting speeches at the beaches. Huge footprints were painted on city footpaths leading to recruiting depots; riderless horses rode past recruiting platforms and volunteers were called to fill the empty saddles.

There were other excitements. A dispute at the government tramway workshops in Sydney was seized by unionists and government for a fight both of them wanted. Strikes spread from one union to the next and in a few weeks there was assembled a large part of a general strike. Railway and tramway workers, miners, wharf labourers, food workers and others went out, often against the wishes of their leadership, in the greatest union uprising since the 1890s. Gas and electricity supplies were rationed, transport was cut, food distribution was limited. The government set up camps for volunteer labour; farmers and their sons hastened to the city to help defeat the strikes; individual workmen stayed at their jobs or drifted back to work. Soon it was clear that the government was going to win. Towards the end of almost twelve weeks' struggle union after union collapsed, all of them maimed, some of them shattered. The broken unions saw themselves as victims of a conspiracy between the government and the Employers Federation, while the government saw itself as victor over revolutionaries (although by then the I.W.W. had all been locked up in jail).

There was another referendum on conscription, more bitter, this time with some ambiguous hesitancies being expressed about the fighting of the war itself. The farmers again voted No. The majority for No slightly increased.

In 1918, as the Allied political leaders and military commanders squabbled about what they would do next, or whether they should just wait for the Americans to do it for them, the Germans moved 35 divisions from the Russian front and with this extra strength smashed at the Allied line, trying to push the British up against the English Channel and destroy them. The Diggers found themselves advancing through an Allied retreat, past deserters, stragglers, looters.

At home some questioning of the assumptions of the war were beginning to show in the Labor movement. In an atmosphere in which the war was seen as a war of benefit to the rich, a relatively easy assumption in Australia where 70 per cent of its cost was carried by loan money rather than taxation, some Labor Councils were becoming restless. In June the Federal Conference of the Labor Party passed a motion favouring a negotiated peace and attached conditions to continued support for recruiting. However, the war was still seen as a great cause by even the anti-conscriptionist political leaders of the already split Labor Party: to save a second split a ballot was called for November. But although it was a time when articulate opposition to the war was growing in other countries there was still little articulate opposition to it in Australia—apart from ambiguities from some Irish clerics—except in the trade unions. Although the ordinary people were confident of the achievements of the Diggers, even this expression of national pride was doubted by some more conservative Anglophiles as a kind of disloyal expression of superiority over the Old Country.

There was new occasion for national pride in the two Anzac cavalry divisions fighting in Palestine (one of which had carried out a two-mile charge through shrapnel and machine-gun fire against the Turks at Beersheba with nothing to wave at the enemy but bayonets). It was an Australian general who commanded all the allied cavalry that broke out into the valley of the River Jordan. In this dry, grim desolation epidemics plagued the Australians but they were riding on to Damascus and towards the fall of the Turkish Empire. On the Western Front when an Australian general—Monash, son of Polish-Jewish immigrants—was given command of the Australian divisions the Diggers felt safer with their own general between them and the British. They admired the thoroughness with which he gave a new kind of care to planning the co-ordination of tanks, aeroplanes and infantry. His first set attack made a big enough mark to earn an immediate visit from Clemenceau. The Diggers boasted that the British command took over Monash's methods.

Then it was over. Out of a population of less than 5,000,000 more than 400,000 had volunteered to fight on the other side of the world. Of those who took the field, almost one in two was wounded and one in five was killed. There was hardly a family group which had not feared the knock of the telegraph boy or the clergyman. There was supposed to have been some reason for it all. The Empire was safe . . . the war had been fought to end war . . . but the deeper feeling was that the Diggers had "established the name of our country amongst the foremost of all brave nations". By their fighting they had decided what Australians were.

The name of the country now demanded further establishment. Although Hughes's Cabinet thought it an unnecessary impertinence that Australia should have a seat of its own at the peace conference, Hughes successfully kicked up a fuss in support of the Canadian demand for separate representation, and his face was to be there among the others, in the official painting of the signing of the peace treaty at Versailles. As 137 different ships on 176 separate voyages brought the Diggers home, Hughes fought the peace single-handed, declaring at one stage in Paris that "in certain circumstances Australia would place herself in opposition to the opinion of the whole civilized world".

He secured the co-operation of President Wilson in discarding a Japanese move that a declaration of race equality should be put into the preamble of the Covenant of the proposed League of Nations and he became enough of a nuisance for a "C" class mandate to be invented ("a 999 years lease") to satisfy him that the Australian control under the League of Nations of the former German colony of New Guinea would be given a special freedom. Hughes added the last of the claims to nationhood when he announced on his return to Australia that it was by having separate recognition at the peace conference that "Australia became a nation".

What kind of a nation? The human qualities apotheosized by the Diggers in their desperate comradeship found only a small place in the new official rhetoric; the old, confident boasts of the Improvers had gone. Australia was no longer going to solve the riddles of the sphinx. The best that Hughes could think of when he got home was that Australians had volunteered to die "to maintain those ideals which we have nailed to the very topmost of our flagpole—White Australia, and those other aspirations of this young Democracy". What the other aspirations were was not stated. Corpses rotted in the fields of France and Belgium and in the deserts of Palestine and maimed men began to draw their pensions at a time when Australians were losing official direction as to what their aspirations were supposed to be.

Chapter 14

THE END OF IMPROVEMENT
1919-1939

The returned men

Now that the dead Diggers had to be commemorated there was not a town or a suburb of any size that did not set up a wayside shrine. In churches lamps of remembrance were installed, often in special soldiers' chapels, and in almost every institution rolls were set up with the Diggers' names in gold. Large temples were dedicated to their honour in the capital cities. The trophies of war were dispersed throughout the public parks, and the Australian War Museum became a sacred place of national self-definition. Worship of the Diggers was a dominant cult.

A Repatriation Department, with six State branches, 800 local committees and its own hospitals and artificial limb factories, served the disabled with treatment and a quarter of a million pensions. "Repat" became a sanctuary not only for the immediately disabled but for many of those who later fell by the way: prayers for solace were offered to it in the form of claims that illnesses had been caused, however remotely, by the war. Money was available for "Returned Men" to buy houses, and just as Roman legionaries claimed land when they gave up fighting, Returned Men could gain farms (half of which, in the Australian manner, thereupon failed). Preference in employment to Returned Men was accepted as such a sacred necessity in the Commonwealth Public Service that the regular recruiting of juniors ceased until 1933: the Returned Men got almost all the public service jobs. The only other main form of entry was to be taken on as a messenger boy and try to work your way up.

The Returned Soldiers and Sailors Imperial League of Australia (the R.S.L.) developed an influence perhaps greater than that of the veterans' organizations in any other country; its representatives sat on each of the main boards in the "Repat", deciding to whom these secular monasteries would dispense alms, and R.S.L. officials were a lobby all politicians respected. Although attempts to form a soldiers' party ("above politics") failed, several passing political movements, all of a conservative and at least one of a fanatical kind, had much of their origin and support from R.S.L. members; and even in the more orthodox parties, especially in the country, the R.S.L. mystique could be significant. Between strangers a combination of an R.S.L. badge and a masonic handshake could make a weighty greeting.

Outside the Labor Party, the sacrifice of the fallen Diggers became more sacred than the White Australia Policy and largely replaced it as an ideal appealed to in speech-making. In 1929 a strongly R.S.L. government in New South Wales banned *All Quiet on the Western Front*. In 1930 the R.S.L. called for ". . . the prohibition of war books which defame the soldiers of the Empire" and sought to arrange "that all war books should be censored by the official war historian before being admitted to the Commonwealth". War had become a mystery that to many was greater than the Christian faith—and the R.S.L. was its prophet. As the 1940s approached, when many Returned Men met each other they had nothing to talk of except their war service. Even when they were with those who had not been to the war almost any conversational opening might remind them of an incident at Bullecourt or Pozières, Beersheba or Fromelles.

Australia at last had a national day—Anzac Day—with the R.S.L. as custodian. A day marking "the irresistible entry of Australia among the nations of the world . . . sanctified by the lives of those who made the great sacrifice", "essential as a crystallising point in the evolution of a national pride and consciousness", Anzac Day became Australia's secular Easter: in the morning sacrifice was honoured in marches and religious services (with the Catholics breaking off after the march to go to their own church rather than join the others in a common mourning); in the evening the resurrection of the nation was declared in drunken suppers. Apart from New Zealand,

Australia was probably the only modern nation to celebrate its nationhood by recalling with solemnity and pride an overseas military expedition. What was celebrated was the purifying flame of war, the self-realization of brotherhood, the fortitude of sacrifice.

The first suburban nation

With the spread of the motor bus, suburbs began to sprawl farther into the bushland away from railway lines, and when the Californian bungalow was adopted as the most commonly desired Australian residence, houses were spaced farther from each other. The six capital cities, which held half the total population, were uniquely suburbanized, covering a greater area for their population than any other cities in the world.

In the new streets of dark purple brick bungalows, "set low and close to the ground as a fortress", the suburban Australians were realizing by regular instalments some parts of their ideal of what life was about. It was not an ideal all could afford, nor that all yet wanted—in the slums there was still a counter-style of cheeky gregariousness; but for most Australians outside the rural areas (by 1939 two-thirds of the population) "a home of one's own" set in its garden seemed to represent the end of that searching for dignity and independence that had failed in so many rural land reform schemes, and that had first driven many of the "bloody emigrants" from the industrialized cities of the British Isles with dreams of a return to a simple arcady that seemed, however mythically, to be their birthright.

Australians were suburban in ways as complex as their history. There were many displays of respectability, but the drive to respectability had been endemic since the first convict got his ticket-of-leave; at the same time suburbanites could still see Australians as larrikins, sometimes approvingly, sometimes not. Some saw their fellow countrymen as lazy boozers, some as Bible-banging wowsers. The ideas of mateship, articulated in the 1890s, were maintained in the unions and in another way in the R.S.L., even if they were not usually expressed in suburban streets. At the same time the individualistic self-assertion of the eighteenth century was still there, as old as the Emancipists and the early traders. Often it was a view of the Australian as a gambler that gave a suburbanite a feeling of national distinctiveness, even if he himself didn't gamble. Three large lotteries flourished (two Government run) and the racehorse was seen as "the one great symbol of events that carried one outside the deadly round of daily toil".

Good fishing was never far away from most suburbs. Many ran alongside the water. Others were near stretches of bush. There was a craze for hiking, access to sport continued to increase (the number of golf courses quadrupled), surfing became even more popular, summertime sunburn even more fashionable, the strutting lifesavers demonstrated the idea of the Australian as bronzed Anzac. For their holidays suburbanites dreamed of camping in the bush or roughing it in a coastal weekender, feeling real again. To those who had a motor car, or knew someone who did, a "spin" to a stretch of nearby bush, and a lunch of lamb chops grilled over a fire and washed down by tea boiled in a billycan was a reminder of what it was like to be an Australian.

Suburbanites accepted the collective restraints of modern metropolitan life more than most of the other peoples who were congregating in cities. In the various ways in which people rub up against each other in cities Australians were usually self-restrained and orderly without outwardly imposed discipline. If naïvely, D. H. Lawrence wondered at how "they ran their city very well. . . . There seemed to be no policemen, and no authority, the whole thing went by itself, loose and easy, without any bossing". "Our street" had become the unit they belonged to and in their streets they combined helpfulness when it was really necessary with a care not to destroy the sense of independence they gained from their privacy. They seemed born to suburbanism, as often, by now, they were. Sometimes "their aggressive familiarity" startled visitors, but usually it was only when rights or dignity were threatened that some became touchy. When this happened they could be devastatingly sarcastic. However, an inner violence was more usually tamed into sardonic wit, or in "chiacking", a kind of chaffing that threatened offence without meaning it, like the fighting games of animals. Their openness of manner was seen by foreign visitors as a freedom from servility, a humbling of the mighty in which taxi-drivers preferred passengers to sit next to them in the front seat as a token of equality. Lawrence noted "that air of owning the city which belongs to a good Australian". That the people should walk around their city as if they owned it seemed remarkable.

As Spanish Mission was added to Californian bungalow and then as architectural styles fragmented into a new diversity, even the competitiveness in style of suburban houses seemed to affirm the dignity of those who lived in them. Contempt was felt for the dull uniformity of the old streets of terraces close to the city, jammed wall to wall, all monotonously the same, without gardens to spend the weekends working in. Brick became such a symbol of the new age that many councils in Sydney and Melbourne forbade the building of houses in any other material. Comfort and self-content could be found in the adoption of new fashions in home furnishing, made possible by time-payment schemes. Dressers and other "old-fashioned" kitchen furniture would be replaced by "breakfast room suites", for example, or a craze for "built-in" furniture would develop. Black fuel ranges were replaced by gas or electric cookers in white enamel; wood-burning coppers began to be replaced by gas; gas water heaters appeared in bathrooms; shiny electric toasters, hot water jugs and irons sprouted in kitchens; brooms were replaced by carpet sweepers, carpet sweepers by vacuum cleaners. The consumption of gas doubled; the consumption of electricity went up five times. Just as exhibitions held in the late nineteenth century showed those who strolled through them new machines like the lawnmower and the sewing-machine, the Electrical and Radio Exhibitions of the 1930s promised new forms of liberation. When confident façades of chromium plated steel and shiny black glass were put up to hide Victorian façades in the cities there seemed no end to the prospects of modernity.

The mode for private lives without public occasion showed itself in new limitations on the diversions of suburbanites. Hotels ceased to be general meeting-places. Because of licence reductions, half of them ceased to exist and, in the three States that kept the six o'clock closing-time imposed during the war, "all around the bar a heaving mass of men elbowing, pushing, trampling on each other's feet" shouted orders for enough beer to fill their bellies in the "six o'clock swill". In Sydney, a small fashionable café society developed around two night clubs and a hotel within a few minutes walk from each other ("night after night the same two hundred dance, laugh and gossip"); a bohemian life was maintained at King's Cross; four or five speak-easies bribed their way into survival; but otherwise night life disappeared. In the other cities there was no sign of it. Hardly any city restaurants stayed open at night and those that did were forbidden to serve drink; diners-out could bring their own bottles but they had to empty them by a specified hour. The police raided hotels and restaurants to make sure they were keeping the law, or they were bribed not to do so.

After the arrival of the talkies only three "live" theatres survived in Melbourne and only one in each of the other capital cities and they contented themselves mainly with revivals of the musical comedy successes of earlier decades. With reproduction marble statues, reproduction oil paintings, reproduction chandeliers, reproduction coats-of-arms and reproduction antique furniture, the most ambitious of the new city picture palaces provided much of what was available in the visual as well as the performing arts. (In the latter category as well as "the pictures" there were full orchestras, stage shows and Wurlitzer organs.)

By day, most visitors to the cities were suburban women seeking "nice things" in department stores and bargain shops. Other than this, the cities—now seen by some as "too Americanized"—were centres from which novelty ideas such as hamburger shops and milk bars slowly spread to the suburbs, later to be some of the few places apart from dance halls where young people could meet.

For many, keeping their gardens neat and their houses in running order became their chief diversion. For those who liked reading, popular magazines were developed, newspapers produced bolder display, more pictures, shorter paragraphs, readers' contests and comic strips, and novels could be borrowed from small private lending libraries in suburban shops, or from the Schools of Arts (whose old ideals were so forgotten that people wondered at their funny name). But it was the wireless that now dominated home entertainment. By the end of the 1930s there were more than a million wireless sets, and 130 broadcasting stations; some of the best known Australian performers on the wireless were as famous as Hollywood film stars. At breakfast time the wireless saw grown-ups off to work and children off to school; it entertained housewives during the day; the whole family would group around it at night. It was now an unnecessary exertion to wind up a gramophone or pedal a pianola.

A sense of belonging was to be found on the beaches, at spectator sports, and at the suburban picture shows. Since in the suburban shopping centres everything shut down at six o'clock, the packed suburban cinemas were the main opportunity for the people from a suburb to gather together and look at each other; this was the only kind of night out most of them knew. Other than these, the suburbs provided no sense of community, not even good shops. Although millions of pounds of loan money now went into public works in the cities it was even difficult to keep the water and sewerage pipes up with suburban development. New lines of criticism of Australians appeared: "Sydney is not so much a city as an agglomeration of small municipalities grouped around a semi-Americanized core and the real estate offices of a score of professional boosters." Suburbanites were seen as fragmented by "stereotyped forces . . . conveyor-belt systems".

Some found a certain drying up of spontaneity. Men lorded it over most leisure pursuits, but women expressed themselves in the neatness and taste of "the home", which in extreme cases could become a sacred place, parts of it unsoiled by use. The shrivelling of opportunities for men and women to publicly enjoy themselves together seemed sometimes to shrivel their other relations with each other and the growing dominance of family life by women sometimes made a man a kind of guest in his own house. Some of the men continued the aggressive assertions of maleness of a society in which there had once been several times more men than women and active homosexual relations had been common. Now "poofters" were despised, but behind the displays of masculinity there sometimes seemed compensating anxieties. A fearful holding-back would drain affection; a deep inner reserve could "make a man go blank in his with-held self"; in extreme cases this defence of privacy could mean that there was little privacy left to defend.

Some families lived in almost complete isolation from everyone else; for others their only home entertainment was within extended family groups, usually on a Sunday (in their best clothes). Those who did not have cars and lived in suburbs distant from each other might have to make three or four transport changes before they got there, and then go through it all again on the way home. Some kept up wider fields of home entertainment (some of the poor and some of the rich most successfully)—women developed the rituals of afternoon tea (dainty sandwiches and many varieties of sponge cake) into a complex art—but for most, if privacy and a removal from a sense of community other than that of family and close friends was what they wanted, they had got it.

Even if, like any other success, it had its disappointments, part of what Australians had most desired from the Improvement had now been obtained. Many were happy. What was unexpected was that, in its public expression, the sense of Improvement had suddenly died.

"Development", not Improvement

From being a pioneer country in social and political reform, Australia had become backward. Even the British, not an advanced nation in social security, had medical benefits, widows pensions and unemployment insurance schemes: Australia had no national provision for any of these. In 1928, after five years of Royal Commissions, special committees and reports, a Nationalist government had proposed a compulsory contributory scheme of national insurance with all employees paying 1s. a week each and employers contributing equally. It came to nothing. Ten years later another non-Labor government proposed a similar scheme, along with a medical benefits panel system. This also came to nothing. In 1937 there were Commonwealth-State discussions on unemployment insurance. These came to nothing.

Australia's history was defeating it. The friendly societies, themselves expressions of Improvement, attacked the schemes as destroying the spirit of independence and thrift. Used to the idea of the government as a provider that went back to the convict period, employers attacked national insurance as too costly, and the Labor Party attacked it because it didn't appear to be "free". Still retaining the nobbishness of the early days, the doctors rejected the panel system as an assault on their dignity.

The drive for political reform also petered out. The preferential system of voting was introduced in five States and the Commonwealth (with Tasmania preferring the proportional system), and voting was made compulsory, first for the Queensland parliament and then for the others, but that was all. There was gerrymandering of electorates in some States and in all of them the Legislative Councils remained stockades of the old nobbishness; but only Queensland got rid of its Legislative Council and Labor governments were among the worst gerrymanderers. The nineteenth century liberal and radical programmes for political reform had nothing much left over for twentieth century Australia.

As part of the general puritanism of the English-speaking nations at that time there was a triumphant impetus to the old drive to respectability. As well as the halving of hotel licences, the restrictions on trading hours, the prohibitions on serving drinks with meals, on off-course betting and on almost any organized Sunday activity, there were attacks on birth control (the size of families had halved), living in flats, swimming trunks for men, smoking, twin beds, trousers for women, the depravity of modern art, the wearing of lipstick. Even spectator sport was attacked as undermining the nation's morals. From ignoring literary censorship (up to 1928 only three literary books had been banned although 120 seditious works, mostly Bolshevik, were impounded), the Commonwealth Government, applauded by church bodies, women's clubs and the R.S.L., launched a campaign to protect the values of the patriotic family man. By the mid-1930s 500 works of serious intent had been banned as "filth". Flim censorship was instituted. There were exhortations that sport was not to be enjoyed: it was to be pursued as a national duty.

That people should want to live in cities seemed even more evil than it had in the 1890s, and as country life declined in economic importance praise for it became more anxious. Australia was said to ride "on the sheep's back". History books presented the wool industry with an earlier and more consistent importance than it had, and John Macarthur, an early woolgrower, was made one of Australia's principal heroes. When Australians wanted to admire themselves they could look at a picture of a merino ram. Yet although wool was important as an export item, contributing 38 per cent of total exports from 1935 to 1939, it had never regained its late nineteenth century pre-eminence.

There was no hope for the cities in the "society" that coagulated at the top of them: it was much the same as the "black-hat" society of the 1840s, with gentlemen's clubs as its most important meeting-places, the Legislative Councils as its unique political expression, the fee-paying schools as its main training grounds, and the Government Houses as its principal sources of honour. The squatters and such "ancient nobility" that each State could muster dominated the clubs, along with leading doctors, lawyers, professors, financiers and merchants, while a blackball awaited retailers, Catholics, Jews and others who were not "the right type".

From being mainly radical or liberal, the Press became mainly conservative, although parts of it, most notably the Sydney *Daily Telegraph* in the late 1930s, gave expression to a contemporary philosophy of Improvement: having overthrown stodgy bumbledom and the Mrs Grundies that gave Australia a bad name overseas, Australia would rise again with airmail services, films for schools, modern marketing, a mature film industry, light wines in cafés, air defence, modern art, uniform railway gauges, parent education, dress reform, slum abolition, music concerts for children, traffic safety, art for the people, the training of unskilled workers, the cultivation of science, free shop trading hours, tuberculin testing for cows, the abolition of examinations and homework, rent control, better treatment of the Aborigines, lower tariffs, the legalization of betting, the sponsorship of the arts, the cultivation of tourists and the removal of restrictions on wearing swimming trunks on beaches.

Within politics the once more-or-less prevailing agreement on the values of Improvement withered now that Australians had achieved their version of the two-party system political theorists had demanded since the 1850s. Although the Nationalists inherited some of the liberalism of men like Deakin, they didn't do much with it, becoming more cohesively and openly a party of special business interest, in reaction to the special trades union interest of the Labor Party. The Nationalists were not even in control of their own finances: independent groups did their fund-raising for them, making much of the Nationalists as an "insurance against Bolshevism", a belief for which some sustenance had been provided when a Communist Party was formed in 1922, mainly out of trades union leaders. Through its overwhelmingly trades unionist nature, it sometimes influenced factions within the Labor parties, and it attacked all the institutions of Improvement as weapons against the workers. In reply the Nationalists denounced the "small minority of foreign extremists who have managed to capture the trades union movement".

At the end of the 1920s, Australia, for its population, was losing more working hours in strikes than almost any other country. The greatest sense of threat had occurred when the Victorian police went on strike in 1923; the centre of the city was in the control of looters until Returned Men volunteers intervened, summoned by appeals at the city cinemas. But there was also violence (and even more talk of violence) in Sydney during the timber workers' strike and the waterfront strike when the Commonwealth Government tried to deport two union leaders (the High Court stopped this) and then introduced coercive legislation that almost destroyed the union. Direct government intervention in big strikes, initiated in the late 1880s, had become routine and the governments usually won. In the 1928-29 coalfields lockout (exports of coal had collapsed) the N.S.W. government secured a victory at Rothbury that shocked Australians when police opened fire and launched baton charges; one man was killed and nine were wounded.

While "working class consciousness" in occupational groups such as the coalminers and the wharf labourers was growing strong enough to be an irritant, it was too weak to achieve anything except successful government retaliation and a further weakening of Improvement. The Nationalists denounced the big strikes as foretastes of Bolshevik revolution and warned voters against putting Labor into power in the Commonwealth parliament lest the "red raggers", through their influence in the Labor Party, gain control of Australia. In such political melodrama there was no place for a shared belief in social progress.

In some States it was the Labor parties, not the Nationalists, who came to seem the natural governing party. In Queensland, where Labor governed from 1916 to 1929 and then returned to power for what was to be twenty-five years, its attitude seemed "more moderate, more positive and apparently more attractive than that of the opposition". With twenty years office in twenty-three years, Labor developed a similar reputation in Western Australia; in Tasmania, after five years government in the 1920s, it re-assumed government in 1934 and stayed in power for thirty-five years. Such support for Labor seemed to indicate a continuing hope among voters for social progress, but the State Labor governments did not achieve much. They were hampered by the nobs in the Legislative Councils and by the puzzles of a federal system; but in any case, whatever their practice, much of their precepts made up a doctrine for situations that did not exist. The Labor parties had discarded most of their doctrines without finding anything to replace them. Prompted by trades-union pressure, they still instituted a reform now and again, but often their aim was simply to look more normal than their opponents. With agreement on social values gone, they were now the parties of progress, but they did not progress and their opponents were no longer prompting them to Improvement. In some Labor parties more than half the members were Catholics; this produced much heady plotting and counter-plotting, but it did not induce Improvement.

Public expression of the belief that Australia would show the world how to live was replaced by the philosophy of the real estate speculator. There were boosters' dreams of an Australia of a hundred million people or more (all white), clothing the world and feeding it, but there was no longer any special reason for these people being there, except fear. ("We must populate this country or we shall never be able to hold it.") Australia was "Unlimited", but it had ceased to be a place in which there was bold talk of social changes; instead, optimism narrowed to a belief in economic activity for its own sake.

As it happened, much economic activity was uneconomic. The professedly expansionist idea of "Men, money and markets" was the great slogan of the 1920s, but of the 500,000 British immigrants hoped for in ten years, only half arrived— and unemployment ran at eight per cent over the decade; of the £225 million raised in the London money market much was wasted; new markets were obtained, but only by a high cost in subsidies or special concessions. The word "development" had assumed great emotive content, but it was "development" without consideration of cost. The assumption was that the "vast resources" of Australia were all "natural resources". What was to be unlimited was Australian farming. Governments, still seeing themselves as the prime innovators, assisted immigration, paid for closer land settlement schemes for immigrants and Returned Men, and built huge irrigation systems and other public works. But by 1928 half the money advanced to rural settlers throughout Australia had been written off.

Some irrigation schemes had been instituted in a remarkably carefree spirit: the Hume Weir, for example, was partly built before thought was given as to how it was to be used. Even where irrigation schemes seemed to be making a return on the money outlayed on irrigation works, the return could diminish or disappear when the cost of other public works was added. When the birds that had previously eaten grasshoppers' eggs on the dry plains found better food in the irrigation channels, grasshopper plagues threatened the wheat areas.

As in the United States and Canada, the rise of wheat farming continued to produce new groups of discontent. Governments set up bulk handling facilities for wheat and government research developed new strains, but the wheat farmers wanted that place of honour in the nation they had begun to imagine in the late nineteenth century, combining with small graziers and the dairy farmers to promote the idea that the small settlers of rugged independence and integrity ennobled the whole land. To most Australians it was still unbelievable that small farmers should receive any respect—a serial called *Dad and Dave*, making fun of a family of cockies, had become a hit on the wireless—but the small settlers took themselves seriously enough to promote Country Parties (sometimes with an R.S.L. flavour added) that in four parliaments became an important part of the political system. In these four parliaments Australia was back to a three-party system, but this time the alliances were not those of progress.

Even the history of Australia as a mineral-exporting country was neglected in favour of dreams of agricultural expansion. Although there was some promotion of oil searches, surveys of mineral resources were ignored. Ironically, it was in the 1920s that the trend of investment moved clearly in favour of the cities. At the very time when governments gave renewed emphasis to rural areas, Australia was taking off as a manufacturing power—without anyone noticing.

The Improvisers

When the Australians were organizing themselves for the Great War the Governor-General had written home, half-patronizing, half-admiring, that "happy-go-lucky methods" were typical of "this people". There was "a grasp of realities, an astuteness and energy" in them: "extremely adaptable, they quickly seize on every device that suggests itself for accomplishing desirable ends". This happy-go-lucky but practicable adaptability was shown in a wartime expansion of manufacturing which by 1921 saw New South Wales, now the leading industrial State, with nearly a third of its workers engaged in industry. The most marked advance was in heavy industry and the metal trades, where New South Wales was pre-eminent, even more so when a second steel plant was built, this time at Port Kembla. The war had broken the remote control by German cartels of much of the Australian minerals industry, and Australian-owned smelting and refining plants had been established. After the war the B.H.P., protected from imports (and after it bought the Port Kembla plant, from domestic competition), was, in the 1930s, to produce the world's cheapest steel.

In the 1920s manufacturing expanded perhaps by a third, in the next decade perhaps by 40 per cent, but the uniform success in heavy industry was not accompanied by an equally uniform success in making consumer goods. For instance, although motor vehicle assembly and the production of motor bodies and tyres was well under way in the 1920s, no Australian-designed car was being manufactured by the end of the 1930s. Such initiative as there was had come from the government's offering a bounty and proposing, as a form of protection, to put the assembly of foreign cars under licence; but none of the proposals submitted to it were economic.

There were difficulties. In the 1920s (although not in the 1930s) wages were as much as 50 per cent, even 100 per cent, higher than in Britain and working hours were less, producing high internal costs; the population, not reaching 7,000,000 until 1940, was small, and with Australia so far away from the rest of the whites this small population seemed the only market. Manufacturers, both Australian and those foreigners, mostly British, who had been persuaded to set up in Australia, fell back on the government; a Tariff Board had been set up in 1921 to recommend protective duties, and while higher protection encouraged efficiency in some cases, of which the B.H.P. was the most notable, in others it simply supported high prices.

While this period saw investment in manufacturing becoming significant, most factories apart from the heavy industries were still short of capital. The banks were the main regulators of capital, and bankers were very conservative. The Commonwealth Bank, although its board was government-appointed, was given an independent status by the Nationalists and, if anything, it turned out to be even more conservative than the private banks. The whole financial machine was still partly that of a farmers' and merchants' society, and while governments were still big investors they in fact distorted investment by putting so much money into uneconomic rural programmes.

Australia was industrializing without developing some of the social characteristics of an industrial society: it was sufficiently like the innovative industrial societies in other countries to be able to take over their innovations into a high-cost system protected by tariffs, but this occurred so relatively easily that it did not throw up strongly all the new institutions and types of people usually produced by industrialization.

Technical education, although more prominent, went prominently backwards. As modern industry's increasing diversification made the apprenticeship system even less efficient than it had been, it was the apprenticeship system that became the main basis of technical training in Australia. In 1934 a Royal Commission reported on the "shocking inadequacies of the entire system" of technical education; in 1939 another Royal Commission said that most efforts were "half-hearted and belated". There were no courses in management or marketing or schools in industrial design, or any indication that the making of business decisions might require training of any kind. And although non-Labor parties seemed to put as much trust in government intervention as the Labor Party, no special attention was given to the recruiting of government officials. Until 1933 there was no provision for admission of graduates, although some State public services instituted small cadet schemes. The Commonwealth Treasury was run by accountants, and when things went wrong the Government had to appoint a committee of university economists to see what had happened; it had no economists of its own.

Australia was still failing to provide a wide educated class with a confident sense of its own importance. Expenditure on education was less than in the United States, Britain, Canada and New Zealand. By the end of the 1930s, when the United

States was planning that all children between 14 and 18 should be at secondary schools, in Australia the proportion was less than a quarter; in Queensland it had dropped from 17 per cent in 1921 to 13 per cent in 1939. In the schools and universities between 1920 and 1940 there were hardly any curriculum or even textbook changes. In 1935 a U.S. expert reported that Australian libraries lagged behind those of most civilized countries; at an international New Educational Fellowship conference in Canberra in 1937 most of the visiting speakers attacked Australia's backwardness.

There was an extra difficulty: Australia was industrializing at a time when British enterprise had run down. The lack of interest in vocational education was British, the very amateurishness of some Australian decision-makers was British (if without a classical education, and sometimes tempered by more astuteness, energy and adaptability). Although some Australian leaders knew of the importance of science in German industry and of the importance of education for businessmen in the United States, they could not impose these ideas on a British-derived education system in which honour was given to uselessness. Among the decision-makers, Nationalist or Labor, business boss or union boss, education was so little considered that not even its uselessness was honoured; that education could be useful seemed even more ridiculous.

There was a slow but important development as 500 committees with 5,000 members set about the long task of co-ordinating industrial standards, looking for what was best in current practice, and chemists', engineers' and physicists' institutes were formed; but with very few exceptions there was no serious research in private firms. Even the steel industry sponsored little private research. The pattern of Australian industry was that the parent company told a foreign-owned firm what to do, and an Australian-owned firm bought ideas from other countries.

The post-graduate schools of science and technology were weak, so, in the manner of colonial governmentalism, a government research body, the Council for Scientific and Industrial Research, set up in 1926, became the dominant force in Australian science. It at once established its acceptance by destroying the prickly pear, which had infested about 60 million acres, in some cases smothering whole districts. Tests had revealed that the caterpillars of the *cactoblastis* moth from Argentina and South Brazil would do the job; by 1930, 3,000 million of their eggs had been distributed with such effectiveness that hundreds of square miles of prickly pear could be destroyed in a few months. But the C.S.I.R's general research, although very valuable in providing a better basis for established rural industries and opening out opportunities for new ones, such as timber-growing for paper manufacture, was mainly concerned with farming.

A class of business men now demanded all the esteem of industrial innovators. But in fact they were not innovators, although sometimes they were improvisers. Bombast about the importance of "private enterprise" was strong, but the ideas behind the enterprise were of foreign origin and its practice usually by virtue of government support and protection. Sometimes the very stridency of these claims seemed an expression of the half-realized anxieties of people who claimed a status they had not earned, and that, by and large, would not be given by the ordinary people, who, if they were going to bestow it on anybody, still preferred to bestow status on doctors, squatters and other nobs. In a nation in which the styles of industrial activity were rapidly becoming significant, the pretences of "enterprise" spread through significant parts of Australian society, perhaps helping to corrupt it with an atmosphere of derivativeness and second-ratedness.

"The greatest Test Match of them all"

At first when two Australian loans failed in London early in 1929 this appeared merely a matter for the banks, but by the year's end stock-market values in the United States had fallen by $26 billion and the world's economy seemed stricken by plague. Australia was so quickly and drastically infected (wool prices dropped by half) that its whole financial system appeared about to collapse from this new and mysterious rottenness. For several months, with a Treasury Department run by bookkeepers, the Commonwealth Government didn't know what to do. Then it put together a "tariff wall", which blocked half Australia's imports and started a "grow-more-wheat campaign"; this was followed by a disastrous fall in the price of wheat. On its own initiative a private bank devalued the currency. The crisis extended to government budgets and for several months the N.S.W. government defaulted, with the Commonwealth paying its debts. Then, in March 1931, governments agreed, in the "Premiers' Plan", to cut salaries and pensions by 20 per cent (except old-age pensions which went down 12½ per cent) and to increase taxes and reduce interest rates. After two years Australian governments had worked out a policy for what was now known as "the Depression"; but by then unemployment was up to 27 per cent. By 1933 nearly a third of breadwinners were out of work.

Thousands of the unemployed hit the track as swaggies; in "happy valleys" on the outskirts of cities the evicted built shacks from scrap timber and galvanized iron; people waited in dole queues for coupons for milk, bread, meat and groceries; relief work was on such a small scale that it offered only one or two days' work a week for those who could get it. The rest of the unemployed stayed on the dole, and even for many of those still in jobs work was rationed to share it out. Over the depression period the population declined by 10,000. One by one, each of the country's seven governments was thrown out of office. The Commonwealth Labor government, baffled by its own divisions, by Treasury ignorance, by a hostile Senate and by the intractability of the Commonwealth Bank, split in three directions before it fell.

It was a time of hopeful slogans . . . "Grow more wheat", "Share the burden", "Balanced budgets and more employment". There was a battle of plans . . . "The Theodore Plan", named after the Federal Treasurer, urged a mild deficit expansion; the "Lang Plan", named after the N.S.W. Labor Premier, urged default; the "Premiers' Plan" decided on deflation. Appeals were made to wartime memories ("Let the whole world know that the heart of Australia is sound, that her people possess the same fighting spirit in peace as they showed in war") and to the love of cricket ("The greatest Test Match of them all—to be won").

Right-wing revolution threatened New South Wales when Jack Lang attacked the "shylocks of London" and tried to turn the depression into a great drama of his own righteousness. A

"New Guard" formed to put out "the bushfire of Langism", a secret paramilitary organization claiming 100,000 members, mostly Returned Men, organized in zones, divisions and localities, each with its own commander, with orders ready for mobilization. Plans were made by cliques of Returned Men and others in country towns to set up provisional governments for three secessionist States, which would proclaim rebellion when coded telegrams came from Sydney. As it turned out, although fighting the Commonwealth with a second default and seizing documents and funds to keep things going, Lang went when the Governor dismissed him.

The imaginative Theodore Plan was one of the few constructive ideas put up by a member of government anywhere in the world at the time, containing some of the style of what was to be known as "Keynesianism", but both left and right moved in to destroy it. Appeals to sacrifice were preferred. When a newly formed "United Australia Party" took over from Labor (the Nationalists under another name, but with Joe Lyons, one of the men who had split from Labor, as leader) it proclaimed those principles of "sound finance" that the banks had forced on it. Remembering the disgrace of the Australian bank crashes of the 1890s and terrified of the German kind of financial disintegration if the politicians took over, the banks pressed only for policies of debt servicing. In a time of despair, when people gathered in city halls to keep up their spirits with community singing, when as many as a hundred thousand could attend a protest meeting, and when the world was so absorbed in its own misery that it had no time to remember Australia, the idea of paying interest on debts seemed something to cling to. To some it was a test of "Australia's good name", in which the fate of the unemployed represented their individual sacrifice, as, earlier, had the deaths of the Diggers. There was a great deal of self-congratulation by those concerned that the "Premiers' Plan" had balanced the budgets. Men had not lost their jobs in vain: Australia's reputation was again good in the city of London.

It seemed obvious that cuts in wages and other costs would help the farmers, in whose hands Australia's future still lay, and when the world prices of farm products again went up, prosperity would be found around that elusive corner which was now the subject of so many jokes. But although governments looked to the farms for recovery, as they had looked to them for development, recovery came earliest, strongest and quickest from the factories, a trend hardly noticed by governments. It was expanded industrial production, stimulated by the rise in protection, by the restriction of imports and by cuts in domestic costs, that put men back into work.

Despite whatever moves there were towards a sense of national unity, the Depression heightened the policies of envy. Western Australia saw the Depression as a plot from the East and voted for secession. South Australia developed a State nationalism, with plans for attracting enough industry to bring its population of 600,000 up to Queensland's million. Tasmania hoped by re-afforestation and hydro-electric plants to at least keep its quarter of a million population from drifting to the mainland. Victoria, with less than two million people, envied New South Wales its two and three-quarter million. Melbourne, which now saw itself as "the most British" of the cities, attacked the "Americanization" of Sydney. But in both States there was a mood of such dispirited caution that even envy could not re-arouse hope for any sense in constructive policies.

Even as the rates of unemployment began to fall to the 1920s' level ("prosperity") shock and uncertainty remained. For many the Depression had been as critical an experience as the Great War and, although no granite monuments went up to it, it remained a despondent memory in unions and Labor parties and in many individual hearts. "Development" now seemed as dead as Improvement. Frightened of their budgets, governments kept silent on questions of hospitals, schools, slum clearance, city transport and social security; although industry was expanding, politicians and writers, traditionally bound to see Australian expansionism as a rural matter, ceased to speak of Australia's future. Immigration had stopped. There were forecasts of a decline in population. A book, *The Myth of the Open Spaces*, helped some Australians to see themselves as a nation that must necessarily remain small for ever, a country hemmed in by difficulties and limitations, in which nothing very new could be done.

Chapter 15

TUNING IN TO BRITAIN
1919-1939 (*cont'd*)

The creed of the black hats

The simple stoicism of Anzac Day and its democratic nationalism that turned the ideal Australian into the Digger, with much the same characteristics as the earlier bushman, became weakened by its forms of ceremony. What came to seem most Australian about it were the drinking and chiacking that took place when the formal rituals were over. In the ceremony itself, Protestant clergymen brought to the Diggers' knowledge of the laconic whims that had prompted them to war, and the desperate comradeship they had found in battle, the certainties of the British Empire God of "Onward Christian Soldiers", so that Australia's national day became partly imperialist.

This was part of a much wider pattern. Many Australians still distrusted "the poms", and when the English developed bodyline bowling as a cricket tactic with the ball bowled not at the wicket but at the batsman's body, the perfidy of the poms was there for all to see; but except for occasional outbreaks from the Labour Party it was the creed of the black hats that usually prevailed in public rhetoric and display—even literally: a criticism of Lang and other Labor men was that on formal occasions they refused to wear top hats.

Englishmen were still appointed archbishops and headmasters; Stanley Bruce, the Nationalist Prime Minister of the 1920s, had been educated in England, had gone to the bar in England, had taken his wartime commission in an English regiment. Loosely connected groups of Anglophiles were sustained both by a self-interested belief that Australia's prosperity depended on Britain and its very existence on the British Navy, and by a mystical belief that the ideals of the late nineteenth century British version of the new imperialism represented the greatest degree of civilization known to man. They commanded most of the high places of national aspiration. At times their fellow countrymen appeared barbarians who must be kept pledged to the distant imperial metropolis. Against the apparent thinness of Australian life and the assumed mediocrity of Australians were set the challenges of sacred words . . . the Throne, the British heritage, the Mother of Parliaments, the Bank of England.

There were affronted outbursts when it became known that the Commonwealth Labor Government wanted an Australian as Governor-General, and it was only after Prime Minister Scullin threatened King George V with an election or a referendum that Scullin won. Sons of King George toured Australia in 1920, in 1927 and in 1934 (along with the English Poet Laureate and the band of the Grenadier Guards). Canada abolished British honours in 1935, but only the Labor Party opposed them in Australia. In 1920 a Labor member was expelled from the Federal Parliament because he criticized British policy in Ireland; even some book censorship was directed against works that blasphemed the Empire. At the founding of the colony in 1788 Phillip and his officers drank two toasts—one to the king and one to the colony's success; at the luncheon celebrating the building of Canberra there was no toast to Australia—the one toast (in fruit cup) was to the British king.

Only the British (in the "Empire Settlement Scheme") were sought as immigrants, although the Italians and Yugoslavs who came in unsought were more suited to the ideals of closer settlement since they actually wanted to be peasants. In the North Queensland canefields and in some irrigation districts in the southern States, Italians were the principal successful settlers but their success—more widespread when Italian immigration to the United States was restricted—stirred a sense of threat and envy. In 1934, at Kalgoorlie in Western Australia, miners looted Italian and Yugoslav shops and clubs and burned down fifty houses, then for three days conducted a "dago hunt". Even the "Yanks" were criticized—for taking so long to ge into the war, for being bad soldiers, for rejecting the League of Nations, for causing the Depression. "Americanization" was attacked, but the United States promise of independence to the Philippines was also attacked—as a Yankee desertion of the West Pacific.

Labor had had enough of a world whose wars and depressions brought party splits, but the Nationalists and then the U.A.P. put their trust in the idea of "Empire defence". This belief was fostered by the 1923 Imperial Conference decision to build a naval base at Singapore for Pacific defence, a belief that still survived when the base was finished in 1939, although it was a base without a fleet. The Department of the Chief of the General Staff of the Australian Army was called "Australian Section, Imperial General Staff". At the end of the 1930s British officers were at the head of the Australian army, navy and air force. The Irish Free State and Canada set up independent diplomatic services, but Australia did not even adopt the Statute of Westminster, which offered it independent status, until 1942. The Nationalists and the U.A.P. believed that Britain should consult Australia on matters of foreign policy but only because, as Bruce said in the 1920s, "We have to try to ensure that there shall be an Empire foreign policy."

The United Australia Party's slogan was "All for Australia and the Empire", and when Joe Lyons, its leader, fought his first election, he added a contemporaneous touch with another slogan—"Tune in to Britain". As well as being a partner in "Empire defence", Australia was part of "the Empire as an economic unit". The over-riding concern for meeting overseas debt payments during the Depression at the cost of so much extra unemployment had come from a sense of loyalty to London: most of the world's other debtor countries had suspended debt payments or reduced them and then negotiated a moratorium, but the Australian Government had invited a governor of the Bank of England to come to Australia and tell it what to do. In the 1920s when the Queensland Labor government put up the rents of government grazing land the London money market boycotted a new Queensland loan: The Queensland government campaigned against the "absentee capitalists" and "money lords of London", then gave in. London loan money resumed—a quarter per cent higher in interest. The whole Empire Settlement Scheme idea that had prompted the development fiascoes of the 1920s was British, formalized in a special Imperial Conference in 1921: if the Empire were to be an economic unit, "a redistribution of the white population of the Empire" should be made from its heart to its periphery, where it could grow things for the British to eat. Australia's role was to support Britain's industrial might by its farming policy.

The most extraordinary expression of Australia's "loyalty" came with the 1935 trade diversion policy when, after representations from British commercial interests in Australia, the Commonwealth Government prohibited the import of certain goods outside the British Empire except under licence. Imports from the United States and Japan were restricted in the hope that this would benefit British manufacturers. Japan was Australia's second-best customer for wool, and cheap Japanese imports were to Australia's benefit; but imports from Japan were against British commercial interests, Japan having replaced Britain as Australia's largest supplier of textiles. So, in response to the British textile lobby, Australia risked its own exports by imposing heavy duties on Japanese textiles. The United States administration was merely bemused, but the Japanese at once banned the import of Australian wool and wheat. Having lost one of their best customers, the Australians gave in. However, the incident had frightened the Japanese, and when they resumed purchases from Australia it was at a smaller rate, and they increased their research into substitutes for wool.

A nation without a mind (1919–39)

Although there was now no Deakin or Hughes to give meaning to political action, Australians did not lack national heroes or a national sense of achievement. Olympic swimmers and Wimbledon tennis players were seen as carrying on the work of the Diggers in putting Australia on the map, and the aviators, in their desperate flights across oceans and continents, competing for prizes or sponsored by governments or businessmen, sometimes finding death, sometimes tens of thousands of cheering people, seemed as great as sporting stars. Of the two greatest Australians, the cricketer Don Bradman and the racehorse Phar Lap, Bradman was the symbol of equality of opportunity, the boy from the bush whose effigy stood in Madame Tussaud's, and Phar Lap was a symbol of Australian gameness: when he died his heart was put on display in Canberra.

In school histories the national heroes, apart from merino rams and the Diggers, were the explorers. Australia was a place notable for being "discovered" and for the fortitude of those who explored it. The explorers' journeys were learnt off by heart and the maps of their expeditions memorized and reproduced at examination time. Other than the explorers, there was little in their history of which young Australians were taught to be proud. The government schools saw the real basis of Australian liberty in Magna Carta, Simon de Montfort's parliament, the English Civil War, the Great Rebellion of 1688, and other victories by English oligarchs. Young Australians learnt nothing of their country's history as a pioneer in social and political reform, nor any distinctive views of themselves as Australians, except as explorers or fighting men.

But while the ethos of mateship was not in school texts, the idea of the Australian as bushman or as larrikin still had commercial success. Australian-made movies had titles like *The Hayseeds*, *On Our Selection* or *The Squatter's Daughter*, and in the vaudeville chain of the Tivoli theatres comics such as Stiffy and Mo and George Wallace maintained a larrikin humour that could be seen as vulgar by suburbanites. A new publication, *Smith's Weekly*, based much of its success on the idea of the Digger as larrikin and while *The Bulletin* changed from the most radical publication to the most reactionary, it still looked to a rural Australia. In painting, the impressionist rebels of the 1890s also became reactionary; two became knights and, now successfully dominant in their emphasis on bush landscapes, they rejected modern painting as "elaborate and pretentious bosh". Book publishers pursued policies that made a 1920s writer complain of "the absence of publishers interested in anything but bushranger yarns, south-sea romances, or studies of flying foxes". Because they were popular in the 1890s, black and white jokes, short stories and impressionist landscapes were seen as the three distinctive Australian art forms, fixed for ever.

The novel *Such is life* by Joseph Furphy ("temper democratic;

bias offensively Australian") although published in 1903, did not come into its own until the 1930s, by when it was an inspiration to new novelists trying to give an idea of what it might be like to be an Australian, a concern at that time largely confined to novelists. The Australian they discovered was not usually a suburbanite—if he did live in the suburbs he was unhappy about it—and mateship was still likely to be his creed, sometimes intellectualized into an Improver's liberal humanism, but with its belief in human goodness now rendered impotent by scepticism about the possibility of successful action. (Some of the greatest opportunities for goodness were seen in the accommodations of the unsuccessful to lack of success.) A composer sought a vocabulary of Australian sounds in bird cries and the other noises of the bush, and in the late 1930s the "Jindyworobaks", an Adelaide-centred group, sought Australian-ness from the Aborigines, writing poetry that adopted Aboriginal words and explored Aboriginal legends.

(There was no advance in the treatment of the Aborigines, beyond the fact that they were no longer being massacred, but there was at least a beginning of an understanding of the extent of the destruction of their society, mainly through anthropologists' work. There were occasional Press attacks on their treatment and in 1939 there was at last a humane statement of policy—by the new Minister for the Interior, John McEwen—which urged "the raising of their status so as to entitle them by right and by qualification to the ordinary rights of citizenship".)

On the left the Eureka Stockade was still a pivotal point, particularly to Marxists; perhaps because through an error in translation, they thought Marx had written about it. Some saw the unions and the Labor Party as the main, or the only, agents of progress in Australia's history: as part of this purpose the 1890s shearers' strikes were given a special significance, and political history was interpreted so as to turn the Improvers into agents of reaction. Some Melbourne intellectuals began to believe that they were the repository of an Australian democratic tradition that had flowered in the 1890s.

In Sydney a countervailing cosmopolitanism decried as provincial all that was traditionally "Australian" and claimed for itself a unique international excellence. Christopher Brennan, a Sydney professor, was described as "the only genuine *symboliste* poet in the English language". Around the artist Norman Lindsay in the 1920s gathered a number of people who proclaimed a renaissance of world culture in Sydney with artists who had "gay hearts and the courage of their desires"; and around the philosophy professor John Anderson in the 1930s was a group that saw Sydney University as the only significant centre of philosophy in the contemporary world. (Even Jack Lang was pronounced by his Sydney followers to be "greater than Lenin".)

There were strong desires for greater "maturity" and "sophistication". In the theatre, apart from the struggling little theatres, all that was offered in ten years was a season of Noel Coward plays and a tour by Sybil Thorndike; but in music the government-sponsored Australian Broadcasting Commission set itself up as a large concert agency, establishing permanent concert orchestras in each State capital, and launching "celebrity concerts" with imported conductors and performers. And in painting, after a bitter battle, with modern art becoming a transcendental issue, a Contemporary Art Society was formed in 1938, encompassing all contemporary schools. In 1939 one of the best collections of post-impressionist painting ever assembled toured Australia. By the end of the 1930s the Sydney poets Kenneth Slessor and R. D. FitzGerald were seen as a literary establishment, and poets who wished to contest their position were grouped around university magazines in Sydney and Adelaide. Several specialist academic journals were established; a few books on Australian history appeared, although the subject was regarded as too thin by some university historians; an annual Political Science Summer School gave some small, beleaguered scope for those who saw themselves as having an intelligent interest in politics. Campaigns continued for the admission of graduates to the Commonwealth Public Service and in 1938 provision was made for 10 per cent of recruits to be graduates (a decision criticized by some Sydney philosophers as an assault on the honorific uselessness of knowledge).

Two internationally minded groups became important in intellectual life, although neither could be described as cosmopolitan. In the second half of the 1930s, as part of the general Popular Front strategy, the Communists began to gain control of a number of unions, by 1940 almost controlling the Australian Council of Trade Unions. In a war of concealed party tickets and expulsions, they tried to penetrate the Labor Party, for a short while actually controlling the N.S.W. branch. They also set up "fronts" with some influence on intellectual life, the peace movement, and some church groups. On the other side, a Catholic lay movement had developed. Beginning in University Campion Societies, it started as anti-capitalist ("the greatest force in spreading communism at the present time is the failure of capitalism"), and when the monthly *Catholic Worker* (rising to 55,000 sales) was started in Melbourne it, too, was at first concerned with social issues of a Belloc and Chesterton kind—the decline of the birth rate, the virtues of family and rural life, the evils of capitalism and State control; similarly when a National Secretariat of Catholic Action was set up in 1937 it was concerned with social issues. But the Spanish Civil War and the Popular Front were causing a change in direction. In 1938 small informal Catholic-dominated groups began to conspire against Communist conspiracies in the unions, and in both Sydney and Melbourne open campaigns against the Communists had begun, especially in the universities, where they were noted more for enthusiasm than for accuracy of aim. Both Communists and Catholics were opponents of Improvement, and with the apparent failure of liberalism in both the Depression and in the League of Nations it became not uncommon for such intellectuals as there were to feel that they must choose between the Communists or the Catholics: "Only [these] two organizations in Australia grasped the total situation as a crisis in liberalism."

The bohemian groups of the 1920s frequented a few coffee shops and wine bars, a few Chinese and European restaurants, and a few clubs, and fabricated a sense of a separate community where the search was "the party to end all parties". When Brennan was sacked from Sydney University, "usually very dirty, smelling like a stale brewery", bumming drinks in pubs, his memory became a symbol for those who saw themselves as outside their society. In this atmosphere of dispossession all politicians and businessmen could seem crooks and the whole society worthless—"the shop-window dummies of standardized neatness, the nitwits of patent leather hair, the good-timers with a repetitive gramophone record of slang for the brain, the gigolos of jazz, the shaven gorillas of the old-school ties". The suburbanites, "so meek and mild", were betrayers of the nation.

While intellectuals in the 1890s tried to find things in

Australia that made it the best country in the world their successors in the 1930s sought evidence that it was the worst. Australian society was "jerry-built"; there was no real nation, no sense of mission except for "the platitudinous rhetoric of the Millions Club"; "if any cry reform we shriek 'Red-ragger' ". The censorship system was seen as one that "neither the English nor American people would tolerate". In Melbourne the Book Censorship League, formed in 1934, became a gathering point for some who saw the shoddy in Australian public life. Some of the best Australian novelists were believed to be the expatriates who had sought a more sympathetic climate to warm their talents. Canberra, intended to be a symbol of national aspiration, was seen as "a city of eight million trees and not a single idea", an absurd white elephant.

Educated persons began to blame the mass of the Australian people for their predicament. Those who accepted the values of the black-hat society were contemptuous of the "mediocrity" of their fellow-countrymen, rather than of themselves. A people "whose attention is divided between beauty competitions, the racing and betting news, and the latest of inane revues" were seen as "a fraternal but rather drab company of one-class passengers". Even some who rejected the standards of black-hattedness might also blame the people, even democracy, for their sense of exclusion. Following a pattern set by Lord Bryce in his *Modern Democracies*, they detected in the ordinary Australians a destructive jealousy so great that "exasperation" was dominant in the public life of Australia. "Where other distinctions are absent, and a few years can lift a man from nothing to affluence, differences in wealth are emphasised and resented . . . the more because they often seem . . . due to no special merit in the possessor." Ignoring the long history of Australian nobbishness and overdoing the "classlessness" of Australians, they blamed the destructive jealousy of the people for the weakness of intellectual life, rather than the dominance of black hat values and the weaknesses of educational institutions. Overestimating Australia's democracy and egalitarianism, they could believe that "in Australia nobody is supposed to rule, and nobody does rule. . . . The proletariat appoints men to administer the law, not to rule." By such arguments it could seem that the weaknesses of Australian administrative and intellectual leadership were not those of the administrators and intellectuals, but of the people.

To some, D. H. Lawrence was seen as the true interpreter of Australia: "This is the most democratic place I have *ever* been in. And the more I see of democracy the more I dislike it. It just keeps everything down to the mere vulgar level of wages and prices, electric light and water closets, and nothing else. You *never* knew anything so nothing, Nichts, Nullus, nients, as the life here. . . . They are healthy, and to my thinking almost imbecile. . . . Yet they are very trustful and kind and quite competent in their jobs."

Not like last time

"Unhappy looking men in long greatcoats, generally carrying an attaché case and in a hurry" were by 1938 being seen in King's Cross and elsewhere. They were the "reffos", the first of the 5,000 refugees from the new European totalitarianism whom the Commonwealth Government had decided to let into Australia each year. Also in 1938, 274 German and Austrian citizens living in Sydney boarded a German freighter, sailed outside the three-mile limit, voted by 272 to 2 for union between Germany and Austria, then came back for dinner.

In a country which commemorated its nationhood by celebrating a military defeat the question *Will there be another war?* came naturally enough with each new threat—the Japanese invasion of Manchuria, the rise of Hitler, the Italian invasion of Abyssinia, the Spanish Civil War, the Japanese invasion of China, the German seizure of Austria. This was the familiar world of Anzac Day. But there were not the same responses in the country's leadership.

In the U.A.P. only Hughes spoke the language of the Diggers. Others saw Communism as a greater threat than Nazism; a few defended Hitler as a man putting his house in order. Most tuned in to Britain, listening to the static. Where Britain went they went. When the Munich agreement was announced Lyons called for a day of thanksgiving. The U.A.P. still spoke of Empire defence, and brought it into the 1937 election to confound Labor's lack of policy, but the Australian army's equipment was still mainly what the Diggers had brought home in 1919.

Many members of the Labor Party saw the causes of war in trade rivalries and the conspiracies of armament kings: in this view war with Nazi Germany would be merely a fight between rival camps of capitalists looking for world markets. Others attacked "scaremongers": Japan would never be aggressive; the seizure of Austria was an expression of the self-determination of peoples. Within the union movement the Catholics and Communists were fighting on foreign policy: to have chosen one side or the other would have split the Labor Party.

The Communists and those who followed them stirred the unions sufficiently for the Australian Council of Trade Unions' conference (which had opposed sanctions against Mussolini in 1935) to support collective security against Hitler in 1937, although the rearmament that could make sense of collective security was still seen as a plot of the arms kings. The Labor Party remained unimpressed: many of its Catholic members supported Mussolini and France and saw Hitler as a bulwark against Communism. "Absolute isolation, strict neutrality" and withdrawal from the League of Nations was proclaimed as Jack Lang's foreign policy when the expediencies of N.S.W. faction-fighting led him to seek Catholic support against the Communists.

But there were two promptings to new policy, one from the U.A.P., one from Labor. The U.A.P. was taking up, if in fear, the idea of Australia as a Pacific power that earlier had been taken up in boastful confidence. At the 1937 Imperial Conference Lyons had suggested a Pacific Non-agression Pact. With no diplomatic service, he became his own envoy, approaching the ambassadors of a number of Pacific powers while he was in London. The Russians, the Chinese and the French said they were interested; the Japanese were hostile, the U.S. indifferent, the British cool. A small External Affairs Department was re-established in 1935; goodwill missions were sent to countries in Asia; in 1939 it was decided to establish legations in Tokyo and Washington. When R. G. Menzies became Prime Minister he said: "We will never realize our destiny as a nation until we realize that we are one of the Pacific Powers." Of course Australia would not act as "a completely separate power" but as "an integral part of the British Empire"; nevertheless "what Great Britain calls the

Far East is to us the near north".

The Labor Party was deprived by its divisions of any opportunity of defining a foreign policy, but for the same reason it was able to put up a more original approach to military planning than "Empire defence". Labor urged a strong air force and a flotilla of defence ships, including submarines, thereby bringing into public life the private discontent of some Australian officers who saw as a hoax an Empire defence that consisted of a base in Singapore which in wartime the British could never adequately man.

"Great Britain had declared war . . . and, as a result, Australia is also at war." To the old Diggers it seemed just like last time, except that it was now the turn of their sons to show what Australia was made of and they had already shown some of this when after the German occupation of Prague a recruiting campaign for the militia brought in 70,000 volunteers in three months. But last time the Japanese had been allies. Now doubts about what it might really mean to be a Pacific power penetrated the government. It took almost a fortnight to decide to raise a special military force of 20,000 men (instead of "the last man and the last shilling", in the first week of war Menzies proclaimed "business as usual") and then it was left open whether the force would stay in Australia. It took until November, and then perhaps only after prompting from New Zealand, to take the risk of deciding to send this new 6th Division to the Middle East and most of the Australian navy to the Mediterranean. It was to take another four months to decide to send anyone else.

Early in the new year trains ran through the suburbs of Sydney and some of the 6th Division embarked on four converted luxury liners on their way to the Middle East. Many had known or feared that this was why they had grown to manhood. But it was not to be like the last time.

Chapter 16

THE ORPHANS OF THE PACIFIC

The 1940s

Convoys sailed off across the Indian Ocean, soldiers posed for their photographs in front of the Sphinx, but, after two years, volunteers were only 188,000 out of a population of seven million, compared with 307,000 from a nation of only five million in what was now spoken of as "the first war". For many the reality of the war flickered in newsreels.

It was twelve months before Australian soldiers saw action, and when it came it was confusing. Victory over the Italians was clear in the two months' push into Libya—the newsreels showed men wrapped against the desert cold advancing in the dawn light on shattered white buildings, but a month later the Germans pushed everyone back where they had come from. Within a few months towns never before heard of had become names for both victory and defeat. By then Australians and New Zealanders were in Greece; they arrived in spring sunshine on 3rd April 1940; as a nostalgic gesture they were given the name "Anzac Corps" on 12th April; seven days later they were defeated. All except two thousand prisoners scrambled out, some to Cyprus where, a week after the Germans had infected their positions with paratroopers, they again evacuated, and this time three thousand prisoners were taken. Yet after only a fortnight's action in Syria against the Vichy French victorious Australians, like their fathers before them, were marching through the streets of Damascus. But it was the 242 days siege of Tobruk that seemed most familiar. Trapped in the

German advance, with an Australian general in command of the allied garrison, Tobruk held the newsreels with a constant story of unlikely survival. This was more like Anzac.

Although imperialist, or perhaps because they were, the U.A.P. government had failed to arouse the open fervour expected of Australians in wartime. Most Australians were concerned about the war, if more sceptically than before, but they were not prepared to make a fuss, and the government's belief in Empire loyalty could make an appeal to national feelings seem "disloyal". Seeing the war primarily in terms of defending the Empire in the Middle East, with Singapore as Australia's inner defence, the government even adopted a subdued approach to Japan's proclamation of a "Greater East Asia" policy, despite its earlier uncertainties about sending troops away from Australia. It asked Churchill for a fleet in Singapore—as a kind of naval metaphor, he dispatched two ships—and itself sent a division to Malaya; but Malaya seemed an exotic kind of place for Australians to be. One question asked was whether Australians were psychologically suited to such garrison duties.

In the early months the incompetence of the public service had been of the greatest assistance in sustaining the dilatoriness of the government. With a public service staffed mainly by Returned Men over the age of forty-five, and promoted messenger boys, it took four months even to make a decision to manufacture new field guns to replace the guns of 1914-18. It was only when a number of businessmen and graduates were pushed into departments that decisions began to flow. When the U.A.P. government went to the polls in 1940 it almost lost the election. In 1941 it collapsed from its own sense of inadequacy. Labor took over. The imperial call had come, but the U.A.P. had failed to make a political success of answering it.

Troops in Australian army camps woke on 8th December 1941 to discover that Japanese aircraft had poured bombs into the U.S. naval base at Pearl Harbour (wherever that was) and blown up much of the U.S. Pacific fleet. By nightfall many of the troops were moving to improvised battle stations here and there on the 12,000 mile coastline. At dawn they stood to, facing sand and sea. The Japanese invaded Malaya and the Philippines; after two days they sank Churchill's two warships and seized Guam; a fortnight later Hong Kong surrendered; five days more and the Americans evacuated Manila; another two weeks and Australian soldiers were fighting to defend the approaches to Singapore; a fortnight after that they withdrew to the island of Singapore; a week later the Japanese attacked. A week later Singapore fell, and into the smoke and flame of its quick destruction went the whole edifice of Empire defence. With a loss in prisoners-of-war proportionate to 100,000 British or 300,000 American, to some Australians the disasters of Singapore signalled British chicanery and rottenness.

Surprise air raids on Darwin left blazing oil tanks, sunken ships, broken buildings: the Australian Chief-of-Staff warned that a Japanese invasion in the north might be expected early in April and an attack on the east coast in May. In Japan General Tojo mocked Australia as "the orphan of the Pacific, helplessly expecting Japan's attack". Guerilla groups formed and there were suggestions for squads of blacktrackers and bushmen. Some harbourside flats in Sydney emptied. Barbedwire and sandbags went up on its beaches. Signboards were pulled down, small boats impounded; 80,000 cattle were overlanded from the north to the south so that the Japanese couldn't eat them, and there were discussions on a scorched earth policy.

Two of the volunteer divisions were brought back from the Middle East, and another 114,000 men were conscripted to add to the 132,000 already drafted into the militia, but there was a soreness about both the dispersal of forces come from Empire defence and the inadequate equipment and training of the home forces. The home army had only half the trucks and a sixth of the anti-aircraft guns it needed, only eighteen tanks, only six days' supply of anti-tank ammunition. Some of the men who went to battle stations in December had had no weapon training. In theory the air forces had thirty-two squadrons but their main equipment was trainers, and they were drastically under-crewed. It was decided that planes and men for sixty squadrons were needed.

Lines were drawn on maps. Not maps of France or the Middle East this time, but maps of Australia. The Newcastle-Sydney-Port Kembla area was to be held, and if possible, the 1,000 mile stretch from Melbourne to Brisbane; there would be garrisons in Darwin, Port Moresby and a few other places. There was a certain amount of hope when General Douglas

Macarthur arrived in March from the Philippines to be appointed Supreme Commander in April, and by June Australia had assembled, with varying degrees of equipment and training, almost half a million men in uniform, to which the U.S. added another 88,000. But by then Japanese submarines were sinking ships on the Australian east coast and had seized most of New Guinea. What was left of New Guinea was seen as the last stronghold from which to fight "the battle for Australia".

Credibility was first given to the possibility of this battle's succeeding when in the Coral Sea in May a U.S. naval force that had two Australian cruisers attached turned back a Japanese fleet moving to invade Port Moresby as part of a general plan to seize New Guinea, New Caledonia, Fiji and Samoa, isolate Australia and New Zealand from these bases, and attack key points in both countries to frighten them out of the war. The American repulse of this Japanese invasion force provided instant and enormous sustenance to Australians. They had lost Singapore, but they had gained the U.S. Navy.

In July the Japanese seized Gona and Buna, pushed on to Kokoda, and threatened Port Moresby. In August they attacked again, at Milne Bay, on New Guinea's extreme eastern tip, seeking its airstrips as a base for their end-game. They landed among Milne Bay's sago and mangrove swamps, but after a week's confused fighting in relentless rain, each side lacking maps and blundering into the other, the Australians won. It was the first land defeat the Japanese had known. Field-Marshal Slim was later to say: "It was the Australian soldiers who first broke the spell of the invincibility of the Japanese army."

On the newsreels the mud and rain of the Battle of the Owen Stanley Ranges now placed it alongside Tobruk as a continuing cinema story. Two small armies confronted each other, both weakened by malaria, strung out in the slush of tracks that cut a path through sweltering jungle. The Australians conquered the mountains and gorges, then the flat swampy country, then took their two bases back from the Japanese. It was 1943. Who would win the war still remained to be seen, but the feeling had begun that Australia was no longer in immediate danger. It was again part of something bigger. It no longer had to fight for itself, but for an ally.

Despite what had seemed a direct threat to Australia's survival, there had not been much appeal to national sentiment. Australians wanted to save themselves, but there was little speech-making about what they were supposed to be saving. In one of his first war speeches, staying with the prevailing fashion, John Curtin had said, "We shall hold this country . . . as a citadel for the British-speaking race", as if Australians were holding their nation for King George. There was shock when he came out more realistically: "Without any inhibition of any kind I make it quite clear that Australia looks to America, free of any pangs as to our traditional links or kinship with the United Kingdom." The habit of wars being an occasion for imperial rhetoric was so strong that this speech (privately denounced by Churchill as "flaunted round the world by our enemies") was treated as a stab in the back for Britain. The Archbishop of Brisbane said: "The most audacious piece of Fifth Column activity hitherto seen in this country has been the effort to belittle Britain's part in the war." Other changes, such as having more Australian and fewer B.B.C. commentators on Australian radio and attempts to make "Advance Australia Fair" the national song, were seen as further blows to Australia's patriotism. What summed up the laconic wartime faith of Australians was a sentence in a union newspaper: "It is not in the Australian make-up to squib a fight." But this was not the language of speech-making.

Soldiers could still call each other "mate" or "Dig", as if they were their fathers, but this time within the army there was no sense of building a nation. The division between volunteers and conscripts caused much bitterness—there were two armies, not one—and there was not much pride in the despairing scramble to throw brigades into New Guinea, or in the lonely fear of fighting in some of the world's most difficult country, with malaria, dysentery and typhus greater killers than the enemy. As the war settled into shapes of possible victory, the Americans sailed north after prestige, leaving the Australians with the humble but debilitating and dangerous role of mopping up left-over Japanese. The Australian war machine was now working so vigorously that it became overheated: men began to be released from munition-making and fighting to maintain Australia as a supply base for the Americans.

This time it was in the arena of world politics that the war and its aftermath gave intimations of nationhood. Dr Bert Evatt, the External Affairs Minister, threw himself with a showman's enthusiasm into creating the drama of an independent Australian foreign policy. He issued a warning to the great powers that Australia might be small in the world but it was big in the South-west Pacific: to make this sound real Australia entered into its first independent treaty. All it could find was New Zealand, but Evatt discovered a bigger stage in the San Francisco Conference of 1945, called to settle the constitution of the United Nations. He appointed himself champion of the smaller powers, fought hard against big power domination, and achieved some reforms and a fairly wide personal reputation.

With a rough-and-ready drive, sometimes with the single-minded impatience of a revolutionary, he threw up around him a bigger, if disordered, External Affairs Department to carry out his "bustling diplomacy": Australia now had fifteen diplomatic missions; it was one of the four nations on the Allied Commission in defeated Japan (where it represented Britain and India): an Australian commanded the British Commonwealth Occupation Forces; Evatt became chairman of the U.N. General Assembly. Menzies attacked "the utter independence of Australian thought and action—which, for seven million people in a small island continent is more pretentious than sensible—as if no special British relation assisted at all", and even Evatt's Australian style was derided as "a sort of larrikin strain in Australian foreign policy, a disposition to throw stones at the street lights just because they are bright". But Evatt was driven on by the adventurous ambition of making Australia one of mankind's consciences, determined on a fair go among nations, "in the forefront of the councils of the world", with a policy on everything.

Although there were no Australian diplomatic missions in South-east Asia there was a feeling of concern for an area where European colonialists, knocked over by the Japanese, were trying to put themselves back into place; there were attacks on "outmoded, reactionary and feudal forms of government" and hopes for "a harmonious association of democratic states in the South-east Asian area". When the Dutch started their first "police action" against the Indonesian nationalists Australia brought the conflict before the Security Council, and Indonesia appointed Australia as its representative on the three-man

Committee of Good Offices. With the second "police action" Australia moved on the U.N. for the expulsion of the Dutch, and when Indonesia entered the U.N. it chose Australia as one of its two sponsors, and saw Australia as one of its greatest friends.

But Australia did not feel big enough to face the future. "Asian countries will undoubtedly be looking at us," said Ben Chifley, who succeeded Curtin as Prime Minister, "and there will be increasing pressure for an outlet for their populations." Unless Australia quickly got more people these Asians might come and take its empty spaces. To fill them up, Australia could not be too fussy: for the first time in its history, it now had to buy immigrants who weren't British. At first there was a hope that "for every foreign migrant there will be ten people from the United Kingdom". But the British were harder to get than that. The government turned to the International Refugee Organization and contracted to give large numbers of "displaced persons" free passages. As 170,000 Poles, Balts, Russians, Ukrainians, Hungarians and others from the refugee camps came to Australia these "D.Ps." began to outmatch the British immigrants. Immigration agreements were signed with other countries; assisted Italians, Germans and Dutch joined the D.Ps.; the target of 70,000 a year for immigration went up to 150,000.

Many of the immigrants were tied for two years to working where they were sent and this gave the government a chance to send them to jobs Australians didn't want; but in a country which had always hated its immigrants there were fears of new outbursts of prejudice and hostility. The name "New Australian" was invented to reassure Australians that even Balts and Italians were fellow creatures, but for safety's sake the Immigration Department set up an Assimilation Branch in the hope that as quickly as possible these foreigners could be made look like Australians. However, the immigrants' labour broke bottlenecks in steel production, housing, public works, transport. Things began to move again. There were tentative returns to the hope that if it could be "developed" Australia might again be Unlimited.

This hope was nowhere stronger than among the businessmen who during the war had gone into the departments and improvised an armaments industry. Because of the confident strength of the B.H.P. and its associates, along with several other monopolies or near monopolies, there had been enough engineering and management tradition for remarkable examples of wartime resourcefulness. The manufacture of the 4,000 component parts of the first field gun was farmed out in two days and the gun was being produced within seven months. The British had said it would take two years. Optical glass was manufactured against British warnings that the task was beyond Australia and against a boycott by the British manufacturers. An aircraft industry was thrown up that produced 3,500 aircraft of nine different types. Destroyers, corvettes, frigates, merchant ships and 33,643 small craft came from Australia's shipyards. The B.H.P. developed 140 specialist steels. Machine tools, not made on any scale before, were produced in great number and variety. Improvised technical training mass-produced tens of thousands of skilled tradesmen. There was not much of a science base to most of this, nor much technological invention—it was mainly a case of getting the instructions and having a go—but there were many inventive modifications and overcomings of difficulties.

With this further onrush of industrialization and the broadening of experience in the production of capital equipment, when the war was finished an impressive number of buildings, skills and machines went off into private manufacturing; but an equally important product of the crash war programme was an emergent type of businessmen who saw themselves as "the real life-savers that Australia always needed", and who had "got into habit of relying on their own resources on practically all occasions . . . accustomed to making decisions all round". They now saw themselves as the backbone of the forthcoming development.

The war had also given Australia its first complex national administration, parts of which also saw themselves as the backbone of national development. The number of departments had nearly doubled, the number of employees had trebled, and new powers had come to the Commonwealth: a virtual monopoly of income tax had been gained from a High Court decision and full powers over social services from a referendum. All except one civilian department gained new heads during the war, several in their thirties, one aged only thirty-two, others in their forties; the public service had become younger and much more ambitious in its sense of what it could do.

Some of the university-educated people who had pushed themselves into the departments stayed after the war and within them a smaller group, "the planners", showed the same talents as the businessmen for hard work, devotion and improvisation, the same self-belief and resourcefulness, the same confidence that they could do anything without thinking about it very deeply. Attacked as "long-hairs", they acquired special strength in the Post-War Reconstruction Department and as "the Chifley men"—a group of advisers who surrounded Ben Chifley. At their most cohesive, this devout group saw themselves as the agents of a social revolution based on the joint ideas of rationality and welfare; they represented another attempt to bring Australia into a state of Improvement through colonial governmentalism. With a stronger momentum and a more definitive sense of purpose than their Labor Party patrons, they became the principal initiators of policy. No field of endeavour seemed outside their talents: Government support for the arts, higher education, town and regional planning, were on their list along with economic growth, full employment, immigration and social welfare.

When the bustle subsided, what most permanently remained from the excitements of adventurous improvising carried out under the name of planning was that Australians regained some of the position in social welfare of which they had earlier been so unexpectedly deprived. A comprehensive social security programme emerged, based on "non-contributory" methods. In a five-year battle, doctors sabotaged a proposed free medical scheme, but there were now widows' pensions, unemployment and sickness pensions, pharmaceutical, hospital and funeral benefits, an employment service, a housing scheme.

Colonial governmentalism produced bodies to control the stevedoring and coal industries and the marketing of farm products; it nationalized international telecommunications and the Australian overseas airline Qantas, and it set up a government-owned internal airline, a shipping line, a whaling industry and an aluminium industry. The idea that mankind might be saved by public works and irrigation projects reached its apotheosis in the Snowy River Scheme, one of the largest engineering works in the world. An Englishman was brought out to advise on the setting up of a national theatre.

But there was an extension to older expressions of government enterprise: it was now hoped, as had happened at the very beginning of New South Wales, that it might be the government that controlled initiative in almost everything. The hopes of the planners reached their highest points in the last six months of 1944 when they were drafting a White Paper on full employment. A product of both the politicians' bitter memories of the Depression and the planners' ideals of rational conduct, the White Paper was to provide the theoretical basis for all future achievement. Its first draft was ready by December 1944; its seventh draft reached Cabinet in April 1945; by the time the politicians had finished with it, it had been re-written enough for some planners to think about going back to their universities; but it was nevertheless seen as a "unique and historic prospectus". By then there had been defeat for an attempt by referendum to gain to the Commonwealth all the powers it needed for controlling all the activities it wanted to control, and two more limited attempts were then also defeated, but the spirit of the White Paper remained: with initiatives coming from the government, Australia would expand and develop through industrialization and immigration so that there would be jobs for everyone and fair shares for all.

"The planners" were part of a more general hope for an intellectual break-through. New painters in Melbourne wanted to apply to Australian complacency "incessant waves of shock"; in the Melbourne-Adelaide magazine *Angry Penguins* there was a sense of literary and intellectual apocalypse; in the Melbourne-Brisbane magazine *Meanjin Papers* old democratic voices took new literary forms. As part of the revulsion against the savagery of the Depression, the drabness that followed it, and the near-disasters of the war, for a while the Labor Party had the aura of social change: it had won by such a landslide in the 1943 election that the already disintegrating U.A.P. was smothered, and a new party, the Liberal Party, had to be formed out of its wreckage. New horizons seemed to break out; there were new senses of the possible. New men were seen as relevant to new occasions.

But things could also get back to seeming the same. "I am a refugee from Australian culture," said Albert Tucker, one of the new Melbourne painters, when he left Australia in 1947. Some of the planners did go back to the universities. Despite the noise, a dullness fell over focal points of political struggle. Chifley called for a "golden age" but people could not find out which way he was looking. In a period of shortages and shoddiness, they wanted not distant goals of "national development", for which austerely puritan sacrifices were said to be necessary, but something to go on with after the shortages and shoddiness of an economy debauched by war. Political debate sank into trench warfare: from prepared positions increasingly intense barrages on both sides concealed a lack of movement. Newspapers engaged in "constant propaganda to show that all politicians are knaves and fools, all Government enterprises hopelessly inefficient, all civil servants bumbling idiots tied up in their own red tape". When Chifley abruptly decided to try to nationalize the banks he was cartooned alongside Hitler and Mussolini as one of the "National Socialist leaders of the 20th Century". From these crudities Chifley retreated to the over-simplifications of his planners. The businessmen who had shared much of the experience of the planners and had much the same improvising adventurous spirit began to retreat to the other side, joining the more conservative financial and professional interests who had been there all the time. In a situation in which there was on both sides an impatience with complexity and a brutalizing of debate, and in which the government seemed to be running out of ideas anyway, Labor was defeated by the new Liberal Party in the 1949 elections. But to many it seemed obvious that Labor would be out of office only long enough to fix itself up and come back fighting again.

To this time of bitter dispute when men could see all light on one side and all darkness on the other (anti-planners sneering at the planners' "road to serfdom", planners sneering at the "freedom to starve") melodrama was added by the Australian Communists who saw themselves in a world in which total victory was near. They had made spectacular advances in the trades union movement, in their righteousness rigging ballots, smearing, threatening violence; and in 1945, with some help from non-Communist supporters, they gained control of the Australian Council of Trade Unions.

With 60 per cent of its caucus Catholics, the Labor Party counter-organized. "Industrial Groups" were formed in the unions to fight the Communists, taking strength from earlier anti-Communist organizations including a "Catholic Social Studies Movement" known to its followers as "the Movement", which had already gained practice in getting the numbers at union meetings. In an atmosphere hot and sticky with suspicion of the intrigues of the "Commos" or of "Catholic Action", Labor fought back, recapturing some key unions and the A.C.T.U.; the government jailed two Communist leaders for sedition and set up a security service to find out what the communists were doing.

Giddy with their general world success, the Communists denounced the Labor Party as "just as anti-Labor as Hitler and Mussolini and the Japanese imperialists" and proclaimed (in its own code) that the time had come to take over the labour movement. As a first step in this absurd adventure, they engineered a miners' strike that was meant to be an exemplary struggle showing the miners that the gains they had made under a reformist Labor government didn't amount to much, and showing the rest of the union membership what true militancy looked like. The Labor government raided Communist Party headquarters and froze the funds of the Communists unions; when union officials took money out of their banks seven were jailed. More than 500,000 were thrown out of work. Train and tram services were severely cut. Electricity was rationed. Gas was down to an hour's supply a day. At this stage the government put soldiers in to work the mines. The strike collapsed. The normal betrayal of the revolution had happened again.

No Australian government had ever launched such attacks on the Communist Party, so the Liberal Party denounced the government as soft on Communism and campaigned for a complete ban on the party. Communist armies were in seven European countries. A Communist army was winning in China. Communists were leading the guerilla war against the British in Malaya and the nationalist war against the French in Indo-China. To many Australians it seemed that the world was again about to fall to pieces. In 1948 an opinion survey in ten countries showed that it was Australians who had the highest expectancy of another world war. The orphan of the Pacific looked to its turbulent north from which only a few years ago had come invasion fleets, armies, bombers, submarines.

Chapter 17

THE LUCKY COUNTRY
1950-1970

The Australian style

The first post-war aim of tens of thousands of young Australians was to join their parents and grandparents in "owning their own homes". Building costs had risen twice as high as other living costs; labour was scarce, slapdash and expensive; and materials were in short supply; so many young people, in a return to an 1850s form of individualism, built their own houses. They would live in a garage for two or three years, and in their spare time construct a house alongside it. To cheer up houses that costs kept down to essentials, their owners looked to cans of paint, turning from the 1930s gentility of cream to the brightness of the paint cards of suburban shops. With fireplaces gone, "feature walls" were created to keep some ancient memory of centredness. But, although romantic in their use of colour, houseowners also dreamed of rationality: their urges to human perfectability turned to the "dream kitchen" where careful planning of cupboards, space, work benches, cooker, refrigerator, stainless steel sink and easily cleaned surfaces, would provide a more efficient basis for life. But neither housewives nor their children were always rational enough to use dream kitchens according to instructions. Among those with money, hopes then moved to the "open plan", houses without the mere decoration of internal walls. The rationality of this idea also affronted mere human-ness.

Under the heroic acres of suburban roofs where both romance

and reason were proving inadequate, there was still scepticism about the amount of money and jobs around, and a balance-of-payments recession in 1952 had a familiar ring. Then things picked up, and from about the mid 1950s, despite occasional dips, the belief began that all this might last. The new generation had no doubts. Use of hire purchase became more confident. Already the greatest house-owning nation and the most urbanized, the 12 million Australians became the third greatest car-owning democracy, with as many cars as all Russia. Motels and caravan parks extended holiday choices along the coastline. Collapsible furniture and "esky" cold boxes made picnics more comfortable. Drive-in cinemas, drive-in bottle shops, and the new supermarkets and shopping complexes with their parking areas, gave some of that sense of community and importance to the suburbs that previously they had lacked.

After 1956, with the spread of television, houses again acquired an indoor ceremonial centre; now they acquired one outdoors. The hopes that had looked to feature walls and dream kitchens turned to "outdoor living". Paved terraces spread across lawns; garden furniture and barbecues became good selling lines. The idea of the "patio" began to express a new sense of progress. There was a wide relaxation in suburban life. The use of gardening as a self-discipline began to be abandoned. Backyards lost their rows of vegetables and their hen runs and were simplified to make a more casual setting. Electric lawn mowers whisked away grass and circular metal hoists where clothes were hung when they came out of electric washing-machines were erected as monuments honouring progress. With gardens no longer in their Sunday best, easy-going native trees and shrubs began to appear. Those with enough money put in swimming-pools.

In this more relaxed style, even some of the nationalist certitudes of sport weakened, with more tolerance of simple pleasure and less concern with moral fibre. Australia won the Davis Cup so often that it lost interest; one cricket season many Australians wanted England to win. There was usually some new achievement to gain attention—Olympic swimming, the mile race, the Americas' Cup challenge—but now Australians could follow sport simply because they enjoyed doing so, without the old feeling that the nation was on trial. Worship of surf lifesavers declined, sales of surfboards went up. Skiing and sailing were democratized to join tennis and golf and a whole new range of water sports.

As part of the general moving away from the idea that self-denial was necessary for respectability, enforced puritanism broke up and things returned to what had once been normal. Sabbatarianism was relaxed; restaurants again served liquor; hotel trading hours went closer to what they used to be, with night entertainment in some hotels, just like the old days; off-course betting became legal. Eating-places improved and proliferated; rules against men and women publicly enjoying themselves together were eroded. The holiday business (and the length of holidays) expanded and a new city—the Gold Coast, south of Brisbane—and a number of towns grew up in dedication to the pleasures of holidays and retirement. In New South Wales poker machines were made legal and in the suburban centres and country towns big clubs, belonging to the ordinary people and designed like U.S. resort hotels, were financed out of their profits. The biggest, $3 million of it, had eight bars, squash courts, indoor bowls, billiards, gymnasia, sauna baths, 200 "pokies", and 20,000 members. As the gold of the Diggers had once brought international performers to appear in Ballarat, the suburban clubs brought international performers to appear in their cabarets.

The new generation took this easier life for granted. The young could be seen by some as a threat, but by others belief in them became a salvationary cult: "They are sharp, up to date, ambitious, image-conscious, materialist—and more than anything else they are *aware*: aware of ideas, fashions, cults, overseas trends, music, business techniques, in a way very few groups of Australians have been before." They at least seemed greater masters than any earlier generation of the easy manner so long sought by Australians, but frustrated by their other traditions and by their own uncertainties. "In certain ways—especially in the emphasis on naturalness and on a relaxed, open style, and perhaps in a greater feeling for democractic equality—the young became more 'Australian'."

Outside Australia, the word "affluence" now described this new state of affairs, and in other countries it had produced marked strains in social relations. But the cohesiveness of Australian society meant that Australians adapted to "affluence" with perhaps less strain than any other country. They had been getting ready for a long time to accept that ordinary people should enjoy the privileges of the rich. And while the economic changes that provided the basis of affluence meant many upsets in other countries, as people were forced to find new jobs, or lost jobs altogether, the cohesiveness of Australian society—the uniformity of much of its education and, except for the Aborigines, its lack of depressed groups—meant an ability to adjust with comparative smoothness to changing technological demands. A desire for everyone to have a job seemed so deeply stuck in the general consciousness that this, along with luck, meant that unemployment was usually as little as one per cent or less, and if it began moving towards two per cent there was a political crisis. A forty-hour working week was made statutory in 1948; later provisions extended paid holidays and sick leave and made long service leave a compulsory charge on employers. An unusually large proportion of incomes were near the average, and both the proportion of poor and the gap between rich and poor was one of the smallest in the world.

In the 1950s a national health scheme at last developed—contributory, with a government subsidy—to be expanded in 1970. But social services policy was most directed to the bottom. The emphasis was on minimums and, with the exception of the health scheme, on a non-contributory principle which made social services look as "free" as largesse handed out by a colonial governor. As time passed this meant that Australia was again falling behind other prosperous countries in its social services for middle reaches of income. In the country which by the 1960s had only one in ten of its people regarding themselves as "working class", the social service system still ignored contributory national superannuation schemes and other income-related plans that had developed elsewhere. However, there was not much discontent, since, until such schemes were hinted at in 1969, it was not widely known that they existed.

Still walking around their cities as if they owned them, the deeds of their houses held by their savings banks, insurance companies or building societies, and their barbecues in their backyards, most ordinary Australians were moving towards fulfilment of that dream of dignity of the common man first manifested by the Emancipists and Natives and then by the mutual societies of the Emigrants. In his own regard, almost every worker would have been a gentleman if the word "gentleman" had not fallen out of use. Australians held much of their achievement to be in their access to material things and to the privileges of leisure, but they also cultivated an openness of manner and a cult of informality that, its aggressiveness now less evident, had in it some seeking towards a common humanity, even if its rituals could conceal or even frustrate differences between individuals. Remarkably similar in some ways to early descriptions of the Currency Lads, it was for better or worse, the Australian style. You could like it, or hate it. It was what there was.

With Australians' length of experience of high urbanization, their long concern with social cohesion and their established moderation in the use of social violence, the cities remained remarkably stable at a time when cities in other countries were seen as symbols of disorder, or even doom. Australians could be violent in their individual relations—the larrikin was still in many of them—but except for the destruction of Aboriginal society their history had been relatively peaceful: social disturbances were so rare and insignificant compared with the violence embedded in almost every other country's memory that some history-writers, affronted by such abnormality, tried to make these incidents larger than they were.

One of the oldest threats to the sense of being one people was now fading. The Irishness of the Catholic Church had been taken away, and even if the church remained more sensitive to the Vatican than other national churches its clergy and hierarchy became Australian. As late as 1929 Archbishop Mannix could still say "the more deeply they breathe the Irish atmosphere the stronger and more vigorous will be the Australian faith"; but in the 1930s Australian-trained priests were moving in and a few were made bishops; in 1937 one of them became Archbishop of Hobart, another, Norman Gilroy—so Australian that he had been a telegraph messenger boy and had then served at Anzac—became Archbishop of Sydney in 1940 and was later made a cardinal. Other appointments followed. But although better represented among the well-to-do and the university-educated, Catholics still seemed to challenge cohesion with the exclusiveness that had marked them since Pius IX. To some their talent for conspiracy threatened the very basis of society. The Catholics' own sense of persecution eased when, to get Catholic votes, Liberal governments began to subsidize Catholic schools, partly returning to the policies of a hundred years before, the abandoning of which had caused so much bitterness. General community attitudes to Catholics changed when Pope John and the Second Vatican Council began to look for the Christianity in other churches. When Pope Paul came to Sydney in 1970 Sydney felt almost as honoured as when Queen Elizabeth, President Johnson or the film star Elizabeth Taylor had visited it.

The old hatred of immigrants also began to fade. With more than two million immigrants and only 40 per cent of them British, Australia was a multi-national society, with Turks as well as Dutch, Chileans as well as Germans, Mauritians as well as Finns. Altogether one-fifth of the population were immigrants; in Sydney, Melbourne and Adelaide immigrants made up one-quarter of the population; in the two biggest cities they provided half the shopkeepers and most of the restaurants. The contents of Australian delicatessens became the most varied in the world. In some inner suburbs immigrants formed minority national colonies; in some outer suburbs they outnumbered the natives. Many worked in heavy industry, building and construction; some as businessmen, skilled tradesmen, professional men; as owners of restaurants, art galleries, specialty shops, they helped smooth out the affluent life. All of them gave the Australian cities a much greater diversity and richness of texture.

The Australian dislike of admitting that strangers were entering their country that had earlier made them call immigrants "emigrants" now produced the euphemism "migrants"; but fears proved false that ordinary Australians would turn their historic intolerance on the "migrants". With so little unemployed, "migrants" provided no economic threat, and the balance of nationalities was well-proportioned, with no dominant nationality making a critical challenge. The chance of immigrant children to rise above their parents' economic station was higher than in most immigrant countries. Whether or not Australians loved their new neighbours, they learnt to tolerate them. The Assimilation Branch of the Immigration Department was renamed the Citizenship Branch.

Attitudes to the Aborigines were slower to change. Throughout the 1950s and into the 1960s there was an official policy of "assimilation", first declared in 1951; but, while legal discriminations were removed, few Australians seemed interested in the brown Australians most of them never saw until, in the mid-1960s, the treatment of Aborigines in country towns burst into controversy with "freedom rides" conducted by students on the U.S. pattern. There was continuing controversy after that. In a referendum in 1967 an overwhelming majority of Australians voted for the Commonwealth Government to take over the Aborigines question and by the end of the decade Aborigines themselves had begun agitating.

In the remote areas of "colonial Australia", as in Alaska and Northern Canada, old values were in varying degrees maintained. Elsewhere, their original society destroyed, the Aborigines lived in a fringe culture, made up of memories of some of what they had lost along with difficulties in adjusting to—or getting anywhere near—what they were now supposed to gain. In sad parody, they often became more "Australian" than the other Australians, their new culture a makeshift memory of the bush culture of the 1890s.

An industrial society

In one sense Australia had finished its industrialization by the late 1950s. By then it had one of the world's most industrialized farming industries and one of the smallest proportions of farm workers. C.S.I.R.O. research and the fairly rapid spread of scientific findings, along with advice from State Agriculture Departments and news of labour-saving machines, had helped major farming industries to remain among the world's most efficient. In a spectacular follow-up to the 1920s destruction of the prickly pear by the *cactoblastis*, the C.S.I.R.O. in 1950 introduced the myxomatosis virus and soon millions of rabbits were dead. At the same time, the expansion of wartime manufacturing skills along with the special protection import licences gave in the 1950s encouraged an unparalleled expansion of investment in manufacturing.

The motor industry boomed after a General Motors subsidiary produced an Australian car, the "Holden", and there was expansion in electrical goods, petrol refining, chemicals, plastics and other industries. Much of the finance came from foreign investment, but this time, unlike the 1920s policy of "men, money and markets" or the nineteenth century "spirited policy of public works", governments did not channel foreign money into Australia in an attempt to keep the economy predominantly rural: foreign money came because foreign companies established new manufacturing firms in Australia or bought out old ones. The amount of manufacturing activity rose to figures that indicated a fully industrialized nation; thereafter it was the proportion of activity in tertiary industries that went up; it was becoming one of the world's highest.

Government investment had a new concentration on the cities. With pipes, wires and concrete there was an attempt to make up deficiencies caused by earlier refusals to accept the nation's predominantly urban nature. From the mid-1950s, especially in Sydney, there began what was to prove the most expansive period of private city building Australia had known. Height restrictions were eased, and shining new prestige buildings rose high above the renaissance-palace commercial styles of an earlier age. In marble, mosaics, oiled timber, bronze sculptures and garden forecourts self-belief flourished. Architectural novelty spread to churches and government offices; new city fountains were constructed in the new styles; the Sydney Opera House, which was to cost about $100 million because the N.S.W. government had accepted a sketch without inquiring whether it was feasible to construct the building, prompted other cities to put up their own temples of culture.

With flat-dwelling acceptable because flats could now be owned by their occupants, there followed a boom in residential towers and smaller blocks of flats. There were experiments in medium density housing. The older examples of this—the now dilapidated terraces ringing the central city areas—were restored and painted light colours by "migrants" and by middle-class people looking for urban living. By the late 1960s almost one in five of households in the Sydney metropolitan areas lived in flats; in some districts they constituted 75 to 100 per cent of all new building. To this extent the first suburban nation was again becoming citified. Guesses went out that the population of the Newcastle-Sydney-Wollongong urbanizing area might reach seven million by the end of the century, with five million of them in Sydney. By 1970 there was a boom in talk about town planning, civic design, traffic control and the newly popular word "pollution".

For much of this period the old rhetoric about national development revived, still with the idea that there was "no price too high to pay" to bring natural resources into production. Closer settlement schemes continued, governments still scattered public works around the countryside with the traditional disregard for economic considerations, and subsidies to farmers became greater. To the idea that it was immoral to leave natural resources unused was added the idea that it was dangerous—some other country might come and take them: in the late 1950s and early 1960s a "develop the north" movement became popular since the north was the part that was closest to other countries. But as time went on and markets became less certain belief in rural expansion disappeared. Money spent on farming and rural areas became defensive: rural public work projects degenerated into isolated attempts to maintain country votes; rural subsidies (despite beliefs to the contrary) were in fact less than in many other prosperous nations; by 1970 closer settlement schemes had been abandoned and with the new slogan of "get big or get out" there were plans to get small farmers off the land.

Despite the efficiency of most farming industries, increasingly protectionist policies in other countries had narrowed markets. But for some time this was scarcely noticed because Australia was again becoming a great mineral-exporting nation. New South Wales was producing the world's cheapest coal and Japanese industrial expansion gave the coal industry relief from its long slump; there was expansion in a wide range of other minerals, some of them metals whose very names had been unknown; drilling rigs spouted oil; pipes were planned to carry natural gas hundreds of miles to the cities.

The explosion of activity in iron ore became the symbol of all this new activity. Until 1960 Australia had a constipated approach towards iron-ore exports—whatever it had it would keep. When this policy broke down survey work was stimulated. Huge new resources were found. At the same time technology was now available to bring this iron ore profitably from outback to coast, and the Japanese "economic miracle" provided a customer. Railways were flung across sunburnt country; new ports sprang up on desolate coasts; pens signed huge contracts; 100,000-ton iron-ore carriers began to shuttle between Western Australia and Japan. In the stock exchange casinos people gambled in mining shares until the market collapsed.

Australians had for a while seen sheep as their symbol of initiative and prosperity; now television documentaries of the caravans and drilling rigs of geological survey parties and the bulldozers that scooped away mountains provided new symbols of enterprise and nationhood. But, as with the nineteenth century wool rushes and gold rushes, it was mainly a matter of foreign markets and foreign money. Foreign firms with their own capital carried out almost all the early mineral expansion. The Australia financial and business system had proved too conservative for new circumstances.

This foreign domination of the minerals boom along with increasing foreign domination in manufacturing raised many doubts about the capacity of Australian businessmen. *The Lucky Country*, a best-seller of the 1960s, suggested they were "racketeers of the mediocre who have risen to authority in a non-competitive community", "a provincial generation exhausted by events". The mineral boom caused extraordinary prophecies, mainly from visitors, of coming prosperity; but there were worries about economic growth rates as commentators disagreed in interpreting the statistics now become fashionable. In international tables of comparative prosperity Australia seemed to be slipping. Would the new managers be able to keep up with what was being described as the "technological age", to distinguish it from the "industrial age" in which Australians had successfully adapted other people's ideas?

Following the theories of the time about the relation between education and prosperity there were considerable doubts about whether enough educated people were being turned out and whether those who had been educated had received the right education. There were shortages in all administrative roles, from managing director to foreman. Discussion of new techniques in city planning raised doubts about the capacities of the government departments and the government-owned corporations who largely controlled city development. If Australia were "a lucky country run mainly by second-rate people who share its luck", would its prosperity pass with the industrial age that was now passing? Or would Australians continue to scrape through, with their ability "to change course quickly, even at the last moment, and seek a quick, easy way out"?

The rise of the executives

With the defeat of the 1940s planners; confidence in the hope that rationality might be applied to human affairs had been lost; but by the 1960s it had been revived—in ideas surrounding the words "management" and "executive". This time it was applied to officials of the business bureaucracies as well as the bureaucracies of government, and sometimes it was businessmen who most extolled it.

A product of large, depersonalized organizations, at his most romanticized the new "executive" was a "technician of general ideas" with such perfect techniques of policy-making and administration that he was able to pass from one bureaucracy to the next applying the same general principles of behaviour. He was a man of merit whose qualifications, based on education, challenged the privileges of wealth or seniority, and he was a man of reason, whose mastery of mathematical techniques and programming brought the orderliness of science to human affairs.

In this ideal form the "executive" was not believed to exist in Australia; in imagination he lived in the United States; or, for a few, in Japan; for even fewer, France. But some young Australians were trained in U.S. business schools; U.S. companies that extended into Australia brought their organizational methods with them; and the monopolist or semi-monopolist tendency in Australian-owned firms produced bureaucracies large enough to adopt some of these approaches. Gradually special management courses were introduced into Australia. Some big government-owned corporations began to look at these new ideas. Smaller, talent-based firms—advertising agencies, architects, town planners and so forth—adopted them with different orders of enthusiasm. Within business firms there were now long, irritating struggles, with new ways confronting old.

The idea of the man of merit and reason, specifically based on university education, had fuller victory in the Commonwealth public service. In the wartime improvisations of virtually creating a new public service graduates had usually proved fitter to their tasks than those who had entered the departments as Returned Men or messenger boys, and after the war an appetite for them developed to the stage that Australia's single most important organization in the 1960s developed something like a meritocratic élite. There was extra pay for university degrees, special entry for particularly promising graduates, and a recognition that second division public servants constituted a corps of top administrators, generalists able to move in their upward progress from one department to the other.

A nation that had shown a unique lack of interest in relations between economic progress and education was now changing profoundly as it scraped together a larger education system which, although it had other professed aims, was to service this new demand. In 1939 there were only six universities and only a few hundred scholarships; in 1970 there were 15 universities and thousands of scholarships. In New South Wales in 1939 there were only 46 high schools; in 1970 there were 288. A greater number of children stayed on at school; full employment developed tastes for privileges previously restricted to only a few, and new careers offered by the new bureaucracies of government and business demanded higher educational standards. For the first time education became a general means of getting jobs with status beyond those of the traditional professions.

This reversal of attitudes was for a time blind, moving in one direction when it thought it was moving in another, seeing itself as a cultural, or personality-moulding, or democratic advance, without specific relation to changes in jobs. Its relation to jobs was clearest first in technical education which, after so many defeats, began to make up for lost time with greater emphasis on higher education; old snobbish habits set in train in the 1850s at the foundation of the first two universities could still inhibit progress, but towards the end of the 1960s government enthusiasm partly turned from the universities towards colleges of advanced education, which were more vocation-based than the "pure" faculties of the universities. It remained to be seen whether they would conquer the traditions of 120 years, or be taken over by them.

What was almost unnoticed was that to the high standards of training of engineers, doctors, dentists and other specialists had been added a high training of scientists. With one in sixty world scientific break-throughs occurring in Australia, it was reckoned that Australia ranked tenth in the world in its contribution to world science. Photographs of Australia's biggest radio telescope appeared in tourist pamphlets; there were television documentaries on Australian research into viruses; two medical scientists shared Nobel Prizes; when the U.S. space programme reached its most spectacular moments there were news angles on the part played by the Australian space-tracking stations. But these attracted small attention and prompted little pride. On the whole, business firms undertook very little research and between 80 and 90 per cent of the best scientists remained in universities or government research institutions, among which the C.S.I.R.O. provided a huge refuge with its 80 laboratories and research stations.

With public services seeking graduates, subsidizing them in further university work and providing in-service training, and with many business executives or would-be executives studying part-time or sometimes being subsidized by their firms for full-time study, it might have been expected that academies would develop, as they had long since in almost all other prosperous countries, to specialize in educating those who seemed most likely to be good at running big organizations. One result of this was that although there was an Australian style in administration it was hard to say what it was. It was easy to attack those ways in which Australian styles did not meet the ideal standards of some other country: it was difficult to praise those ways in which they suited Australia and, by idealizing them, improve them.

The rise of the intellectuals

"Australian audiences heard for the first time in their lives Australian characters on stage speaking the Australian idiom of the streets." Words like these hailed the success of the play *The Summer of the Seventeenth Doll* in 1956 as the beginning of an Australian national theatre. In the 1950s such prophecies of artistic maturity were commonplace. Renaissances were detected in all the arts and in fact the general achievement was superior in quality and much more diverse than in the 1890s, the last time Australians had believed in their own artists. The tedium of some of the intervening decades was drifting away.

The first drama "renaissance" lasted little more than four years (it coincided, although quite independently, with outbursts of anger on the London stage), but in the other arts Australia began to seem a place where things continued to happen. In writing and in the composition of music a belief developed in established Australian practitioners, to whose existence other practitioners could react. Lists were made out, hierarchically arranged in the classroom fashion, according to guesses about how their work would "last". In painting acceptance of achievement was so wide that it attracted the rich and there was a harvest of dealers' galleries, art openings and prizes from business firms. Belief in Australian painting spread: offers of prints became a promotional device of newspapers and magazines. And at last in the late 1960s there eventuated those government subsidies to the performing arts first urged in the 1840s, although this time the inspiration was found in Canada, not ancient Rome.

With many more graduates coming from the universities and more belief developing in education, Australians interested in ideas and concepts began to speak of themselves more confidently as "intellectuals". From the late 1950s onwards, beginning with the magazines *Voice*, the *Observer* and *Nation*, new publications emerged to serve the emerging intellectuals, and, more generally, the educated; some of the older publications changed. There was a flourishing of conferences, seminars and travel grants, and government money began to sponsor research in the universities (whose staffs were now known as "academics"). Some who moved in among the old terraces of the inner cities were intellectuals; they felt more at home there than in the suburbs where they had been born. Young people began to find it less difficult to display their talents; starting a new publication was almost as easy as it had been in the nineteenth century. There was at last a new middle class of intellect and taste where an intellectual could feel he belonged (or to which he could react) even if the old sense of isolation and threat could also remain.

The idea of the Australian as bushman or Digger had been altogether overthrown. *The Summer of the Seventeenth Doll* questioned mateship; *The One Day of the Year*, a successor play, questioned the values of Anzac; the rise of the poets James McAuley and A. D. Hope as literary figures was seen as a defeat for literary nationalism (if also for literary modernism); in painting the old bush impressionism had shrivelled away; even *The Bulletin* was taken over and modernized. The traditional naturalistic style was questioned: Patrick White's novel *The Aunt's Story* was praised because it showed that "the Australian novel is not necessarily the dreary, dun-coloured offspring of journalistic realism"; and as soon as the first drama renaissance got going it was attacked as "backyard realism", and a second renaissance—of anti-naturalism—was proclaimed. In novels there developed a fashion in disjointed prose. The old subjects appeared to survive most confidently among some painters, but new styles had created new "subjects". Russell Drysdale's landscapes offered a thinner and more qualified hope than Streeton's, and Sidney Nolan's tentative Ned Kelly seemed emptied by his own wanderings.

Most of this activity, along with increased publication by academics and improvements in journalism, were seen as the cutting edges of a new sophistication. Once again Australia had come of age, but this time in pigment, not in blood. Even attacks on Australian life could be part of this new maturity. (For some they were its main matter.) In these attacks old themes were renewed: the first volume of verse published in Sydney, in 1819, had seen Australia not as part of the initial creation but "an afterbirth, not conceived in the Beginning"; now A. D. Hope saw Australia as "the last of lands, the emptiest". Charles Harpur had written of the "dead murky level" of the "intellectual grossness" of his fellow countrymen; James McAuley now wrote of "white Australia, as she hugely squats, above her pint-pot, fly-blown and resigned". There was a recurrent belief that the country was so spiritually dried out that it would crack into pieces to be picked up by Asian powers. In a wave of satire, with Australia being savaged as a uniquely barbarian land, the R.S.L. became the most hated symbol of out-dated Australian provincialism, the paradigm enemy of the new sophisticates. Beginning with *The Australian Ugliness*, a criticism of Australian design that was seen as a general onslaught on the Australian condition, there developed a market for books making comprehensive attacks on Australia; but with the new sophistication self-criticism became so quickly institutionalized that two of these books, *Australian Civilization* and *The Lucky Country*, were soon set as school texts.

To some of those who saw Australia as "an unimportant

country which has contributed little or nothing of a distinctive character to the world", flight seemed the only escape from its frustrations. Usually they went to London, where colonies of Australian expatriates formed, their view of their country sometimes summed up in the comic strip character "Barry McKenzie", an amusing apotheosis of the stalwart follies of Dinkum Aussiness. Somewhat like lost Russian intellectuals in the nineteenth century, others remaining in Australia were "expatriates in their own country": Some still looked to London as the world cultural centre, others, projecting Anglophilia into a new cosmopolitanism, saw the rest of the world ("overseas") as if it were all one place, all of it better than anything in Australia.

In the manner brutally articulated by D. H. Lawrence and others in the 1920s and 1930s, the "expatriates", whether at home or "overseas" were likely to blame their predicament on the ordinary Australian people. In a sad misunderstanding of their sense of isolation, making them hate those who should not have been blamed, they attacked the "apathy" and "intolerance" of the common man for inadequacies of intellectual life in Australia. In the 1840s the "fatal facility" for making money had been seen as a corruption of the people; now it was the "affluence" of the suburbs that aroused uneasiness. Patrick White's play *The Season at Sarsaparilla*, a study in suburban vacuity, was taken to be a study of the whole nation; "Mrs Everage", a caricature of shallow suburban optimism, was seen both as typical of Australia and unique to it.

The ordinary people were being blamed for a failure to take initiatives that were beyond the reach of the common man in any country. Sometimes the fate of disappointed intellectuals was due to a failure they could meet anywhere, but when frustration came from being Australian it was not always realized that it came from the colonial origin of the country, not from its democracy. Most obviously it came from the weaknesses and derivativeness of the education system, which for a long time produced very few educated people, and those usually Anglophiles. But even the fashion of disjointedness in Australian prose, although partly a product of a general world uncertainty in style, may also have come from the uncertainties of educated ex-colonials caught between the "reality" of an acquired culture and the "reality" of their own society, which could seem so unfamiliar ("She has no gods, no songs, no history") as not to be worthy of art, or even investigation. A situation in which both Australian society and the learnt-off culture could seem unreal made even many educated Australians "anti-intellectual". Taught ideas and values that did not grow in their hearts or reflect values around them, they became sceptical of all ideas.

A. D. Hope may have seen Australia as a "river of stupidity", but he also suggested that from this "Arabian desert of the human mind" might spring "some spirit which escapes the learned doubt, the chatter of cultured apes which is called civilization over there". McAuley had complained of Australia's citizenry that, "For it, Plato's a horse, Socrates a dog. Surrounded by its vast domain it sleeps; a pigmy in the iron bed of Og"; but when he grew older he wrote a sequence of suburban poems that gave poetic form to some of the common stuff of Australian life. Social critics also began to give a more sympathetic treatment to the suburbs. A number of autobiographies searched childhood and youth in the 1920s, -30s, and -40s, seeking some of the springs of contemporary existence.

In yet another revival of the drama, the political vaudeville *The Legend of King O'Malley* (which gave a brilliant dramatization of how in the debaucheries of the Great War the ideal of a nation showing the world how to live was replaced by the ideal of a nation showing the world how to fight) began a fashion for bouncy expeditions into Australia's past. It was beginning to look as if many Australian intellectuals could accept the conditions of their existence. Among many of the young, that they were Australians seemed an increasingly natural assumption.

Some intellectuals again began to have hopes of improving things. After the belabouring received by the planners, intellectuals for many years had detached themselves from matters of policy; but as their strength grew, some set out by their own standards to modernize Australia. In a society where culture had been seen as "a policeman's beat, who, having learnt to bully honest whores, is let out on the Muses for a treat", one obvious target was censorship: censorship laws had proved such a symbol of Australian depravity that they began to be demolished in a series of strategic retreats. Abortion was made legal in South Australia; in the States where hanging survived it almost caused riots; there were campaigns for reform of the laws on homosexuality; the fate of the Aborigines became a popular intellectuals' cause. Street protests had for long been the traditional form of new political action in Australia, but they had fallen into disuse; now they were revived (as a new idea from "overseas") and hundreds of students and others were sometimes arrested in mêlées with the police. Civil liberties groups systematized protest; panels of volunteer lawyers defended those arrested in protest demonstrations.

Other intellectuals, both academics and journalists, gave detailed study to aspects of public affairs. The careful work of an Immigration Reform Group in the 1960s helped change the attitudes of influential people. Economists, singly or in groups, raised a flow of new ideas on tariffs, foreign investment, social services, national superannuation schemes, taxation, and the economic effects of immigration. There was increasingly detailed discussion on urban planning. Others gave systematic thought to foreign policy. Contacts grew between intellectuals outside the government departments and those inside them. Australia, for so long living on an exhausted political capital, had found a source of new ideas.

Chapter 18

THE END OF IMPERIALISM
1950-1970

The failure of politics

All the nations that grew from European colonies were "fragments" of European culture lodged in a new land, their future partly set by what came out of Europe in the first place. Charles Darwin quickly saw that the Australian colonies had made more material progress in "scores of years" than Latin America had achieved in "an equal number of centuries". This was because some of the greatest creative impulses in the settlement of Australia were those of the English Age of Improvement: belief in material progress was part of Australia's nature. Although not usually innovating material change, Australia could not help accepting it, and adjusting to it. Something that had been set going did not stop. Steam engines were built. So were radio telescopes.

A belief in general human progress was also part of the Age of Improvement. This "fragment" of one of the conflicting attitudes of British society was also lodged early in Australia, and although at the start it was very weak it grew with the Emigrants and some of the Emancipists. Otherwise born with little faith, the colonists, if they were to believe anything, could believe in human betterment. At first, in a convict colony, many found betterment in access to respectability, and that trend continued. Then they found betterment in the access of the common man to the home ownership, the privacy and the leisure pursuits of the rich, and that trend continued. There was a continuing belief that it could be found in education: very largely, that trend did not flourish. When in the late nineteenth century, Australia at last produced painters, writers and orators who could suggest what Australians might be, there was an expressed belief that betterment was to be found in distinctive human styles and relations. But since this belief was given flesh in the bush-hero and then in the soldier-hero it was not accessible to suburbanites except during picnics and wars, and it seemed inaccessible to women. In any case, the black hats took over Anzac Day and partly turned it to other purposes.

There was another possibility for betterment. With the beginnings of parliamentary democracy there had been hopes that if the people sought conspicuous virtue, it would be by acts of parliament. In the confusion of parliamentary factions of self-seeking men in ill-brushed hats, Australia, by the standards of the age, soon became one of the world's most progressive countries, and one of the most pleased with itself and its ideals, although, with sceptical wisdom, it spared enthusiasm for political leaders for only a few practitioners. Then these impulses grew less. Once so remarkable for the speed with which it could put new ideas into practice that books were written about its progressiveness, its governments now seemed to move so slowly that books were written about its political backwardness. By the 1960s its belief in itself as a political animal was even less than it had sunk to before the second world war.

For twenty years the one government had remained in power in Canberra. At first the victory of the Federal Liberal Party in 1949 seemed merely one of those swings of the pendulum supposed to be essential to the two-party system that Australia had tried to imitate. After its 1940s success Labor had seen itself as the "natural government" of Australia and its defeat as merely an aberration; the theory was held that Labor was the great initiating force in Australian politics, and in the 1954 election it won slightly more than half the votes, only electoral inequalities depriving it of office. But the Liberals still seemed a pleasant change; their victories had restored an emphasis on the pursuit of happiness through the purchase of consumer goods, and Labor's defeat was a reminder to governments that they were not God Almighty. However the Liberals became a permanency when in 1955 the Federal Labor Party collapsed from its own contradictions and lost election after election. Menzies, who had created the Liberal Party out of the wreckage of his earlier defeat, seemed to have become Prime Minister by divine right. The office at first interested him but, as the years went on, his use of it assumed more whimsical meanings.

The Labor Party's collapse had come from its undermining by the greatest of the Catholic conspiracies. The "Movement" had organized Catholic cells in many parishes, forming a secret political machine to act as servicing agent to Labor's industrial groups. These tactics brought success against Communists in some trade unions, but then the ambitions of the "Movement" and some "Groupers" expanded towards political influence in the Labor Party, perhaps control of it. So great was the fear of "Catholic Action" that this extraordinary plot was not exposed until Evatt, the Labor Party leader after Chifley's death, switched sides among the party's factions and, for his own preservation, spoke of what had been happening. The effect of the subsequent manoeuvre was a split that produced the new Democratic Labor Party in an attempt, prompted by what was left of the Movement, to bring the Labor Party low and re-occupy it; from the accidents of internal party warfare and in hatreds, the "left" became stronger in some State Labor machines, distorting the party's balance and taking from it many of its earlier skills in compromise. This disarray, combined with slight electoral inequalities, inadequate leadership (Evatt's brain was failing) and, for some time, a generally backward and Depression-oriented look, seemed to turn Labor into a permanent opposition, one of the mere ceremonies of parliament.

Menzies also looked backwards—beyond the Depression, back to those certainties of the 1920s that had first marked Australia's political decline. There was little talk of improvement but much of "development" (although not with the same disastrous results) and in a party in which there were so many R.S.L. badges and old school ties, political leaders sometimes spoke as if loyalty to the British Empire could still be Australia's saving. In certain ways—including a greater suspicion that social services were merely for the idle and improvident—it was a kind of Federal government that Australia had not previously known. The bureaucracy set up in the 1940s was still there and, although swinging from an over-adventurous spirit to an over-cautious one, it sufficiently reacted to events to save the Liberals from the more florid parts of their declared policy; but the Liberals could not fully exploit this new instrument of administration. Once so marked in its use of government for human betterment, Australia ignored new techniques of government long after they had been tested in other countries. As the 1960s proceeded, much else was changing, but of all of the nation's institutions government was one of the slowest to change. Even most of Australia's successes were not to Menzies' liking, so that the government could not dramatize them and claim them as its own.

Towards the end of Menzies' rule discontent began to be expressed not only against the Liberals but against what seemed to be a general failure of Australian politics to keep moving with the times. When Menzies retired none of his three successors caught for long at the imagination. At the same time Labor was not backed with much enthusiasm. Feelings of discontent had arisen first and most articulately among the new executives and intellectuals; it then spread amongst some of the ordinary people. It reached a climax in the 1970 Senate elections when in every State there was a vote against the whole political system. It was as if Australians understood that their politicians were not reaching out to Australia's new potentialities or even reflecting what Australia now was. Entirely derivative—from upper house and speakers' maces to an imitation of the two-party system—the political system was beginning to seem outlandish. By 1970 the paradox had arisen that Australia was at another pitch of success, but most public talk was of failure.

If, as a fragment of the Age of Improvement, Australia had naturally sought radical change, how could it cease to do so? Partly because it was also a product of the earlier, and contradictory, Age of Authority. Government had not begun with dreams of betterment but with the despotism of a penal settlement. Even with self-government, participatory local government was weak and in a country that was so early in developing large bureaucracies there was a big vested interest in keeping things as they were. In that way they could be quietly administered according to precedent. Government was something provided from above.

For a while, before the imitation of the two-party system, the blunderings of short-term political coalitions had allowed that fairly regular introduction of novelties that made Australia seem progressive. But when the political system became more rigid there was less acceptance of change. Affronted by Labor's apparent "socialism", the non-Labor parties moved from the liberal-radical centre where the power had previously been, and in administrative and economic values increasingly adopted capitalist-Protestant ethics of "free enterprise" that were foreign to the Australian experience. (At least they adopted them in theory; in practice, as in the early days when trading and speculative factions of rugged adventurers had tried to unseat governors, "free enterprise" usually meant the government protection of special interests.) And partly because of strong Catholic influence, partly because of the contrary impulses of a continually unrealizable "socialism", the Labor parties also moved away from the liberal-radical impulses that had earlier seemed to be an essential part of the Australian style.

Reflecting both the contrary impulses of Improvement and Authority, Australian politics can swing between the excitements of adventure and the comforts of caution. By 1970 it seemed to many that caution was now the only style; they had forgotten, or re-interpreted, the whole period of Improvement. But there were signs that contrary impulses might still be there. For more than half a century following its earlier radicalism South Australia had been a centre of conservatism but, with younger men in command, South Australian politics suddenly swung back to a contest over the liberal-radical centre. In federal politics, when one of Menzies' successors, John Gorton, seemed about to adopt a radical approach this seemed something people had been waiting for. His popularity dropped only when it became clear that he had no coherent style of any kind. And although the apparent immutability of the older men in the Federal Parliament remained, some younger ones on both sides of the house appeared to be contemplating the possibility of a return to a more liberal-radical style.

The afterglow of Britishry

Some of the values of the Age of Authority had been strengthened in the Age of Imperialism. There was a waning in the more aggressive excesses of the cult of the New Imperialism after its price was paid in the bloodshed of the Great War, but in its equation of civilization with Britishness it was strengthened in the 1920s and 1930s, and the acceptance of the British Empire as an economic and strategic unit was not even marked by the kind of occasional public criticisms of British policy by which earlier political leaders had partly made their reputation. The cult was full blown, like a dying flower.

In the 1950s, there was an extraordinary revival. Not long after taking over as Prime Minister, Menzies announced that "the British Empire must remain our chief international preoccupation", and even when the red had gone from the map some older Liberals still tried to project the "British Commonwealth" as a political institution. There was an attempt in the mid-1950s to restrict immigrants from southern Europe; a "Bring out a Briton" campaign was announced. (It failed.) In this afterglow of Empire Menzies' annual journeys to London seemed pilgrimages to the Holy Land.

In 1962 even Menzies admitted that "the old hopes for concerted common policies have gone". But although the Commonwealth had let Menzies down there was still an attempt to make Britain itself seem the main centre of civilization. There were ardent proclamations of Britishry ("I am British to the boot heels") and loyalty to Queen Elizabeth ("We are the Queen's men"). Visits to Australia of British royal persons averaged one every two years; when it was announced that Queen Elizabeth's eldest son would spend a year at an Australian school the Australian High Commissioner in London expressed his pleasure by saying that he felt like jumping over the moon; some State governments clung to Englishmen as governors and for most of the period Englishmen were still appointed governor-general; vestiges of the black-hat life of the 1840s regained confidence; "God Save the Queen" remained the national anthem; the Union Jack remained on the Australian flag; the number of royal honours bestowed on Australians increased at four to five times the rate of increase of the total population. There were limits to these excesses. Menzies' Cabinet stopped him from calling the main unit of the new decimal currency the "royal" and there was derision when, confusing royal with profane love, Menzies welcomed Queen Elizabeth with the lines, "I did but see her passing by, and yet I love her till I die." But the Australian political style had become partly one of *tableaux vivants* reconstructing the past as if the present were a garden party.

Yet not only had the Empire gone, and the Commonwealth virtually gone: now Australia no longer looked to the British navy for protection; Britain was no longer the dominant foreign investor in Australia, nor Australia's main source of technological innovation; it was no longer the biggest customer for Australia's exports, nor the second biggest, and with its proposed entry into the European Economic Community its purchases were expected to dwindle further; it was no longer the supplier of most immigrants; London was no longer Australia's only cultural centre; to younger people the old imperial cult seemed hard to imagine.

Except amongst the elderly, Britishness was dying, but, with the old nationalism gone, nothing had replaced it. There were odds and ends of self-assertion: Australian commemorative themes on Australian stamps; Australian faces on the new dollar currency; occasional meaningless boasts; a chic revival of folk songs; a self-amused adoption of some of the words of bush mateship amongst executives and intellectuals. For a moment Gorton thought he was a nationalist, then he seemed to forget about it.

It seemed unlikely that, in the nineteenth century sense, there would be a new nationalism. Australia was already cohesive, and somehow aware of itself even if its intellectuals hadn't become very confident in talking about it. But if there were again some achievement, with political and intellectual leaders to dramatize it, there could again be self-confidence; if there were a great achievement there could be great self-confidence. There was a kind of free, floating self-confidence with nothing credibly lasting to attach itself to.

That Australia would at last get around to electing its own head of State seemed obvious enough, although the timing was less obvious. Perhaps other changes would then accompany this disavowal of political infantilism.

Ten minutes to midnight

For a while the excitements of Evatt's foreign policy revived a latent big-headedness with his hope that Australia might become the conscience of the world, and even after the Liberal victory there remained some dash and independence in Australian diplomacy. Percy Spender, the first Liberal External Affairs Minister, was one of the main prompters of the Colombo Plan for economic and technical assistance to South and South-east Asian countries, and Spender's initiative was mainly responsible for the Anzus Treaty between Australia, New Zealand and the United States, a treaty from which Britain was excluded.

But somewhere in the mid-fifties this public attitude of independence evaporated. Australia had joined a different "empire" —that of the United States. Australians knew that it was the United States, not Britain, that had saved them from the Japanese (they were not even resentful of the United States for saving them) and while politicians still chanted praise to the British lion it was on the altar of the American eagle that they now offered the blood sacrifices of strategy. Australia was the first nation to send forces to the desolate sweeps of mountains and the rivers and rice paddies of Korea, and while Australian troops there later became part of a British Commonwealth Division it was from the U.S. that Australia was seeking rewards for its merit; even its forces in Malaysia and Singapore were seen as part of an offering to maintain U.S. interest in South-east Asia; and when Australia sent a battalion to South Vietnam, and then a Task Force, introducing selective conscription to man it, Queen Elizabeth was required to issue medals to Australians for fighting in a war of which the British Government had no part.

Politics and ideas of what kind of a nation Australia was were debilitated by transferring to "the American alliance" the older excesses of loyalty to Empire. Itself a sensible and prudent arrangement in an uncertain world, the relation with the United States was treated with much of the sacredness that had been so disastrous in dealings with Britain in the 1920s and 1930s. Menzies had announced in 1950 that "we cannot survive a surging Communist challenge from abroad except for the co-operation of powerful friends", but keeping in with powerful friends moved from prudence to something close to sycophancy. Publicly there was never any Australian disagreement on any aspect of U.S. policy and privately the Australian government carried the principle of loyalty to the extreme of assuming that the U.S. could not be reckoned on as an ally in even the most serious circumstances unless Australia did what it was told on even minor occasions. Menzies maintained this inner subservience with some outward dignity—his public acting of the loyal Briton provided a diversion from the realities of the new alliance—but his successor, Harold Holt, transferred to the U.S. the public adulation that had previously been saved for the British, proclaiming to President Johnson that Australian would go "all the way with L.B.J.", while one of his colleagues said: "Where American goes, Australia goes.'- Holt's two successors each carried the Anzus Pact to Washing' ton for blessing as if it were a magic charm instead of a mere document signed by human hands.

For almost twenty years fear played a part in Australian political life, colouring attitudes to the United States. The nation that in 1948 had shown itself most expecting war found it easy in 1951 to believe Menzies' warning that war could break out at any time within three years. In the "Movement" and among some of the "Groupers" it was already "ten minutes to midnight". Estimates were made of how long Australia had to go. ("I give us four years," was a common prediction in the 1950s.) For two decades cataclysm was always just around the corner. With so much cohesion and success at home Australians looked increasingly to the outside world for that sense of threat that could give texture and difference to politics and poignant purpose to life.

But so far as Menzies' warnings were concerned, a gap separated words from actions; he announced that he would put Australia on a semi-war footing, then he let military expenditure slide down to a level lower than in almost any other nation. Until the 1960s, when President Sukarno's "confrontations", domestic criticism, and private U.S. pressure, forced an increase in military expenditure, in their trance-like dissociation between the images of threat and the realities of business-as-usual the Liberals could move from warnings of imminent danger to assurances that expenditure on "national development" rather than the armed forces was really the best form of defence. The result was a corruption of political life by a sometimes hysterical use of language that did not prompt action: Australians were urged to fear, but not to self-reliance. Not long after Menzies was forced into some rearmament he resigned.

At first, as part of the period of cold war, there was a general concern that what was still an international Communist movement under Russian influence would prove even more expansionary than the Nazis. To Australia this world threat was given extra meaning by seeing South-east Asia as "the most unsettled region of the world". Then a more particular sense of threat emerged—from China. To Australians who had so recently known Japan attack from the north it seemed possible that history could be repeated, especially when Sukarno's theatricalities turned Indonesia into an ally of China. At election times red arrows appeared on maps with exhortations to stop the Chinese at the border between North and South Vietnam.

Much of Australia's sense of danger was shared by large parts of the rest of the world, and its fears, when expressed in their more moderate forms, made as sensible a basis for action as any other. But behind specific fears there often lurked a more general—and absurd, but degrading—terror of *all* Asia, as if it were one political entity whose faceless hordes would swoop down on Australia like huns from the steppes wanting more room for their horses.

Australia enjoyed the greatest—and the last—of its imperial moments after Harold Holt was drowned during a Sunday morning swim. From this quick death, symbolic of Australia's pursuit of innocent happiness, there arose an imperial funeral. The President of the United States announced that he would fly to Australia to give the occasion meaning, and Asian presidents, prime ministers and foreign ministers took to their aircraft to be near him. Australia had received the greatest honour for its imperial loyalty: the presence of the emperor himself. For a day Melbourne had fulfilled an old dream. With processions of presidents, princes and prime ministers passing through its streets it seemed an imperial city.

A few months later the president had announced that he would abdicate his power. A few months after that a new president had announced a new doctrine, calling on nations like Australia to do more for themselves. By 1970 Australia was in a world in which the relations between the powers had become so complicated that the kind of unqualified loyalty it had shown first to Britain, then to the United States, no longer had meaning. Many of its promptings were still those of the son looking for an empire to belong to, but it was now doubtful whether a new empire could be found.

Becoming something

Except for the D.L.P., politics was suddenly drained of its sense of external peril. The overthrow of Sukarno had removed much of the credibility of immediate threat and with the announcement of a planned U.S. withdrawal from Vietnam there was a sudden calm in which the government's advisers were heard to say that Australia would face no military threat for ten years, a figure that was treated by some with the certainty once given to the prediction that it was ten minutes to midnight. In this pause, Australia still had several ways in which it could imagine it belonged to something, even if the something it belonged to was short of empire and demanded more self-reliance.

From its earliest days, although seeing itself above all as British, it had also seen itself as a Pacific Ocean nation. In its ambitious moments it could plunder the islands of the Southwest Pacific; in its less assured moods it could fear the Pacific as the ocean of some conqueror. By 1970 Australia was a Pacific Ocean nation in another sense: its economic prosperity now depended above all on a three-way economic relationship between Australia, Japan and North America, the three prosperous industrialized areas of the Pacific. U.S. investment stimulated much Australian economic activity and with it came U.S. technological innovation, the world's best; by 1970 Australia was getting more than two-thirds of its imports of machinery and equipment from the United States. At the same time, just as Australia's prosperity had once been attached to the rapid expansion of Britain, it now became attached to the rapid expansion of Japan, the world's fastest-growing economy. Japan became Australia's best customer, the U.S. its second best. And, while in its relationship with Japan and the U.S. Australia was small its wealth was almost equal to that of all of the South-east Asia which it adjoined. If it wanted to, it could imagine itself as a Pacific Ocean power of some significance.

In its early days Australia had seen itself as "Austral-Asian", South Asian. In the great days of Empire this self-definition withered, but with the destruction by the Japanese of the European colonies Australia began again to realize that it was near some of the countries of Asia. Many Liberals preferred imperial insignificance to national self-recognition, but the idea of Australia as a power in South-east Asia was welcomed by some External Affairs Ministers. Their department (renamed the Foreign Affairs Department to emphasize Australian independence) became one of its main prophets. Of Australia's 68 missions around the world most of those coveted by diplomats wanting to make their mark were in Asian countries, and in the politics of Australia's immediate neighbourhood they showed increasing skill and sublety in finding a path through the intricacies of relationships between Indonesia, the Philippines, Singapore and Malaysia.

At the time when many European intellectuals were finding novelty in the idea of the "African", a number of Australian intellectuals saw liberation in the idea of the "Asian". Moods changed with protests against the Vietnam war in the second half of the decade, but an increasing number of academics and journalists grew to know more about a number of Asian countries. Coverage of these areas in radio, television and Press increased very considerably; some Asian countries became increasingly popular to tourists; some young people preferred to get their "overseas" experience there rather than in London; many executives had contacts with some Asian countries; technical assistance programmes and cultural tours led Australians into areas where they could be confident. There was a slow but accelerating movement towards new horizons by many groups and thousands of individual persons. At home in the 1950s a very slight liberalization of the immigration procedures combined with the presence of up to 12,000 Asian students introduced Australians to the idea that "coloured" faces could appear in their streets without riots. The phrase "White Australia" dropped out of public use—the Labor Party was the last to use it openly—and a more noticeable liberalization introduced by Holt in 1966 meant that by 1970 about 3,500 non-European and 6,000 part-European immigrants were coming each year to Australia, a fact greeted with such indifference that it seemed easy enough to increase these numbers.

Overall, there was enough progress in adjustments to its map for Australia, if it wanted to, to imagine itself not only as a Pacific Ocean power of significance but also as a nation of European origin adjoining an Asian area and therefore able, in hundreds of ways, to show how a prosperous nation could express a sense of brotherhood in helping the less prosperous, how a "white" nation could seek the humanity common to different races, gradually merging its own whiteness, and how a nation of one culture could cross-fertilize with many different cultures.

Even if it wanted still to see itself as a European nation, Australia now had wider choices. A society of such diverse multi-national origin could imagine itself as "European" in a much less parochial sense than when it saw itself as "British". There had always been some understanding of other European cultures; it now became wider and deeper. And there was the prospect that while Australia's economic relationships with Britain would decline even more quickly when Britain went into the European Economic Community, its economic relations with France, Germany and other European nations could grow so that these, along with its economic relations with Japan and the U.S., could allow Australia to see itself as a relatively big trading nation, belonging to the prosperous world, and, if it liked, cosmopolitan.

Perhaps such imaginings would prove nonsense. Other prospects might open out. Prospects might narrow. But by 1970 even the barrenness of Australia's political life could not disguise the way in which there had been an almost complete change in the underlying realities of Australia's place in the world. There were many possible ways in which there could be a release of new springs of action. Even if they were not all released by Australians, Australia belonged to enough worlds for foreigners to release some of them.

Australians' historic ability to change was moderated by other aspects of their history. Perhaps, not sufficiently understanding themselves, they expected more from political activity than they really wanted from it, having contrary values. In achievement and attitudes Australia seemed between the United States and Europe, half new, half old. Australians shared the thirst for materialism of both, although they were earlier to accept access to material goods as a right for all. As Improvers they had some of the U.S. belief that man could master anything, but as a society founded in an age of scepticism and on a sardonic frontier they could settle for less. They did not see either man or the machine as God; they merely expected that things would go on changing for the better—although they were a bit lackadaisical in helping change along. When U.S. self-belief cracked in the late 1960s, the self-belief of ordinary Australians still seemed to survive. It had not set itself such high standards.

To some of their own intellectuals Australia could appear "superficial". This was even seen as a reason for a "lack of depth" in its arts. In some cases this came from comparing some work of modest aims with the work of Rembrandt, Shakespeare or Mozart but, superficially, Australia *did* appear "superficial". Its past had been more peaceful than that of almost every other country and the search for innocent happiness among its people was an affront to a student of history.

When, after a night of thunder, drunkenness and lovemaking, a thousand or so people assembled among the red gums to hear Phillip announce the birth of what seemed a small and remarkably ill-favoured colony, there was no sense of mission, either religious or secular. The foundation of New South Wales was a matter of convenience made in an age of scepticism, and such individual senses of mission as first emerged were among those Emancipists who desired to achieve respectability or those old hands who scorned it. A recurrent theme was the conflict, often within the one person, between the contrary tendencies later personalized as the larrikin and the suburbanite, a conflict so brilliantly and universally expressed in the film *Wake in Fright* that it had a longer run in Paris than in Melbourne. The extension of Australia's frontiers was tedious rather than heroic, producing sardonic wit more than high hope, and with an emphasis on luck as an element of success rather than on hard work (which could seem merely the penalty of failure). When a public sense of mission came it was that of the Age of Improvement—the nineteenth century optimistic materialism of which could be an affront to the intellectual standards of the second half of the twentieth century. All this could make Australia seem trivial or even repellent to those Australians who through their acquired culture had learnt of other things; but this did not make Australia "superficial"—it merely confronted black hats, churchmen, the Protestant work-ethic, and intellectual bearers of an acquired culture. There was no denying it. It was Australia. But so were they.

Bibliography

FURTHER READING

WORLD CONTEXT

It can be disastrous to the understanding of Australia to look at it as if it existed in itself. The most ambitious account of Australia's place as an area of influence of contradictory strands in European civilization is to be found in C. M. H. Clark: *A History of Australia*, vol 1 (1962). Of particular importance to the themes of my book (and partly affecting them) are Asa Briggs: *The Age of Improvement* (1960) and Heinz Gollwitzer: *Europe in the Age of Imperialism* (1969). E. P. Thompson: *The Making of the English Working Class* (rev. 1968) is worth looking at, along with studies of the growth in England of particular institutions that were transplanted to Australia. Louis Hartz in *The Founding of New Societies* (1964) puts up a general argument on the different kinds of "fragments" of European societies that provided the European colonies in the Americas and Australia. (He sees the Australian "fragment" as radical.) Histories of the United States would seem essential reading, for example, R. B. Nye and J. E. Morpurgo: *A History of the U.S.* (2 vols, 2nd ed., 1964), but some acquaintance with two classics on the U.S., Alexis de Tocqueville's *Democracy in America* and F. J. Turner's *The Frontier in American History*, is equally important since so many Australian commentators either directly or at second or third hand have received their views of Australia from these two works.

Detailed studies of particular aspects of relations with Britain in the early period are J. J. Auchmuty: "The Background of the Early Australian Governors", *Historical Studies*, vol 6, no. 23 (1954); J. C. Beaglehole: "The Colonial Office 1782-1854", *Historical Studies, Selected articles, Second series* (1967); Peter Burroughs: *Britain and Australia 1831-1851. A Study in Imperial Relations and Crown Lands Administration* (1967); J. J. Eddy: *Britain and the Australian Colonies 1818-1831. The Technique of Government.* (1969); John M. Ward: *Earl Grey and the Australian Colonies 1846-1857* (1958); David S. Macmillan: *Scotland and Australia, 1788-1850* (1967).

GENERAL REFERENCE

The best short histories are: Manning Clark: *A Short History of Australia* (new ed., 1969) which raises the most ideas; R. M. Crawford: *Australia* (new ed., 1970); Douglas Pike: *Australia, The Quiet Continent* (1962), particularly useful as a reminder of regional history; A. G. L. Shaw: *The Story of Australia* (1962); and Russel Ward: *Australia* (rev. ed., 1967). For browsing, and for reading about matters the historians don't usually cover, there are A. H. Chisholm (ed.): *The Australian Encyclopaedia*, 10 vols (1958) and Douglas Pike (ed.): *Australian Dictionary of Biography* (still being issued). In its own class is Gordon Greenwood (ed.): *Australia, a Social and Political History* (1955). Two longer histories are Marjorie Barnard: *A History of Australia* (1962) and R. M. Younger: *Australia and the Australians* (1970). The first, although generous in impulse, represents a type of interpretation no longer received. The second is a useful compendium. Fred Alexander: *Australia since Federation* (1967) and Trevor R. Reese: *Australia in the Twentieth Century. A Political History* (1964) tell the modern story. Of special interest is Ernest Scott: *A Short History of Australia*, first published in 1916 and revised many times since. It was the first serious attempt at a short history of Australia and was to represent just about all that two generations of Australians were likely to know of the history of their country.

SPECIAL PERSPECTIVES

Works attempting to throw up some special perspectives have been rare in Australian history-writing. The most notable are W. K. Hancock: *Australia* (1930), the most influential of the Tocqueville-style interpretations; Russel Ward: *The Australian Legend* (1958), the best of the applications of F. J. Turner's Frontier Theory to Australia's special conditions; and R. M. Crawford: *An Australian Perspective* (1960), which should be read to offset Hancock and Ward because of its emphasis on non-democratic as well as democratic trends in Australian history, the recognition of which can make present Australian society more intelligible. With it should be read Hugo Wolfsohn: "The Ideology Makers" in Henry Mayer (ed.): *Australian Politics. A Second Reader* (1969). James G. Murtagh: *Australia—the Catholic Chapter* (rev. 1969) is interesting as an expression of the pieties of a Catholic view of the Labor Movement. Geoffrey Blainey: *The Tyranny of Distance* (1966) goes fascinatingly beyond its own special concerns. Sean Glynn: *Urbanisation in Australian History, 1788-1900* (1970), was the first attempt to throw up general theories on Australia's high rate of urbanization, a subject until recently ignored by historians, but now supplemented by "Urbanization in Australia", a special issue of *Australian Economic History Review*, vol. x, no. 2 (1970).

AUSTRALIAN CLASSICS

Australian history-writing did not broaden out until after the Second World War. The earlier histories, e.g. G. W. Rusden: *A History of Australia* (3 vols, 2nd ed., 1897) or H. G. Turner: *A History of the Colony of Victoria* (2 vols, 1904) have little to interest the modern reader. The earliest real achievement was T. A. Coghlan: *Labour and Industry in Australia* (4 vols, 1918, reissued 1969), now coming back into fashion, as can be seen in the comments on it by E. C. Fry in *Historical Studies*, vol. 14, no. 55 (1970) and S. J. Butlin: *Australian Economic History Review*, vol. xi, no. 1 (1971). Apart from Scott's and Hancock's works there was little of significance in general histories. There were however some specialist studies, now become classics: Edward Shann: *An Economic History of Australia* (1930); S. H. Roberts: *History of Australian Land Settlement* (1924, reissued 1968); S. H. Roberts: *The Squatting Age in Australia, 1835-1847* (1935); Eris O'Brien: *The Foundation of Australia* (1937, 2nd ed. 1950); R. B. Madgwick: *Immigration into Eastern Australia 1788-1851* (1937)—see also the comment on this by R. J. Shultz in *Historical Studies*, vol. 14, no. 54 (1970); Brian Fitzpatrick: *British Imperialism and Australia 1788-1833* (1939) and *The British Empire in Australia 1834-1939* (reissued 1969).

NINETEENTH CENTURY CONTEMPORARY ACCOUNTS

W. C. Wentworth: *A Statistical Account of the British Settlements in Australasia* (3rd ed., 1824) was the first account of Australia by one of its native sons. J. T. Bigge: *Reports* (1822, 1823) provide the first attempt at a comprehensive account of Australian society. The two most widely read accounts for the early period are P. Cunningham: *Two Years in New South Wales* (1827, reprinted 1966) and "Alexander Harris": *Settlers and Convicts* (1847, reprinted 1969). A number of visitors gave their impressions: of these the best known are the chapters on Australia in Charles Darwin: *The Voyage of the Beagle* (1839, enlarged and revised 1845) and in C. W. Dilke: *Greater Britain: A Record of Travel in English-speaking Countries during 1866 and 1867* (1868); Anthony Trollope: *Australia and New Zealand* (1873: Australia section reissued 1967); R. E. N. Twopenny: *Town Life in Australia* (1883); J. A. Froude: *Oceana* (1886); A. G. Austin (ed.): *The Webb's Australian Diary 1898* (1965); Mark Twain: *Following the Equator* (1897); Joseph Conrad: *The Mirror of the Sea* (1906). Perhaps the best of them all is A. Métin: *Le Socialisme sans Doctrines* (1901).

Of the impressions of residents in the second half of the nineteenth century, the most interesting are Francis W. L. Adams: *Australian Essays* (1886) and *The Australians. A Social Sketch* (1893) and John

Stanley James: *The Vagabond Papers* (abridged edition, 1969). W. Pember Reeves: *State Experiments in Australia and New Zealand* (1902, reissued with an introduction by John Child, 1969) was the first attempt to provide an overall picture of the colonies as vehicles of Improvement. C. E. W. Bean: *On the Wool Track* (1910) can startle away clichés about rural life at that time. There is a compendium in Werner F. Friederich: *Australia in Western Imaginative Prose Writing, 1600-1960* (1967).

SELECTION OF DOCUMENTS

For those who would just like a taste of how it seemed at the time, C. M. H. Clark: *Sources of Australian History* (1957) and *Select Documents in Australian History*, vol. 1, 1788-1850 (1950), vol. 2, 1851-1900 (1955), provide an illuminating run through, with a rich bonus in the editor's prefatory notes to each section. An idea of the development of city life can be got from Alan Birch and David S. Macmillan: *The Sydney Scene* (1962) and James Grant and Geoffrey Serle: *The Melbourne Scene, 1803-1956* (1957), and of what it was like to be an explorer from Kathleen Fitzpatrick: *Australian Explorers, a Selection from Their Writings* (1958) and C. C. MacKnight: *The Farthest Coast. A Selection of Writing Related to the History of the Northern Coast of Australia* (1969). Contemporary accounts are collected in Russel Ward and John Robertson: *Such Was Life: Select Documents in Australian Social History, 1788-1850* (1969). Its difference in emphasis makes it interesting to compare with the earlier Helen Palmer and Jessie MacLeod: *The First Hundred Years of Australia as seen by the people who lived it* (1954). Some of the heights of Australian rhetoric are found in Ian Turner: *The Australian Dream* (1968). R. N. Ebbels (ed. L. G. Churchward): *The Australian Labor Movement, 1850-1907* (1960) gives extracts from contemporary documents of the working-class movement.

SPECIAL TOPICS

ABORIGINES

D. J. Mulvaney: *Prehistory of Australia* (1969) gives a report on the state of knowledge of this subject up to 1969. Not much that is any good has been written giving an historical account of relations between Aborigines and whites, except for C. D. Rowley: *The Destruc-*

tion of Aboriginal Society (1970), Outcasts in White Australia (1971) and The Remote Aborigines (1970), all of which make up the first real study of the effects of the guerilla war on the brown Australians.

CENSORSHIP

Peter Coleman: *Obscenity, Blasphemy, Sedition* (1962) provides a history of the growth of censorship in Australia, and Keith Dunstan: *Wowsers* (1968) of general restrictions on pleasure.

CULTURE

A (patchy) general introduction is to be found in A. L. McLeod (ed.): *The Pattern of Australian Culture* (1963). On writing, Geoffrey Dutton (ed.): *The Literature of Australia* (1964) and T. Inglis Moore: *Social Patterns in Australian Literature* (1971) are useful. Judith Wright: *Preoccupations in Australian Poetry* (1965) gives a valuable special perspective. On painting, Bernard Smith: *Australian Painting* (2nd ed. 1971) is now supplemented by Robert Hughes: *The Art of Australia* (1970). James Gleeson: *Masterpieces of Australian Painting* (1969) collects reproductions of some of the best known paintings. On music, Roger Covell: *Australia's Music* (1967) provides a sense of social background to its subject, as do J. M. Freeland: *Architecture in Australia. A History* (1968) and Robin Boyd: *Australia's Home. Its Origins, Builders and Occupiers* (1952) on architecture.

ECONOMIC

Although meant mainly as a school text, James Griffin (ed.): *Essays in the Economic History of Australia 1788-1939* (1967) is useful. Special studies are provided in Geoffrey Blainey: *The Rush that Never Ended. A History of Australian Mining* (1963, rev. 1964), Edgars Dunsdorfs: *The Australian Wheatgrowing Industry 1788-1948* (1956) and Helen Hughes: *The Australian Iron and Steel Industry* (1964).

EDUCATION

There are few general histories of education. Useful are A. G. Austin: *Australian Education 1788-1900* (1961); C. Turney (ed.): *Pioneers of Australian Education. A Study of the Development of Education in New South Wales in the Nineteenth Century* (1969); Alan Barcan: *A Short History of Education in New South Wales* (1965); Rupert Goodman: *Secondary Education in Queensland 1860-1960* (1968) S. Murray-Smith: "Technical Education in Australia—a

Historical Sketch", a chapter in E. L. Wheelwright (ed.): *Higher Education in Australia* (1965); and J. J. Auchmuty and A. N. Jeffares: "Australian Universities: the Historical Background", and E. L. French: "The Humanities in Australian Education", chapters in A. Grenfell Price (ed.): *The Humanities in Australia* (1959).

GOVERNMENT

For a country then so noted for its government action there is a remarkable lack of work on the nineteenth century bureaucracies. T. H. Kewley: *Social Security in Australia* (1965) is an extremely useful compendium. R. S. Parker: *Public Service Recruitment in Australia* (1942) tells some of the story. G. E. Caiden: *Career Service* (1965) gives a brief colonial background before describing the evolution of the Commonwealth Public Service. A. F. Davies: *Australian Democracy* (1958, rev. 1964) gives an analytical account of Australian styles.

LANGUAGE

Sidney J. Baker: *The Australian Language* (rev. ed. 1966) is as valuable (more valuable?) for its social comments than its philology, in showing the nation-defining use of language. Recent useful studies are: W. S. Ramson (ed.): *English Transported—Essays on Australian English* (1970) and W. S. Ramson: *Australian English* (1966).

REGIONAL

The only books really worth recommending are Douglas Pike: *Paradise of Dissent 1829-1857* (1957), a study of South Australia; Geoffrey Serle: *The Golden Age. A history of the Colony of Victoria 1851-1861* (1963) and *The Rush to be Rich* (1971); and F. K. Crowley: *Australia's Western Third* (1960). On New Zealand there is W. H. Oliver: *The Story of New Zealand* (1960) and Austin Mitchell: "A political scientist looks at New Zealand history", a chapter in *Politics and People in New Zealand* (1969).

RELIGION

The most interesting general studies are by and on Catholics: Patrick O'Farrell: *The Catholic Church in Australia* (1968); T. L. Sutton: *Hierarchy and Democracy in Australia, 1788-1870* (1965); John N. Molony: *The Roman Mould of the Australian Catholic Church* (1969).

PERIOD STUDIES

PART I—THE AGE OF AUTHORITY

The First Years
There is a profusion of contemporary accounts. Some of the earliest are collated in John Cobley (ed.): *Sydney Cove 1788* (1962), *Sydney Cove 1789-1790* (1963) and *Sydney Cove 1791-1792* (1965). Most popular at present is W. Tench (ed. Fitzhardinge): *Sydney's First Four Years* (1961). There are also the accounts of Hunter, Bradley, Southwell, Bowes, King, White, Clark, Collins and Scott.

General Histories and Biographies
O'Brien's *The Foundation of Australia* and Fitzpatrick's *British Imperialism and Australia* (1939) now give way to C. M. H. Clark: *A History of Australia*, vol. 1 (1962) and vol. 2 (1968) which, as well as being history, have some of the characteristics of a great nineteenth century novel. The best known early period biographies are G. Mackaness: *The Life of Vice-Admiral Bligh* (1931), M. H. Ellis: *Lachlan Macquarie, his Life, Adventures and Times* (1947), *Francis Greenway* (1949) and *John Macarthur* (1955). Hazel King: *Richard Bourke* (1971) gives a picture of Australia's first vice-regal Improver.

Early Society
What was left of old illusions about the convicts were cleaned up in L. L. Robson: *The Convict Settlers of Australia* (1965) and A. G. L. Shaw: *Convicts and the Colonies* (1966). There are interesting small studies in M. Roe: "Colonial Society in Embryo", *Historical Studies*, vol. 7, no. 26 (1956); Ken Macnab and Russel Ward: "The Nature and Nurture of the First Generation of Native born Australians", *Historical Studies*, vol. 10, no. 39 (1962); L. A. Whitfield: *Founders of the Law in Australia* (1969); Kelvin Grose: "William Grant Broughton and National Education in N.S.W., 1829-1836" in E. L. French (ed.): *Melbourne Studies in Education* (1965); J. A. La Nauze: "The Collection of Customs in Australia: a note on Administration" in *Historical Studies*, vol. 4, no. 13 (1949); Hazel King: "Some Aspects of Police Administration in New South Wales, 1825-1851", *Journal of the Royal Australian Historical Society*, vol. 42, part 5 (1956). On different aspects of the frontier the following are valuable: T. M. Perry: *Australia's First Frontier* (1963); H. C. Allen: *Bush and Backwoods* (1959); John M. R. Young: *Australia's Pacific Frontier* (1967); M. Roe: "Australia's Place in the Swing to the East, 1788-1810" in *Historical Studies*, vol. 8, no. 30 (1958); and Geoffrey Blainey's emphasis on the sea frontier in *Tyranny of Distance*.

Economic

S. J. Butlin: *Foundations of the Australian Monetary System, 1788-1821* (1953) has already become a classic. G. J. Abbott and N. B. Nairn (ed.): *Economic Growth of Australia, 1788-1821* (1969) provides a good, comprehensive run through. D. R. Hainsworth: *Builders and Adventurers* (1968) clears up some old mysteries about how a convict settlement quickly became a get-rich-quick society and presumably ends old historians' squabbles about the Rum Corps. Margaret Kiddle: *Men of Yesterday, A Social History of the Western District of Victoria, 1834-1890* (1961) and Marnie Bassett: *The Hentys, An Australian Colonial Tapestry* (1954) give human accounts of the squatting age. Special aspects of the wool rush are taken up in E. H. Beever: "The Origin of the Wool Industry in N.S.W.", in *Business Archives and History*, vol. 5, no. 2 (1965); K. Buckley: "Gipps and the Graziers of N.S.W.", in *Historical Studies*, vol. 6, no. 24 (1955) and vol. 7, no. 26 (1956); D. W. A. Baker: "The Squatting Age in Australia", in *Business Archives and History*, vol. 5, no. 2 (1965). Some of these test some of the approaches in S. H. Roberts's *The Squatting Age in Australia*.

The Coming of Improvement

A new interest was given to the second quarter of the nineteenth century (long neglected, except for rural life) by George Nadel: *Australia's Colonial Culture* (1957); Michael Roe: *The Quest for Authority in Eastern Australia, 1835-1851* (1965); and John Barrett: *That Better Country. The Religious Aspect of Life in Eastern Australia 1835-1856* (1966). All three—referred to in Paul F. Bourke: "Some Recent Essays in Australian Intellectual History", *Historical Studies*, vol. 13, no. 49 (1967)—help solve the puzzle of the connection between then and now. In fact it was only after reading Roe's book that I realized that it was possible to write this book. L. J. Hulme: "Working Class Movements in Sydney and Melbourne before the Gold Rushes", *Historical Studies, Selected Articles, Second series* (1967) gives another example of the transplant to Australia of English institutions of Improvement. Glimpses of some aspects of Australian intellectual and social life are provided by J. Normington-Rawling: *Charles Harpur, An Australian* (1962). A. C. V. Melbourne: *Early Constitutional Development in Australia* (1963) gives an overall framework, and Margaret Kerr: "The British Parliament and Transportation in the Eighteen Fifties", *Historical Studies*, vol. 6, no. 21 (1953) gives the background to the crisis with Britain; but Ruth Knight: *Illiberal Liberal. Robert Lowe in New South Wales, 1842-1850* (1966) brings it all splendidly to life and Terry Irving and Baiba Ferzins: "History and the New Left: Beyond Radicalism" in Richard Gordon (ed.): *The Australian New Left* (1970) makes an attempt at comprehensive theory.

PART 2—THE AGE OF IMPROVEMENT

Gold and Melbourne
The gold rushes are no longer seen as decisive in Australian history as they were in *The Eureka Centenary Supplement, Historical Studies* (1954). Useful sidelights are given in G. Blainey: "Gold and Governors", *Historical Studies*, vol. 9, no. 36 (1961) and "The Gold Rushes: the Year of Decision", *Historical Studies*, vol. 10, no. 38 (1962), Bruce Kent: "Agitations on the Victorian Gold Fields, 1851-4", *Historical Studies*, vol. 6, no. 23 (1954) and D. R. G. Packer: "Victorian Population Data", *Historical Studies*, vol. 5, no. 20 (1953); but full accounts are given in Serle's *The Golden Age* and Blainey's *The Rush that Never Ended*. Charles Bateson: *Gold Fleet for California* (1963) describes the rush out of Australia. For the continuing story of Melbourne, see the excellent chapter "Melbourne, a Victorian Community Overseas" in Asa Briggs: *Victorian Cities* (1963); and for Melbourne's downfall Michael Cannon: *The Land Boomers* (1966).

Economic
Much background analysis is given in N. G. Butlin: *Investment in Australian Economic Development 1861-1900* (1964), a book that liberated thinking about economic development in this period, not least the importance of urban development. Other background can be found in Alex Hunter (ed.): *The Economics of Australian Industry* (1963) and F. G. Davidson: *The Industrialization of Australia* (1957, second ed. 1960). Special studies can be found in Helen Hughes: *The Australian Iron and Steel Industry, 1848-1962* (1964); Alan Barnard: *Visions and Profits. Studies in the Business Career of T. S. Mort* (1961); Alan Birch and David S. MacMillan (ed.): *Wealth and Progress. Studies in Australian Business History* (1967); A. H. Morris: "Echuca and the Murray River Trade", *Historical Studies*, vol. 4, no. 16 (1951). On wool: Alan Barnard: *The Australian Wool Market 1840-1900* (1958). D. W. A. Baker: "The Origins of Robertson's Land Acts", *Historical Studies*, vol. 8, no. 30 (1958), and N. G. Butlin: " 'Company Ownership' of N.S.W. Pastoral Stations, 1865-1900", *Historical Studies*, vol. 4, no. 14 (1950), both raised new theories about old subjects.

Education
The annual publication *Melbourne Studies in Education* (M.S.E.) shows continuing interest in this period. For the long fight over the system of education: A. R. Crane: "The New South Wales Public Schools League, 1874-1879", in *M.S.E. 1964*; Kenneth E. Dear: "Bishop Perry and the Rise of National Education in Victoria, 1848-1873", in *M.S.E., 1965*; Mary Raphael Leavey: "The Relevance of St. Thomas Aquinas for Australian Education", in

M.S.E., *1963*. For something of the quality of education: G. E. Saunders: "Public Secondary Education in South Australia—The Nineteenth Century Background", in *M.S.E.*, *1968-1969*; A. M. Badcock: "The Vocational Fallacy in State Secondary Education in Victoria, 1900-1925", in *M.S.E.*, *1965*; C. Turney: "The Rise and Decline of an Australian Inspectorate", in *M.S.E.*, *1970*. For the general secularist background: J. S. Gregory: "Church and State in Victoria, 1851-72", *Historical Studies*, vol. 5, no. 20 (1953).

Labour Movement
The story of what until recently was one of the most significant unions in Australia is told in Robin Gollan: *The Coalminers of New South Wales. A History of the Union, 1860-1960* (1963). More general accounts are given in Robin Gollan: *Radical and Working Class Politics. A Study of Eastern Australia, 1850-1910* (1960) and Ian Turner: *Industrial Labour and Politics. The Labour Movement in Eastern Australia 1900-1921* (1965).

There are special studies in Helen Hughes: "The Eight Hour Day and the Development of the Labour Movement in Victoria in the Eighteen Fifties", *Historical Studies*, vol. 9, no. 36 (1961); N. B. Nairn: "The Role of the Trades and Labour Council in New South Wales, 1871-91", *Historical Studies*, vol. 7, no. 28 (1957); L. G. Churchward: "The American Influence on the Australian Labour Movement", *Historical Studies*, vol. 5, no. 19 (1952); N. B. Nairn: "The 1890 Maritime Strike in N.S.W.", *Historical Studies*, vol. 10, no. 37 (1961); A. A. Morrison: "The Brisbane General Strike of 1912", *Historical Studies*, vol. 4, no. 14 (1950). Some of the story of Catholic influence in the Labour movement is told in: Patrick Ford: *Cardinal Moran and the A.L.P.* (1966); Celia Hamilton: "Irish Catholics of N.S.W. and the Labor Party 1890-1910", *Historical Studies*, vol. 8, no. 31 (1958), and "Catholic Interests and the Labor Party: Organized Catholic Action in Victoria and N.S.W. 1910-1916", *Historical Studies*, vol. 9, no. 33 (1959). The story of the unsuccessful export of Australian utopianism to Paraguay is told in Gavin Souter: *A Peculiar People; The Australians in Paraguay* (1968). A counterblast on traditional views of the nature of the Labour movement (or what he alleges them to be) is found in Humphrey McQueen: *A New Britannia* (1970).

Politics
The groundwork of finding system in the apparent mess of the faction period in politics was provided by A. W. Martin: "Henry Parkes and Electoral Manipulation, 1872-1882", *Historical Studies*, vol. 8, no. 31 (1958), and P. Loveday and A. W. Martin: *Parliament,*

Factions and Parties; The First Thirty Years of Responsible Government in N.S.W. 1856-1889 (1966). Sidelights on this period are provided in Brian Dickey: *Politics in New South Wales 1856-1900* (1969). The story is continued in Joan Rydon and R. N. Spann: *New South Wales Politics, 1901-1910* (1962). Cyril Pearl: *Wild Men of Sydney* (1958) gives an idea of how tough Australian politics could be. There are several particular studies: J. M. Main: "Making Constitutions in New South Wales and Victoria 1853-1854", *Historical Studies, Selected Articles, Second Series* (1967) and Joy E. Parnaby: "The Composition of the Victorian Parliament 1851-1881", *Historical Studies, Selected Articles, Second Series* (1967). An extraordinary sidelight on fringe politics is found in Henry Mayer: *Marx, Engels and Australia* (1964).

Nationalism and Imperialism

The main paintings of the Impressionist school can be found in Alan McCulloch: *The Golden Age of Australian Painting* (1969). There is a background to the uses of bushrangers as proto-Australians in R. B. Walker: "Bushranging in Fact and Legend", *Historical Studies*, vol. 11, no. 42 (1964). Vance Palmer: *The Legend of the Nineties* (new ed. 1963) is interesting as an example of what was once believed. K. S. Inglis: "Australia Day", *Historical Studies*, vol. 13, no. 49 (1967) is relevant to Australians' difficulties in deciding what they were going to be nationalist about. B. Mansfield: "The Background to Radical Republicanism in New South Wales in the Eighteen Eighties", *Historical Studies*, vol. 5, no. 20 (1953) records a failed movement. It should be read in conjunction with Charles S. Blackton: "Australian Nationality and Nationalism: The Imperial Federationist Interlude 1885-1901", *Historical Studies, Selected Articles, Second Series* (1967). For other imperialist episodes, see Marjorie G. Jacobs: "Bismarck and the Annexation of New Guinea", *Historical Studies*, vol. 5, no. 17 (1951); and "The Colonial Office and New Guinea", *Historical Studies*, vol. 5, no. 18 (1952); B. R. Penny: "The Age of Empire: An Australian Episode", *Historical Studies*, vol. 11, no. 41 (1963) and Barbara Penny: "The Australian Debate on the Boer War", *Historical Studies*, vol. 14, no. 56 (1971). For English attitudes and the relation of defence to federation there is Luke Trainor: "British Imperial Defence Policy and the Australian Colonies, 1892-96", *Historical Studies*, vol. 14, no. 54 (1970). For the collapse of nationalism, Charles Grimshaw: "Australian Nationalism and the Imperial Connection 1900-1914", *Politics and History*, vol. 3, no. 2 (1958). On immigration policy: A. T. Yarwood: "The 'White Australia' Policy: A Re-interpretation of the Development in the Late Colonial Period", *Historical Studies*, vol. 10, no. 39 (1962) and Myra Willard: *History of the White Australia Policy to 1920* (1923).

Federation
Why the Australian colonies federated still tends to mystify historians. There was an attempt to raise new issues in R. S. Parker: "Australian Federation: The Influence of Economic Interests and Political Pressures", *Historical Studies*, vol. 4, no. 13 (1949); but the quick reply by Geoffrey Blainey: "The Role of Economic Interests in Australian Federation", *Historical Studies*, vol. 4, no. 15 (1950) seemed to end the discussion until A. W. Martin (ed.): *Essays in Australian Federation* (1969). However a significant biography of the man most notably associated with the articulation of the new nation came out in that period—J. A. La Nauze: *Alfred Deakin*, 2 vols (1965). Deakin's own account, *The Federal Story*, was not published until 1944. Since then, there has been a selection of his newspaper dispatches in Alfred Deakin: *Federated Australia. Selections from Letters to the Morning Post 1900-1910* (1968). That he was anonymously acting as Australian political correspondent to a newspaper in London while he was Prime Minister, even commenting on his own actions, gives Deakin a unique niche in the world history of statecraft. A contemporary account of the beginnings of the Federal Parliament is provided in Henry Gyles Turner: *The First Decade of the Australian Commonwealth* (1911).

PART 3—THE AGE OF IMPERIALISM

Of the "state of Australia" books in the 1960s, the first was John Douglas Pringle: *Australian Accent* (1958). This was followed by Robin Boyd: *The Australian Ugliness* (1960), Peter Coleman (ed.): *Australian Civilization* (1962), Donald Horne: *The Lucky Country* (1964, rev. several times but the best edition to give a picture of the period is the first rev. ed., 1965); Craig Macgregor: *Profile of Australia* (1966); Donald Horne: *The Next Australia* (1970) and Ronald Conway: *The Great Australian Stupor. An Interpretation of the Australian Way of Life* (1971). Of a different type are A. F. Davies and S. Encel: *Australian Society. A Sociological Introduction* (2nd ed., 1970) and S. Encel: *Equality and Authority. A Study of Class, Status and Power in Australia* (1970), valuable both for its information and some of its ideas.

Of the autobiographies that became fashionable in the 1960s the most useful for social insights are Jack Lindsay: *The Roaring Twenties* (1960), Hal Porter: *The Watcher on the Cast Iron Balcony* (1963) and *The Paper Chase* (1966), Donald Horne: *The Education of Young Donald* (1967), and George Johnston: *My Brother Jack* (1964) and *Clean Straw for Nothing* (1969).

Egon Kisch: *Australian Landfall* (1937, reissued 1969 with a foreword by A. T. Yarwood) and H. G. Wells: *Travels of a Republican*

Radical in Search of Hot Water (1939) bring together many of the moods and discontents of the 1930s. The most widely quoted account is D. H. Lawrence: *Kangaroo* (1923). A source book of many of the criticisms of Australians is J. B. Bryce: *Modern Democracies* (1921).

Economic
Colin Forster (ed.): *Australian Economic Development in the Twentieth Century* (1970) covers the field. C. B. Schedvin: *Australia and the Great Depression* (1970) is a useful special study. W. D. Forsyth: *The Myth of Open Spaces* (1942) and B. R. Davidson: *The Northern Myth* (1965) give contemporary expression to two moods of disillusion. There is an account of the greatest of the industrial men of will in Geoffrey Blainey: *The Steel Master* (1971).

Foreign Policy
W. J. Hudson (ed.): *Towards a Foreign Policy 1914-1941* (1967) gives a quick run through. E. M. Andrews provides a special study in "The Australian Government and Appeasement" in the *Australian Journal of Politics and History* vol. 13, no. 1 (1967). Questions of what kinds of initiatives Australia took in this period are argued in J. R. Poynter: "The Yo-Yo Variations", *Historical Studies*, vol. 14, no. 54 (1970) and a comment on this by W. J. Hudson in *Historical Studies*, vol. 14, no. 55 (1970). Australian-U.S. relations are considered in Raymond A. Esthus: *From Enmity to Alliance. U.S.-Australian Relations, 1931-1941* (1964) and Norman Harper (ed.): *Australia and the United States* (1971). Of the post-war period, probably the best account is Alan Watt: *The Evolution of Australian Foreign Policy* (1967). There are special studies in Trevor R. Reese: *Australia, New Zealand and the United States, 1941-1968* (1969) and Henry S. Albinski: *Australian Policies and Attitudes Towards China* (1965) provides a useful sampling of ideas at that time.

Politics
V. G. Childe: *How Labour Governs* (1923, reissued 1964) is an example of a certain kind of contemporary disillusion. Bernie Schedvin: "E. G. Theodore and the London Pastoral Lobby", *Politics*, vol. vi, no. 1 (1971) give a fascinating vignette of how British pressure could be applied to Australian politics; and Miriam Dixson: "Ideology, the Trades Hall Reds and Lang", *Politics*, vol. vi, no. 1 (1971) provides an example of shifts between faction and ideology. To this can be added Robert Cooksey: *Lang and Socialism* (1971). B. D. Graham: *The Formation of the Australian Country Parties* (1966) and Ulrich Ellis: *A History of the Australian Country Party* (1963) are useful both for their special subject and a general background to the times. A. F. Davies: *Australian Democracy* (2nd ed., 1964), Louise Overacker: *The Australian Party System*

(1952), S. Encel: *Cabinet Government in Australia* (1962), Katherine West: *Power in the Liberal Party* (1965) and Colin A. Hughes (ed.): *Readings in Australian Government* (1968) give analytical accounts. Of the political biographies L. F. Crisp: *Ben Chifley* (1960) and Irwin Young: *Theodore, His Life and Times* (1971) are the most worth reading. W. Denning: *Caucus Crisis* (1937) and Alan Reid: *The Power Struggle* (1969) give accounts of two particular political crises. Robert Murray: *The Split: Australian Labor in the fifties* (1970) gives a fascinating run through on Labor's civil war.

World War I
There is a description of the pre-war anti-conscription battle in L. C. Jauncey: *The Story of Conscription in Australia* (1935, reissued with a foreword by P. O'Farrell, 1968) and of wartime attempts at conscription in L. L. Robson: *The First A.I.F. A Study in Its Recruitment, 1914-1918* (1970). C. E. W. Bean (ed.: *Official History of Australia in the War of 1914-1918*, 12 vols, 1921-37) includes one volume on the home front by Ernest Scott. There is a useful potted history in C. E. W. Bean: *Anzac to Amiens. A Shorter History of the Australian Fighting Services in the First World War* (1946). K. S. Inglis: "The Australians at Gallipoli", *Historical Studies*, vol. 14, no. 54 and vol. 14, no. 55 (1970) gives an account of the beginning of the Anzac Legend. Ian Turner: *Sydney's Burning* (rev. 1969) describes the wartime actions of the I.W.W. and their treatment.

World War II
Of the 22 volumes of *Australia in the War of 1939-1945*, the volumes on civil affairs are Paul Hasluck: *The Government and the People, 1934-41* (1952) and 1942-45 (1970), S. J. Butlin: *War Economy, 1939-42* (1955) and D. P. Mellor: *The Role of Science and Industry* (1958).

INDEX

Aborigines, way of life, xiii-xiv; not understood, 17-18, 54; killing of, 17, 54; dispossessed by squatters, 53-4; "protection" of, 55, 164; attitudes to, 109, 211, 233, 235-6, 247; in literature, 211; referendum on (1967), 236
Abortion, 246
"Academics", 243
Adams, Francis, (quoted), 115, 116, 121, 156
Adelaide, 62, 123, 126
Advocate (Melbourne), (quoted), 175
Aeroplanes, first, 137
Agriculture, 63, 122, 135; improvement in methods of, 106-7, 138; training colleges for, 115; expansion of, 134; and closer settlement, 135; Departments of, 138, 236
Air Force, in World War II, 220
Aircraft industry, 225
Airlines, government, 226
Amusements, 92-3, 231-2
Americans, criticism of, 207-8
Anderson, John, 212
Angry Penguins, 227
Anniversary Day, 65-6
Antarctic expeditions, 157
Anti-transportation League, 73
"Anzac", term first used, 176
Anzac Day, 177, 187, 206, 249
Anzus Treaty, 255, 256
Arbitration, 102, 130, 131, 167
Architecture, 67; in the cities, 137, 237; in the suburbs, 141, 188, 190, 230-1, 237
Armaments industry, 224-5
Army, 208, 256; citizen, 168; in World War I, 178-82, 184; in World War II, 217-22. *See also* Australian Imperial Force

Art. *See* Painting
Asia, the threat of, 257; immigrants from, 259
Auckland, 63
Australia, founding of, xiv-xvii; extent of settlement in 1820, 6; naming of, 16, 61; British claims extended, 25-6; a nation?, 66-7, 69, 122, 152-6; demand for self-government, 74; federation of colonies, 163; its flag, 164; a national capital for, 173-4; and Britain, 206-7, 209; and the United States, 222, 257; its peaceful history 235, 261; and South-east Asia, 255, 256-7, 258-60; as a Pacific power, 258, 259
Australian Council of Trade Unions (A.C.T.U.), 212-3, 216, 228-9
Australian Freedom League, 175
Australian Imperial Force (A.I.F.), *In World War I*, volunteers for 175, 184; at Gallipoli, 176-7; the men of, 177, 179; on the Western Front, 178, 181-2; recruiting for, 182; in Palestine, 184; memorials to, 186, 187; benefits for returned men, 186-7. *In World War II*, volunteers for, 217; in the Middle East, 217, 218-19, 220; in Malaya, 219; in New Guinea, 221, 222
Australian Mutual Provident Society (A.M.P.), 32
Australian Patriotic Association, 56, 57
Australian Subscription Library, 22
Australian Ugliness, The, 244
Australians, described by visitors, 119, 155, 189, 198-9, 215
Australians, qualities in character

of: individualism, 8; respectability, 14, 15, 16, 34, 140-1; self-reliance, 16; snobbery, 20-1, 70, 71; national pride, 24-5, 152, 154-5, 168, 176, 179, 254; independence, 35, 95; tolerance, 35-6, 235; belief in material progress, 41, 132-4, 233-4, 248, 260; sense of mateship or brotherhood, 70-1, 81, 155, 177, 210; radicalism, 71, 72, 73, 147; puritanism, 87, 133; Britishness, 117-18, 142-5, 253; larrikinism, 119, 153, 154, 210; respect for wealth, 128, 129; cult of the bushman, 154, 155, 210; egalitarianism, 155, 189-90, 214; suburbanism, 188-93; devotion to sport, 209-10; pursuit of pleasure, 231-2, 261; informality, 233-4; growth of sophistication, 242-7, 261; self-examination, 244-5, 246, 260-1

Ballarat, 79, 80, 83
Ballarat Reform League, 82
Beersheba, 184
Bigge, John Thomas, 4
Bligh, William, 4
Boer War, 145
Bolsheviks, 195, 196
Book Censorship League, 214
Bourke, *Sir* Richard, 36, 40
Bradman, *Sir* Donald, 215
Brennan, Christopher, 211, 213
Brisbane, 65
Britain, imports from, 89, 110; its immigrants, 97, 98-9, 116; its military garrison withdrawn (1870), 122; Australia's loyalty to, 142-4, 204, 206-7, 208, 250-1, 253-4; criticism of, 157-8; its strategy in World War I, 178, 181-2; financial domination by, 208-9; and the British Commonwealth, 253-4; in World War II, 219, 222; and the E.E.C., 254, 260
Broadcasting, 137, 191
Broken Hill Proprietary Company, 138, 199, 225

Bruce, S. M., 208
Building societies, 34-5
Bullecourt, 181
Bulletin (Sydney), 120, 154-5, 158, 210, 244
Buna, 221
Bushrangers, 51, 119-20
Businessmen, in Parliament, 109; lack education, 200, 201; status of, 202, 224-5, 228; educated in management, 240-2

Cables, the first, 91
Canberra, 173-4
Carmichael, Henry, 40, 41
Catholic Action, 213, 228-9, 250
Catholic Federation, 174
Catholic Social Movement, 256
Catholic Worker, 213
Catholic Workers' Association, 174
Censorship, 194, 214, 246-7
Chambers of Manufactures, Associated, 129
Chief Justice, first, 23
Chifley, J. B., 224, 226, 228
China, fear of, 257
Chinese, on goldfields, 83, 84; hostility to, 102, 158; in Queensland, 123
Chisholm, Caroline, 37
Church of England, 2, 12, 39; the one endowed church, 14, 23; land grants to, 23; ceases to be State church, 36-7
Churches, government subsidies to, 36, 39
Cinema, 133, 191, 192; Australian, 210
Citizen army, 168
Civil Service, becomes Public Service, 140. *See* Public Service
Class distinctions, 70, 98, 110, 128
Closer Settlement, 135, 197
Clubs, gentlemen's, 43, 195; wealth of sporting, 232
Coal industry, 138, 226, 238
Coalminers, 102, 146, 196
Cobb and Co., 90
Cocky farmers, 105-6, 107, 198
Colombo Plan, 255

Commonwealth Bank, 200
Commonwealth Government, 161, 164-5; its functions and policies, 165, 166, 167, 168; in the Depression, 202-3, 204, 205; its subservience to Britain, 208-9; growth of its powers, 225; and social welfare, 226-7; its conservatism, 249-52
Commonwealth Literary Fund, 167
Communist Party of Australia, formed (1922), 195; and the unions, 212-13; and the Catholics, 213, 216, 228; and Nazism, 215, 216; and the Labor Party, 229, 250
Conscription, in peacetime, 168; in World War I, 179-80, 181, 183; in World War II, 220
Contemporary Art Society, 212
Convicts, the first, xvi, 9-10; character of, 10-11; assignment of, 12, 19-20; emancipation of, 13-14; children of, 15-16; outnumbered by immigrants, 30-1; and the wool industry, 53; end of transportation, 73. *See also* Emancipists
Cook, James, xiv-xv
Copper, 62, 138
Coral Sea, 221
Council for Scientific and Industrial Research (now C.S.I.R.O.), founded (1926), 201; its achievements, 201-2, 236, 242
Cricket, 93, 132
Currency, early shortage of, 6-7
"Currency" lads and lasses, 16
Curtin, John, 222
Cyprus, 218

Dad and Dave, 198
Daily Telegraph, 195
Dairying, advances in, 135, 138
Darwin, 220
Darwin, Charles, (quoted), 14, 28, 34, 44, 248
Davis Cup, 156, 231
Deakin, Alfred, 157, 166-7
Democracy and "the people", 11, 71, 72, 98-9
Democratic Labor Party, 250
Depression, the, 202-5
Diggers, in the goldfields, 81, 88; in World War I, 181, 186-8; in World War II, 222
Divorce laws, 130
Dole, the, 203
"D.Ps", 224
Drought of 1902, 127
Drysdale, Russell, 244

Echuca, 90
Education, limitations of, 42-3, 44, 115-16, 128-9, 210; State and secular, 99; secondary, 115, 141-2; lack of technical, 114-15, 129, 220; technical and professional in universities, 137, 138-9; compulsory, 173; in the 1930s, 200-1; advance in technical, 225, 241-2; and the rise of the "executive", 239, 240-2
Eight-hour Day, 86, 96, 132, 146
Electricity, 91, 190
Elizabeth II, 253, 255
Emancipists, 13-14, 56-7, 248, 261
"Empire Settlement Scheme", 207, 208-9
Employers' Federation, 150, 174
Employment, White Paper on full, 227
Eureka Stockade, 83, 155, 211
European Economic Community, 254, 260
Evatt, H. V., 223, 250, 254-5
Evangelism, 15, 87
"Executive", rise of the, 240-2
Expatriates in Britain, 245
Exploration, 5, 45-6, 210; by sea, 6, 26-7
External Affairs, Department of, 216, 223, 259
Eyre, E. J., 46

Factory legislation, 101, 130
Farming, early setbacks to, 5-6; and closer settlement, 135, 197-8, 238; in World War I, 180, 183; in the Depression, 204-5. *See also* Agriculture

Index

Federation, 160-4; attitudes to, 68-9, 161, 162; drafting constitution for, 161, 162. *See also* Commonwealth Government
First Fleet, complement of, xvi-xvii
Fitchett, W. H., 144
FitzGerald, R. D., 212
Fitzroy, *Sir* Charles, 58, 72
Foreign Affairs, Department of, 259
Forty-hour week (1948), 233
Free selection, failure of, 135
Free Trade *v.* Protection, 165
Freemasonry, 174
Friendly Societies, 32
Fromelles, 178
Froude, J. A., (quoted), 94
Furphy, Joseph, 210-11

Gallipoli, 176-7
Gambling, 189
Gaol Fund, 3
Gas, first use of, 190
General Motors Holden, 236
George, Henry, 149
Germans, in World War II, 218-19; as immigrants, 224
Gerrymandering, 194
Gilroy, *Sir* Norman, 234
Gipps, *Sir* George, 57, 58
Gold, discovery of, 79, 80; and the diggers, 80-3; in Western Australia, 126
Gona, 221
Gordon, Adam Lindsay, 121
Gordon of Khartoum, 144, 145
Gorton, John G., 252, 254
Governors, the first, military opposition to, 4, 8-9; power of, 8, 9, 22-3, 56, 57; and the Legislative Council (1844), 57
Governors-General, 164, 207, 253
Grace, W. G., 93
Granlund, Laurence, 149
Greece, 218
Griffin, Walter Burley, 174
"Groupers", 250, 256
Guam, 219

Haig, *Earl*, 178, 181, 182
Hanging, 246

Harpur, Charles, 41, 67-8, 244
Health scheme, national, 233
High schools, 115, 141-2, 241
Hire purchase, 231
Hitler, Adolf, 215, 216
Homosexuality, 11, 51, 192, 247
Hong Kong, 219-20
Holt, Harold, 256, 257
Hope, A. D., 243, 244, 246
Hotel trading hours, 130, 232
Housing, in the detached cottage, 34-5, 94-5; investment in, 88; as progress, 249; for the rich, 110; in the suburbs, 147, 188, 190, 230-1; in flats, 237
Hughes, W. M., 177, 180, 184-5, 215
Hunter, John, 4

Immigrants, first assisted, 29-31; effect of, on the "Natives", 31-4, 56; influence of, 70-1; population increase by (1880), 89; in Parliament, 97; outnumber native born, 117, 119; necessary to progress (1910), 127, 129; in the twenties, 197; only British sought, 197, 207, 253; foreign (European), 215, 224, 235; fading of hostility to, 235; Asians as, 259
Imperial Conference (1923), 208
Imperial Federation League, 143
Imperialism, the concept of, 142-5, 168, 179
Imports, British, 89, 209
Indonesia, 223-4, 257
Industry, lack of education for, 201; stimulated by the Depression, 205; wartime development of, 224-5, subsequent growth, 236-7. *See also* Manufacturing
Insurance, national, 193
Intellectuals, in the 1930s, 213-14; influence of, 246-7; and the failure of government, 251; their view of Australia, 259, 261
International Exhibition (1879), 91
Invalid pensions, 130
Irish in Australia, 11-12, 37, 38, 39; and Catholicism, 111-12, 234-5
Irish Rifle Corps, 149

280 Index

Iron ore, export of, 238
Irrigation, 135, 198
Italians, 207
I.W.W. (Industrial Workers of the World), 145-6, 180

Johnson, Lyndon B., 256, 257
Japan, seen as threat, 168; moves for race equality, 185; duties on its imports, 209; in World War II, 215, 216, 217, 219-20, 221, 222, 223; Australia's best customer, 258
Jevons, W. S., 35
Jindyworobaks, 211
Kalgoorlie, 207
Kanakas, 123
Kelly, *Archbishop*, (quoted), 174, 175
Kendall, Henry, 121
King's Cross, 191
Kingsley, Henry, 117
Kokoda, 221
Korea, 255

Labor Party, emergence of, 148-51; advocates compulsory military training (1908), 168; wins power in 1910, 173; progressive measures of, 173, 174, 193, 197, 226; and the trade unions, 174; supports conscription in World War I, 179; split and defeated, 180, 181, 183; gains power in three States, 196-7; split in the Depression, 203, 204; attitude to Britain, 207; communist infiltration of, 212-13, 228-9; policy on defence, 217; takes over in 1941, 219; defeat of (1949), 228, 249; reasons for collapse of, 250, 252
Labour Electoral Leagues, 148
Land, grants abolished (1831), 20; the desire for, 29-30, 34; absentee ownership of, 49; and free selection, 105-6; and closer settlement, 135; for returned soldiers, 186
Lang, J. T., 203-4, 212, 216
"Lang Plan", 203
Larrikins, 119; as heroes, 153, 210; in suburbia, 261

Law, faculties of, 139
Lawrence, D. H., 245; (quoted), 189, 190, 215
Lead, 138
League of Nations, 185, 216
Legend of King O'Malley, The, 246
Legislative Council (N.S.W.), 22-3, 38; character and membership of, 57, 69, 70, 110; conservatism of, 174, 194
Leo XIII, *Pope*, 149
Liberal Party, formed to combat Labor, 151, 174, 227, 228; and communism, 229; conservatism of, 249-52
Libraries in 1935, 201
Libya, 218
Life-saving clubs, 131-2
Lindsay, Norman, 212
Literature, 66-7, 121, 153-4, 210-11, 212, 243-4, 246
Long service leave, 233
Lotteries, 189
Lowe, Robert, 72
Loyal Orange Lodge, 150
Lucky Country, The, (quoted), 239, 244
Lutherans, 63
Lyons, J. A., 204, 215, 216

Macarthur, *General* Douglas, 220-1
Macarthur, John, 194
McAuley, James, 243, 244, 246
McEwen, John, 211
"McKenzie", "Barry", 245
Macquarie, Lachlan, 3, 5, 13, 16
Malaya, 219, 255
"Management", training in, 240-2
Manufacturing, growth in, 95, 110, 128, 198, 199-200; and tariff protection, 167, 199, 200; in World War II, 224-5; foreign investment in, 237
Maoris, 64, 122
Marconi Company, 137
Maritime strike (1890), 146
Mateship, 51-2, 81, 155; and the A.I.F., 177, 179, 188; as a creed, 211
Meanjin, 227

Mechanics' Institutes, 40-1, 114
Medicine, faculties of, 139
Melba, Nellie, 157, 164
Melbourne, beginnings of, 65, 79; its prosperity, 84-5, 86-7, 92; rivalry with Sydney, 122; financial disaster in, 124-5
Melbourne Cup, 93
Menzies, R. G., 216, 250-1, 255; his attitude to Britain, 253, 256
Methodist Church. *See* Wesleyan Church
Middle East, 219, 220
"Migrants", 235
Militia, compulsory service in, 168, 175
Mill, John Stuart, 98
Milne Bay, 221
Minerals, discovery of, 62; new discoveries, 138-9; neglected for agriculture, 198; boom in, 238, 239
Miners, militancy of, 147
Mannix, *Archbishop*, 180; (quoted), 234
Monash, *Sir* John, 184
Moran, *Cardinal*, 145, 149
Moreton Bay District, 26, 48-9, 65
Motor-cars, 199; manufacture of, 236
Mount Lyell Copper Company, 138
Munich agreement, 215
Municipal Councils, 133
Music, 67, 120-1, 243
Mussolini, 216
Mutual Protection Association, 71
Myxomatosis, 236

Nationalist Party, 181, 193, 195
"Natives", and "nobs", 24, 56; qualities of, 25; and free immigrants, 33-4; pushed aside by squatters, 49-50
Natural gas, 238
Navy, Australia's own, 168
Nazism, 215, 216
"New Australia", 135
"New Australians", 224
"New Guard", 204
New Guinea, claimed for Britain, 118; the Australian mandate, 185; in World War II, 220-1, 222
New Hebrides, 118
"New Protection", 167
New South Wales, self-government achieved for, 74; population (1880), 88; in the Depression, 203, 203-4
New South Wales Corps, 4, 7, 9
New Zealand, 27, 60; first settlement, 63; Maori influence in, 64, 122; gold in, 121-2; central government in, 122; in World War I, 175; in World War II, 217, 218
Newcastle, 6, 26, 139
Night clubs, 190-1
Nolan, Sidney, 244

Old-age pensions, 130
One Day of the Year, The, 243
Orange Lodges, 104, 150
Orphan Fund, 3
Owen Stanley Range, 221

Pacific Non-aggression Pact, 216
Paddle-steamers, 90
Painting, 67, 120, 153, 154, 210, 212, 227, 243, 244
Palestine, 184
Pasteurization, 138
Parkes, Henry, 103, 104, 157
Party politics, 103; beginnings of, 148-51
Pastoral Association (1844), 57
Paul VI, *Pope*, 235
Peace Preservation Act, 146-7
Pearl Harbour, 219
Pearling, 126
Pensions, 226
Phar Lap, 210
Philippines, 208, 219
Phillip, *Governor* Arthur, xv-xvi, xvii, 4
Pius IX, *Pope*, 112
Poker machines, 232
Police, and bushrangers, 119; strike in Victoria (1923), 196
Politics, and the intellectuals, 212-13; failure to promote pro-

gress (1950-70), 249-52, 260
"Poms", 206
Population, increase in the gold rush, 84; growth in (1860-80), 88; in the nineties, 126; increase advocated, 197; proportion of migrants in, 235; of Sydney, 237
Port Essington, 61
Port Kembla, 199
Port Moresby, 220, 221
Port Phillip District, 48; in the 1840s, 65; legislative council for, 68; becomes Victoria, 68
Post-War Reconstruction Department, 226
Pozières, 178, 181
"Premiers' Plan", 203, 204
Presbyterian Church, 15; recognition of, 36; schisms in, 39; its schools, 40; in Victoria, 125
Press, freedom of the, 23; in the eighties, 120; influence of, 152-3; conservatism of, 195
Prickly pear, 127, 201-2
Prince of Wales, 253
Prisoners of war, in Cyprus, 218; in Singapore, 220
Production, costs of, 199, 200
Professions, local training for, 139; only for the rich, 140
Protection, v. free trade, 100, 165; helps local industries, 236, 238; in the Depression, 205
Public Service, growth of, 113; quality of, 114; advantages of being employed by, 140-1; preference for returned soldiers, 186-7; lack of specialist education in, 200, 212; staffing and performance in World War II, 219, 225-6; recruiting of university graduates for, 240-1, 242, 243
Public Service Board, 114; examinations, 141
Punch (Melbourne), 120
"Pupil teachers", 141
Puritanism, 87, 133; in government, 194; decline in, 232

Qantas, 226

Queensland, population (1880), 88, (1890s), 126; founded (1859), 89; Chinese in, 123; Kanaka labour in, 123

Rabbits, 127, 236
Racing, 128, 189
Radicalism, 71, 72, 73, 98, 147; defeat of, 251-2
Railways, in the 1870s, 90; clerical employees of, 140; open up suburbs, 133; effect on rural industries, 134-5
Referendum, on the Federal constitution, 162, 174; on conscription in World War I, 179-80, 181, 183; on Commonwealth powers, 225, 227; on Aborigines (1967), 236
Refrigeration and export of primary products, 107, 138
Refugees, 215, 224
Reid, George, 150
Religion, indifference to, 14, 38-9; evangelism in, 15; tolerance in, 36
Repatriation Department, 186
Republican League, 158
Research, scientific, 241-2
Returned Soldiers' and Sailors' Imperial League of Australia (R.S.L.), 187, 244
Roman Catholic Church, 11-12, 15; subsidies for, 36; growth of, 37-8, 39; hostility to, 38, 111; organizes for political power, 104, 174-5; Irish influence in priesthood, 111-12; its schools, 112, 234-5; and British imperialism, 145; and the Labor Party, 149-50, 228-9, 250, 252; and conscription, 180; and communism, 213, 250; and Nazism, 216; becomes more Australian, 234-5
Rothbury, 196
"Rum Corps", 4
Rum as currency, 7

Sabbatarianism, 87, 93-4, 133, 232
San Francisco Conference (1945), 223

Index

Savings banks, 15, 35
Schools, the Church of England's monopoly, 23; subsidies to all church, 36; government non-denominational, 36; Presbyterian, 40; limitations of government, 42-3, 112-13; withdrawal of subsidies to church, 99; Catholic, 112; private, 115-16; State aid for Catholic, 174, 234-5
Schools of Arts, 40-1, 133, 191
Scientists, their achievements, 241-2
Scullin, J. H., 207
Sealing, 6
Servants, household, 95
Senate elections (1970), 251
Shearers' strike (1891), 147, 211
Sheep, in search of pasture, 46-7; and the 1840s depression, 48; improvement of, 107; effect on of drought and rabbits, 127. *See also* Wool
Shipbuilding, 225
Shipping and trade, 89-90
Silver, 138
Singapore, 208, 219, 255; fall of, 219-20
Six-o'clock closing, 182, 190
Slessor, Kenneth, 212
Slim, *Field-Marshal*, (quoted), 221
Smith's Weekly, 210
Snobbery, 70, 96, 128, 129, 195
Snowy River Scheme, 226
Socialism, and the working class, 145-7; and the Labor Party, 149; in State-owned industries, 173; after World War II, 226-7
Somme, the, 178
South Asian Register, 60
South Australia, its beginnings, 61-3; immigrants to, 63; legislative council for, 68; population (1880), 88, (1890s). 126; progressive measures in, 98, 125-6; in the Depression, 205; liberal-radical conflict in, 252
South-east Asia, 223, 255, 256-7
South-west Pacific, 258
Spanish Civil War, 213
Spender, *Sir* Percy, 255

Sport, for the people, 92-3, 132; as foreign policy, 156-7, 209; change in attitude to, 231-2
Squatters, and the pastoral rush, 46-8; their land-grabbing, 48, 49, 58; their way of life, 49-51, 108, 127-8; power or, 57, 58-9; political ambition of, 70; and the Land Acts, 105-6; improvements introduced by, 107; in the Great Drought, 127; as depredators, 134
Steel, 225
Stephens, A. G., 158
"Sterling" and "Currency", 16
Strikes, and the I.W.W., 145-7; shearers', 147; during World War I, 182-3; in the twenties, 196; government intervention in, 196; communist inspired, 229
"Stump jump" plough, 106
Suburbs, growth of, 133; amenities in, 133; architecture in, 141; working-class, become slums, 147; quality of life in, 188-93, 230-1; in literature, 245, 246
Sudan, military contingent to, 117-18
Such is Life, 210-11
Sukarno, *President*, 256, 258
Summer of the Seventeenth Doll, 242, 243
Superannuation, national, 233
Superphosphates, 138
Supreme Court founded, 23
Surfing, 131-2, 189; and the surf life-savers, 231
Swaggies, 108-9; in the Depression, 203
Swan River Colony, founded, 26; its first 20 years, 60-1
Sydney, first settlement at, xv-xvii; to 1819, 1-4, 5; and Melbourne, 87, 122; in World War II, 220
Sydney City Council, 57, 69, 70; "the voice of the people", 71, 72
Sydney Hospital, 3
Sydney Morning Herald, (quoted), 132
Sydney Opera House, 237
Syme, David, 100
Syndicalism, 145-7

Syria, 218
Talkies, 191
Tariffs, 130; and party politics, 148, 150; protective, 167, 203. *See also* Protection
Tasmania, 73; population in 1880, 88; overshadowed by Victoria, 122; in the Depression, 205. *See also* Van Diemen's Land
Taxation, 130, 225
Teachers' colleges, 173
Teaching, a respectable occupation, 140-1
Telecommunications nationalized, 226
Telegraph lines, first, 91
Telephones, first, 91
Television, 231
Temperance societies, 33
Terraces, restoration of, 237
Theatre, its beginnings, 67, 93, 120; effect of vaudeville on, 132; and the talkies, 191; in the 1930s, 212; a national, 226; 1950-70, 242, 243, 244, 245, 246
"Theodore Plan", 203, 204
Time-payment, 190
Tobruk, 218-19
Tojo, *General*, (quoted), 220
Tokyo, Australian Legation in, 216
Torrens Title, 94
Trades unions, 32-3; growing power of, 102, 132; and the I.W.W., 146-7; aims of, 146, 147; create the Labor Party, 149; in World War I, 182, 183; and the Communist Party, 195; and social reform, 197
Trading, its beginnings, 6-7, 7-8
Trams, steam, 91
Transport, in the 1870s, 89-90; suburban, 192-3
Trollope, Anthony, (quoted), 91-2
Tropical Medicine, Institute of, 139
Tucker, Albert, 227
Twopeny, R. E. N., (quoted), 97

Unemployment, 95-6, 125; government bureau for, 130; insurance, not achieved, 193; in the twenties, 197; in the Depression, 203, 205; fall in, 233
United Australia Party, 204; and Empire defence, 208, 215; its policy in the Pacific, 216-17; in World War II, 219; collapse of, 219, 227
United Nations, 223
United States, in World War II, 219-20, 221; imports from, 209, 258; Australian dependence on, 255-6, 257; its withdrawal from Vietnam, 258; its investment in Australia, 258
Universities, in the eighties, 115; introduce technical and professional faculties, 137, 138-9; the Arts faculties of, 139; entrance to, from high schools, 142; growth in, 241; occupations for graduates of, 240-1, 242, 243
University of Sydney, incorporation of, 42
Upper Houses frustrate new legislation, 111
Urbanization, 153, 231, 234, 237

Van Diemen's Land, 6; killing of Aborigines in, 17, 54; in the 1840s, 64-5; Legislative Council for, 68; becomes Tasmania, 73
Versailles, Treaty of, 184-5
Veterinary schools, 138
Victoria, Legislative Council for (1851), 79; discovery of gold in, 79-80, 84; growth in population, 88; education in, 99; rise of the businessman in, 109-11; collapse of its prosperity, 124. *See also* Port Phillip District
Victoria Cross, 144, 145
Vietnam, 255, 258, 259
Voting, preferential and proportional, 194

Wages, in the 1920s, 199; cut in the Depression, 203, 204
Wake in Fright, 261
War Museum, Australian, 186
Washington, Australian legation in, 216

Wealth, social recognition of, 110
Wentworth, W. C., 24
Wesleyan Church, its first chapel (1819), 14-15; recognition of, 36; growth in strength of, 40; in Victoria, 85, 86
Western Australia, its population, 88, 126; no more convicts for, 123; expansion of, 126; votes for secession, 205. *See also* Swan River Colony
Westminster, Statute of, 208
Whaling, 27
Wheat, in South Australia, 62; growth in production of, 134, 137-8; in World War I, 180; bulk handling of, 198; in the Depression, 203
White Australia policy, 158-9, 166, 185; dropped in public, 259
White, Patrick, 244, 245
Wilson, Woodrow, 185
Wireless sets, 191
Women, as assisted immigrants, 30; votes for, 130; in suburban life, 192

Wool, demand for, 47; in the 1840s, 48; its export value, 88, 108, 194; and the Great Drought, 127; in World War I, 180; worship of, 194; in the Depression, 202; Japan as customer for, 209
Workers' compensation, 131
Working class, status of, 132-4; solidarity of, 147
World War I, 175-85; enthusiasm for, 175; proposed conscription for, 179-81; British strategy in, 181-2; casualties in, 178, 181, 182, 184; volunteers for, 184; its effect on Australians, 184-5
World War II, 215-22; prelude to, 215-17; war declared, 217; volunteers for 218; prisoners of war in, 218, 220; attitude to, 219, 220; conscription in, 220; Australia after, 223-9

Ypres, 181
Yugoslavs, 207

Zinc, 138